Praise for Malc

'With his corking reviews and flair for quips,
His nose has launched a thousand sips'

(Ann Smallman's winning entry in the *Superplonk 99* competition)

'An impressive and accessible guide to what's really worth drinking'

Observer

'The Nick Hornby of the wine world . . . He comes across as the ideal dining companion'

Birmingham Post

'For those intent on drinking their way through the festivities, Malcolm Gluck's *Superplonk* and *Streetplonk* are invaluable stocking fillers'

Solicitors Journal

'If you are a wine enthusiast whose inclination on finding an exciting bottle is to wish to share it with the world and sing its praises from the rooftops – and many of us are – Malcolm Gluck is your man'

Newcastle Journal

About the author

Malcolm Gluck is the *Guardian*'s wine correspondent, writing a regular Saturday column, *Superplonk*. He writes three wine guides a year, each one fresh, fruity and unadulterated by anything but his own singular viewpoint. He has presented his own BBC-TV wine series, *Gluck, Gluck, Gluck*. He is consultant wine editor to Sainsbury's Magazine, contributing a monthly wine diary. He has compiled a double-CD of classical music with wine for Deutsche Grammophon. His guide to wine tasting, *The Sensational Liquid*, has just been published. Other major preoccupations are his children, dead authors, all styles of piano music and relaxing in cemeteries.

Superplonk 2000

Malcolm Gluck

CORONET BOOKS
Hodder & Stoughton

First published in Great Britain as a Coronet paperback original in 1999

10 9 8 7 6 5 4 3 2 1

A CIP catalogue record for this title is available from the British Library

ISBN 0 340 71313 5

Typeset by Palimpsest Book Production Limited,
Polmont, Stirlingshire
Printed and bound in Great Britain by
Mackays of Chatham PLC, Chatham, Kent

Hodder and Stoughton
A division of Hodder Headline
338 Euston Road
London NW1 3BH

To C.S. – whose life and work are an inspiration

'Le degré de la civilisation d'un peuple est toujours proportionel à la qualité et à la quantité du vin qu'il consomme.'

Maurice des Ombiaux

'Whenever a Frenchman puts wine and civilisation in the same breath you can be sure he suffers from halitosis.'

Anonymous Guardian reader

Superplonk 2000

CONTENTS

Superplonk 2000

INTRODUCTION

It was tempting – though the temptation lasted less than a minute – to consider something millennial for this edition of Superplonk. But I am a plonker not a pundit. This book is not an oracle, it is a manual: the detailed record of one man's reasonable abuse of his liver and application of his sensory faculties plus a listing of the thousands of bottles accountable for his condition.

This latter objective is, I hope, entertainingly realised. It is certainly not narrowly or parochially achieved. I drink from every major wine retailer's shelf everywhere in Britain. True, I am a Capitalist residentially but I am pleased, and sometimes humbled, to recognise that the readers of this book live in every shire in the UK and I travel far and wide to meet them.

This is accomplished mainly, though not exclusively, as a result of my national winter book signing tour and my Introductions to various editions of this book have been based on the diaries I have compiled during these tours. This annual jaunt is both a pleasure for me to achieve (only sometimes to endure) and an instructional and refreshing exercise – especially for one who works in an ivory basement – for it gives me food for thought, always one of the more nourishing accompaniments to wine. It is also a reinforcement for my endeavours and insight into the concerns and habits of the British wine drinker – a creature who since the last world war has been turned from a once-a-year Christmas tippler, spending five bob on his celebratory bottle, to a representative of a civilised group – 72% of us Britons now – spending somewhere in the region of £70 a head on average on wine annually. The slaking of this thirst shows no sign of abating.

In such an eager atmosphere, I feel no pressing need to fatuously decorate what I do except to make my words more congenial to swallow. Reporting on wine bottles seems to generate its own heat. Readers enjoy taking a gamble on wines I enthuse about, mindful (and I remind them often enough) that wine which has not come from the writer's own bottle is a gamble, a different wine from his, and it will always be so until we can guarantee every single bottle of wine on sale is 100% fault-free and exactly the same as its relative from the same barrel or tank. If I am to dream up any new-Millennial oracle it will surely be to float the idea that in the century to come more and more wine will be sealed with plastic corks and screwcaps until cork taint is a thing of the past like bubonic plague. The Portuguese will find new uses for exported cork – on floors and ceilings but not in wine bottles except those which can afford in their high cost to absorb the £1 or perhaps £2 per cork cost necessary to guarantee that the inch-and-a-quarter of tree bark is free of the taint which not only spoils a percentage of bottles but also contributes to each bottle of the same wine aging differently (and often so vividly as to be a different wine). I had considered an introduction along these lines but I have covered much of this ground – and gone into certain of the more intelligent responses to the problem – in my new book on wine tasting, *The Sensational Liquid* (Hodder & Stoughton, £17.99 at all bookshops good or bad). But let me say right here that not for one moment have I been fooled, though several of my readers have, by the public relations balderdash of the cork industry in this area. Instead of turning its attention to solving cork taint, the industry has trumpeted that rare birds are at risk from plastic corks if they replace real cork seals. This is patent nonsense. Cork has many uses apart from wine seals and the trees' crop can, with a little effort, be otherwise employed and ensure a continuance of fauna habitation and protection. The only animals at risk from plastic corks are the fat complacent cats of the cork industry and its PR lapdogs.

I also considered, at greater length and with more seriousness than any Millennium idea, the thought that it might be fun to write the introduction to this book and to each of its representative retailers in the style of a particular novel and then invite readers to guess which novel, which hero/heroine, and author of which it was a pastiche. The readers who guessed the whole bunch correctly would receive a case of wine from me. I did not abandon this idea, after a certain amount of work and with great reluctance, on the grounds of the damage it might do to my pocket but due to the disastrous disruption it became apparent it would cause to my working life. I reckoned I might have to cough up the cost of a couple of cases, but not much more than this because I wasn't going to make the solutions soft. I did not anticipate many readers would correctly solve the puzzle of the identity of all thirteen books (one introduction plus twelve retailers). However, when I set to work to fashion what I wanted to say about Morrisons (which I based on Jane Austen's *Mansfield Park*) and Marks & Spencer (*Bonfire of the Vanities*), I realised that my ambitions were beyond me to accomplish. Devoting so much time to such lengthy literary lampoonery – of little relevance to any wine or drinker – would have seriously diminished the time I set aside each week to actually taste wines not to mention the hours I need to write my weekly and monthly wine columns.

Readers may breathe a sigh of relief over this. The Co-op as Jude the Obscure, Safeway in the guise of Madame Bovary, Waitrose – an easy guess this – as Humbert Humbert, and Sainsbury frolicking as Jim Dixon all bit the dust. Similarly, it has been bye-bye to Augie March (Asda). Farewell to Mr Toad (Budgens – whose love of motoring forecourts has become an obsession).

You pay, after all, for my ratings on wines, not for my interest in authors. You are, however, stuck with my diary but this involves you in no guessing game above that of merely wondering to yourself whether the author has got his tongue permanently in his cheek or does he only adopt this posture when he's tasting wines? I make no more enigmatic an apology for my attitude to wine and to writing on the subject than this.

Friday 6th November

Negotiating the odd spent rocket, lying like some exotic canine turd in the road, I cycle across to the canal where it is possible (ignoring the signs forbidding it) to pedal the entire towpath, a short pause to negotiate the stairs at Crocker's Folly excepted, to Bennett country (Alan not Arnold) where the office of Classic FM is situated in Camden Town or, if you're an estate agent, Regent's Park. I suppose Mr Bennett would regard the Dales as more his country but I do not believe his verbal embroidery would be so finely wrought or so delicately barbed if he lived elsewhere than wicked snotty London. I make my contribution to a radio commercial for Morrisons wines and cycle back.

Letter from Majestic Wine Warehouses concerning Beaujolais Nouveau on doormat. It describes this wine as having 'the subtle smell of banana followed by a huge amount of bubblegum and soft red fruit' – a description which had me gagging over my desk. A fiver a bottle for bubblegum!? Well, that's Beaujolais Nouveau for you – or rather, if you have any taste at all, it's not for you. Modern BN is so repulsive a confection that I wonder why anyone goes to all the bother of picking grapes to make it. It could surely be confected in a laboratory from grape concentrate plus a few other fruit-derived chemical substances (bananas and bubblegum being easy flavours to imitate).

Sunday 8th

The 31 bus, half way down Kensington Church Street, suddenly stops, brakes hard and pulls into the kerb. Some sort of loud and urgent message has been crackingly relayed to the driver over his radio. We passengers look at one another and wonder, wordlessly, what kind of exotic situation has occurred to create this unique hiatus. The young and solemn driver (I guessed at him being a Balkan refugee when I negotiated change for the fare) emerges from his cabin and says 'two minutes silence, pleez, for the end of the second world war.' There is stunned compliance from within his vehicle. I want to protest that the war ended on the 11th but then realise today is Remembrance Sunday and the silence is not for the end of the war but for the men and women who died fighting it. A sense of awe settles over the passengers. Even my nine-year-old son sits in a silent daze. On the previous Thursday I'd stood with him and a bunch of American kids and observed the marking of the anniversary of another historical event. But with that one £1500's worth of fireworks went up in pungent smoke and brilliant explosions. I wonder: haven't we got our celebratory expressions the wrong way round?

Later, sitting in a Richoux coffee shop jotting down notes in reply to readers' letters (whilst son plays science fiction wargames in shop across the square), a startlingly attractive young woman asks if the seat opposite mine is free. I confirm its vacant status and she lights up a cigarette. I consider, not for the first time, that I should always carry about my person a self-erecting cardboard sign for placing on public tables which reads 'This is a non-smoking table'.

Tuesday 10th

Oddbins tasting in Battersea. The retailer's charming PRO, Karen Wise, rings up the afternoon before and asks would I mind Jancis gatecrashing and could she book me a cab? I say fine to the first and it depends on the severity of the weather to the second. In the event, the weather is gently unpluvial and so I cycle. Finding myself early I sit on the riverine wall of St. Mary's church graveyard and watch two herons aquaplane the Thames.

In the afternoon I take the train to Cambridge for a signing at Dillons. Sainsbury has donated the wines. Many attendees do not like the tannins in Chateau Carsin or those in the Valdivieso Malbec. Representatives of Wine Rack, looking combative, skulk at the back. Dillons' manager gives me copy of new book on Edward Hopper as a thank-you. Another author, the American linguistician Deborah Tannen, is also signing books on another floor and I buy her book and ask her to sign it. Sitting in the cold London-bound train later, half way through a tuna sandwich (using Hopper, who looks like George Peppard's uncle, as a tray) and beginning Ms Tannen's book, Ms Tannen herself boards my carriage and we chat the whole journey. Is this the first time that a reader has been prevented from delving into a book by the living irruption of its author? She offers me some of her skin salve, which she uses on her hands after book signings to soften the effect of having shaken so many people's hands. I decline, though recognise that I have a lot to learn as an author.

11th

Restaurateur who used to be my neighbour, Dominique Rocher, writes to me from Cairanne and invites me to go truffle hunting in Provence. Decline on grounds of other hunting engagements: for signatures on my books.

Walk up to Paddington for train to Bristol.The woman opposite in the carriage removes her personal stereo earphones and phones her lover to ask where he is and then, three times, tells him she had fallen asleep when he earlier tried to contact her. Meaningless drivel really. What do they find to talk about in bed? A notice by her head clearly forbids the use of mobile phones and personal stereos.

Train pauses at Swindon, which is a derivation of swine town, and an exceedingly smart, spot-lit Majestic wine warehouse, the shape of a seaside retirement bungalow or modern super-sty, glows smugly in the dusk as we negotiate entry to the station. Several men leap up and don raincoats, all the colour of wet cement. This sort of grey is the colour of corporate middle management nowadays and somehow I see all these blokes dropping in to Majestic after they've picked up their Rovers from the car park and buying dull raw claret.

Tannoy voice: 'Sorry, but there will be a wait before we reach the station. We are in a long queue because of brake trouble with a train two trains ahead.' I ask the ticket collector about trains to Bath from Bristol. His parting shot, after he has supplied me with this information, is to wonder aloud if he will be paid overtime for this 20 minute delay. He thinks he is being funny. No passenger laughs.

No taxis at Bristol and large queue. Walk to Blackwells, guessing route. Only have to ask way five times. Wonderful tasting, lots of frisky readers, lively questions. Sainsbury's wines again and the Valdivieso is adored. Manager gives me copy of a biography of Glenn Gould as a present and I have it autographed by staff. Take train to Bath in order – my publisher's wicked idea – to stay at the Royal Crescent Hotel where I am given the Brinsley Sheridan room. With my late supper drink a bottle of 1992 Rolly Gassmann Gewurztraminer – all those delicious tartrate crystals so reassuring to find in the last glass from the bottle (like kisses at the end of a farewell performance). So couth on the tooth is the food, too – delicate, civilised. Can't eat like this every night. Have conversation with American guests re. US actor called George Hamilton (for reasons apparent later). Read, with mounting sense of astonishment, details of Glenn Gould's tortured life. Is it worth paying his price to play the piano so potently?

Breakfast kipper superior. Hotel arranges taxi and umbrella for my trip to Haycombe Cemetery. Note that the taxi, a sedate green Rover, has MCLK as lettered part of its number plate and not for the first time I marvel at the lengths the Royal Crescent go to to make guests feel personally indulged. Lay flowers including a single red rose (for the First World War anniversary) on parents' grave. Continue indulgence theme at Camden Books on Walcott Street by spending more than I would normally consider proper: £10 on *Sydney Smith* by Gerald Bullett, Michael Joseph 1951; £10 on *D.H. Lawrence* by F.R. Leavis, Chatto & Windus 1957; £10 on *The Last Hours of Sandra Lee* by William Sansom, Hogarth Press 1961; £5 on *The Working Novelist* by V.S. Pritchett, Chatto & Windus 1965; and £25 on *In the Beginning* by Norman Douglas, John Day USA 1928, which brings my Douglas collection satisfyingly nearer completion.

Momentary excitement as co-proprietor thinks he may have something on Maine de Biran, but hope dashed.

Go to Waterstone's in Milsom Street. Driver says he'll take umbrella back to hotel for me. Sign 150 books in Waterstone's, each written by me, and leave for lunch at the Hole in the Wall. Drink Pfaffenheim Reserve Gewurztraminer 1996 with Cornish shell fish followed by fillet of mackerel with korma sauce (an ethnically-fused rendition of the E. David classic *macquereau aux façon de Quimper*). £8.50 for two courses seems most reasonable to me. Every other customer, when consulting the menu, asks the waitress what tagine is. Old customers, you see.

Take train from Bath via Bristol Temple Meads to Birmingham New Street for evening signing. Leave Gould's tortured life and listen on my earphones to an old American tape of the original radio broadcast of *Shane* with Alan Ladd.

Ticket collector, with the detached urbanity of a College porter informing a visitor that the lawn is strictly for the fellows, asks me to move seats for a chap in a wheelchair who enters with minder and is forced, in order to be comfortable, to put his booted feet on the table.

Discover there is less ambiguity in the radio version of *Shane* than there is in the film. On radio, Shane clearly sticks around because of Marion Starrett. In the movie, the producers more mindful perhaps that no hero can be a home breaker, there is a mixture of motives; however, in both productions Shane guns down the baddies because he wants to keep a home together by keeping the husband alive and away from the baddies' guns. The tape finishes, and I return to the book on Gould. When Gould gave his first public performance of the Goldberg Variations only fifteen people turned up to the concert hall in Toronto. Hurricane Floyd kept people indoors. Would it not make an interesting magazine article to find out who those brave fifteen were and how Gould performed?

Reach Birmingham and go to Burlington Hotel to be interviewed by Ross Dodd, a local journalist. Have my picture taken with an Aussie red. Book signing at Waterstone's with M&S

wines. Casa Leona Chilean Cab Sauv, Honey Tree Sem/Chard are notably terrific. Lively bunch of readers. Questions on free radicals, flying wine makers, availability in supermarkets, why are these M&S reds thin, is Jilly Goolden past it and 'pushing an act past its sell-by date', and how can I taste so many wines? Defend Jilly (there should be statues to her) and deny anoxeria in M&S reds. Have to tell a small enclave of drunks to 'shut up or go down the pub.' Get letter a fortnight later from Michele Platman telling me how 'irascible' I was but, in the next breath, what a 'wonderful' evening she and her husband had.

Try hamburger on train. Horrible. Buzzing torture in carriage from the light fittings. Read Pritchett. He describes *Don Quixote* as if the book were your typical Chilean cabernet sauvignon: '. . . stoical, not Epicurean; sunlit, not eupeptic; civilised, not merely robust.' I wish I had a bottle in front of me now to take away the taste of the hamburger, the screech of the lights.

Friday 13th

Driven to Sainsbury's Savacentre at Chalcot. Sign a fair number of books. Persuade a reluctant functionary to open for tasting a bottle of Domaine Leroy Richebourg 1992, a snip in Sainsbury's special Christmas shelf at £199.95. Richard Neill, *Daily Telegraph* wine writer, turns up. Wine is slightly volatile. I prefer the Chilean Malbec at £4.49. Mr Neill proclaims the Richebourg marvellous. It might well be, if it wasn't very subtly oxygenated. I cannot credit his enthusiasm for a faulty wine. Perhaps he is in love with the woman who makes it, Lalou Bize, who controls a bio-dynamic wine-making estate which has been called the greatest in Burgundy. Bio-dynamism places emphasis, amongst many other things, on phases of the moon and minimal chemical treatments (except sulphur for oidium and copper sulphate for mildew – both vine diseases). The bloody cork has caused the problem with the Richebourg. It's let air in. If only it had been screwcapped, all that love which went into the wine would have been preserved. (With wines like this, one is irresistibly reminded of a sharp French saw – '*beaucoup de bruit, peu de fruit*' – which might have been coined specifically to refer to many burgundies.)

Monday 16th

Make a decision not to appear on a Grampian TV chat show. I do like Aberdeen and would welcome a chance to see it again (granite and lobsters, smoked fish and malt whisky), but I'm put off by the notion of giving up a large part of my weekend to appear on TV with, amongst others, a 'Scottish gladiator who worships her body'. My wife and children are whom I worship and weekends are my sabbath.

This evening, wishing to see how certain Thresher wines I have tasted in the afternoon will perform with food, I take eight bottles and two book designers to a local BYOB taverna, Kalamaras, and discover how well the smoky elegance of Californian chardonnay is suited to Greek starters. Hugel Vendange Tardive Gewurztraminer 1989 fails to perform remotely as well at the other end of the meal, with a range of the usual honeyed pastries. 'You'd be barmy to pay £60 for it,' remarks one designer, 'aren't you pleased it cost you nothing to find this out?' I shake my head and reply that overpriced underperforming wine always makes me sad. 'I don't like a wine which reminds me I'm drinking wine,' puts in the other designer, which clears the matter up perfectly.

Tuesday 17th

Train to Bradford (Forster Square). Offered tea and complimentary biscuits. An unnerving journey – fog in the Peterborough area as enveloping as a shroud. Mobile phones a constant, unholy (yet paradoxically also sacerdotal) clatter of tiny bells. One conversation, as futile as any in English, is in the speaker's native French and it offers, as far as I can make out, apologies, mendaciously, for lateness. The speaker, I note, has a half bottle of Nottage Hill Cabernet Sauvignon at his elbow. The British mobile telephonists stick to tea. A woman passenger, who proclaims how chilly it is as we crawl into Leeds, wrestles meticulously with her cardigan and puts it on inside-out, the label visible below her dark hair, and I wonder why she didn't think it odd that her sleeves were turned inwards when she struggled so much to slip her arms through?

The train reluctantly stops at Leeds and then goes back in the direction it has come. I wonder why this should be, slightly alarmed that it might return me to King's Cross. 'To do with the electrification,' says the tea lady mysteriously when I ask how it is Bradford is reached by this method. Peterborough's fog, it seems, is all pervasive.

Train does indeed stop, via Shipley, at Forster Square. I put down my exciting read – W.G. Sebald's *The Rings of Saturn* – and find taxi. The driver is none too sure exactly where Waterstone's is, though the building I claim it is in, the Wool Exchange, excites his attention. Completed in 1867, it was once the centre of the whole wool world. In Sebald's book is told the story of Dunwich, a Norfolk town which was also once a significant entrepôt; it traded with all the ports of the globe. Dunwich, however, suffered a real sea-change: it was destroyed by the very element which was instrumental in creating its wealth and most of it now lies beneath the waves. Bradford's transformation is less destructive, being a creative process dictated by human currents rather than the awesome caprices of the ocean. The Exchange has been brilliantly utilised to house one of the most architecturally satisfying bookshops in the country.

Under the robust ribbed roof, refurbished but still clogged with the echoic mercantile murmurings of men who could, apparently, feel a small piece of a fleece and know exactly which part of the animal it came from and where the sheep was raised (from a Pacific island to La Mancha, Shropshire to Sussex). Certain wine tasters also enjoy making such distinctions.

The wines for the tasting have been purchased at Oddbins. Of particular interest are the Fair Valley Bush Vine Chenin 1998 from South Africa and the Norton Cabernet Sauvignon 1997 from Argentina. Lots of spirited questions, especially about how it is possible to find so many flavours in a glass of wine. I respond by saying we wine writers make it up most of the time.

Morrisons' whole wine department, Stuart and Fiona, take me to the Shiraz restaurant which fails, in one respect, to live up to its name since 'because of the religious beliefs held by the proprietors we do not serve alcohol' but they serve up sizzlingly tasty vindaloos, Madras curries, bhunas, kormas and dhansaks. Alas, Stuart's BYOB bottle, Torres Gran Sangre de Toro, is badly corked. Considering we had no corked bottles at Waterstone's this is gallingly ironic.

My publisher has thoughtfully booked the Bradford Novotel instead of something more bijou since it is situated by the motorway and I am to be driven to Manchester the next day to meet an old star of the screen whom I seem to remember my mother, when she was alive, thinking 'rather cute'.

Wednesday 18th

Investigation reveals that I am in a room designated as Comfort. It costs £58 a night. My publisher could, however, have booked a Harmony room, at £59, but she knows how much I hate unnecessary extravagance. The hotel offers a fine outlook on Batleys Cash & Carry from the front entrance; from my bedroom window, double glazed, there is only a bleakly moist panorama of the motorway traffic hissing past. Three jackdaws forlornly peck the startlingly pea-green lawn which glaciates to the swimming pool (closed).

Look at *Daily Telegraph* whilst waiting for car. The issue is dominated by the activities of powerful women – another rich change for Yorkshire. Delia Smith's TV show is responsible for inspiring the sale of an extra 1.3 million eggs a day, Cecilia Bartoli – she of the angelic throat – is tying opera director Jonathan Miller up in knots, and the 87-year-old Louise Bourgeois is expanding the boundaries of modern bullshit, and severely stretching the limits of geriatric chutzpah, with a collection of unspeakably stupid sculpture at the Serpentine Gallery.

Car whisks me across the dales to Manchester. As we go down Leicester Road in Salford I note the names above the shops – Grunwald, Brackmar, Habelstadt. Lot of history here.

George Hamilton, screen veteran, is waiting for me after make-up with a moll in tow called Claudia. George – it seems impolite to use anything other than a familiar term for so avuncular a specimen – is a closet wine collector and cigar merchant. He worries that he might find such cheap wines as the ones I have chosen, or have had chosen for me, disgusting. I tell him he should speak as he finds. When we taste our way through the wines with Claudia (I never discovered her second name or her precise function) he evinces surprise at how agreeable he finds them particularly M&S Argentine Cabernet Sauvignon (£3.89) and Asda's Argentine Bonada at £3.49. He even agrees with me, though he could of course have been acting, that Sainsbury's £2.49 bottle of Oppenheimer Krotenbrunnen Kabinett 1996 is perfectly acceptable sipped whilst lying in a deckchair on a warm day – an activity, I feel sure, with which he is intimately acquainted.

I am pleased to break my journey from Bradford to Harrogate to appear on George's cable TV show. My mother regarded George as a permanently tanned and richly polished individual a woman could clasp to her bosom like a much-loved and well-worn handbag. This would be a more creative use of his talents than this televised infantile proceeding, insulting to every intelligence involved (though by the viewers no act of intelligence is required). Other components of the show involve a vet, a person who reads feet like a palmist, a vitaminist, and a collector of telephones. We all make a circus of thudding mediocrity. Pleased when it finishes and I can get away to normalcy.

Cab driver, Mr Singh, is late due to his ignorance of the existence of Granada TV or its headquartering in an ex-educational establishment. He is, he tells me, new to cabbing.

He takes me to Piccadilly where I get the 4.12 to Leeds and change for the train to Harrogate. I am given the Colefax room at the White House hotel. Do fund raising auction for Marie Curie Cancer Care at Morrisons supermarket. Gallo Bros munificently donates weekend in New York. Boos greet my asking £20 for signed copy of Will Carling's biography. Raise £7,500. Some delightful wines drunk – consume personally far too much of Morrisons' brilliant own-label Cava – and many books sold (which the publisher has generously donated). Supper is Morrisons' finest slices of pork pie and triangles of ham sandwich. Stuart drives me to hotel but declines to come in for nightcap as he is late for his midnight disco dancing class. (The life some of these professional wine buyers lead you simply wouldn't believe.)

Thursday 19th

Kipper splendid. Adequate fuel for walk to station. Lovely train ride to Leeds via Hornbeam Park, Weeton, etcetera – sheep farms, cattle, mud. Take out book given me by the Bradford Waterstone's staff, *Isaiah Berlin – a Life* by Michael Ignatieff.

Leeds train promises to take me to King's Cross. Why do all train announcers start every announcement with 'we are sorry to announce . . .'? Attempt to read Ignatieff on Berlin. The book reads like a press release. If Sir Isaiah could read it he'd spin in his tomb. It is unreadable. Isaiah this, Isaiah that. I felt physically unwell swallowing the prose.

So many things today continue to delay us. It's enough to make one a determinist. 'Once again we must apologise for our delay in our approach to Grantham. This is due to a vehicle striking the road bridge and we are waiting for the inspectors to examine the damage and give us an all clear' says a voice over the loudspeaker.

15 mins later: 'Ladies and Gentlemen, we are now running in to Grantham.' No sign of the car which ran into the road bridge.

Make another stab at Ignatieff. He cavorts in strangulatory prose. Or: the book is like a jelly which won't set; it clots the throat yet offers meagre nourishment. It reads like a paean.

The colour purple springs to mind. Sebald, read yesterday, was crystalline silver in comparison.

Outside the carriage the mist is like a glaucoma over the eye of the day. A thin watery sun is hard put to make any impression. Read some of Graves' early war poetry for light relief.

Get home. Have one hour to deal with answering machine messages. Train to Reading for signing at Blackwells. Turns out to be the worst evening ever. Terrible signing!! Oh dear! Only 2 or 3 genuine customers (who pity me, I think). Shop gives me a book on Hegel as a thank-you.

Friday 20th

Sticking stamps on readers' letters has become less of a saliva-exhausting chore since the introduction of a box of 200 self-adhesive first class stamps in a box. Each stamp neatly pops out in response to a gentle tug. Best thing to come out of the Post Office since Linford Christie.

Enjoy a rather luxurious tasting in the afternoon, which extends into dinner, where the two out-and-out stars are a Rothbury chardonnay '97 and the '96 of Baileys Old Block Shiraz. They make the two most civilised Aussies it is possible to imagine; not cheap nudging a tenner apiece, but excellent value since they are more gripping than many legendary wines with similar grapes I have tasted from France which cost five times as much.

Sunday 22nd

Take the family to Lunch at the Tate. Go completely crazy with the wine and drink Tinel-Blondelet Pouilly-Fume, Gaja Nebbiolo d'Alba and Ch. Coutet with the pud. It's how I spend my money. Better than lavishing it on petrol.

Tuesday 24th

Driven to SavaCentre in London Colney. Stand behind counter with Fred, Wine Advisor, and try to interest shoppers in book.

'Your book is our bible,' says one, accepting a glass of cabernet. Dancer appears. Or rather she is swaying like a dancer. She says: 'I drink two bottles of wine a day unless I'm on the brandy. I don't need your book. I'm already a connoisseur.'

The Fairview Pinotage is faulty, so I give dancer a glass. 'Lovely,' she says and knocks it back. Offer her the Errazuriz Cabernet Sauvignon, genuinely brill and in perfect condition. Santa Carolina Chardonnay goes down superbly too. I drink several glasses. Need them. Cowardly abdication in the face of life (Swann).

Wednesday 25th

Go to new Sainsbury store in new shopping centre in Finchley Road for morning book signing, but no sign of books in wine department so I go upstairs to Books Etc. Am immediately invited to do wine tasting and book signing. Sainsbury's book wholesaler later apologises for absence of books. This company is called Cork International. Always trouble when cork and wine mix.

In the evening there is a launch party for my new books at the Groucho Club. Asda generously supplies the wines and guests comment upon their deliciousness. I remark that Asda has been slated by a chorus of snotty wine critics who are about as in touch with what the drinker in the street calls wine as is an octogenarian C of E prelate with the finer points of rap music. Later, I am taken out to Live Bait where I eat dead fish.

Thursday 26th

Daughter has breakfast TV on and I catch Isabel Allende in a telephone interview talking about General Pinochet. When I get to my desk there is a fax from Chile, from Luis Felipe Edwards, thanking me for a review I've written of his wines. When PR companies do this (well, they don't do it any more since I got shirty about the practice), I feel irritated but when the gaffer writes I can at least understand why he feels the need to communicate his pleasure – though having said that I would die of embarrassment rather than write and say thanks to a benevolent book reviewer. I did, however, once mumble my thanks to Auberon Waugh for his hugely entertaining review of *Superplonk* a few years back; he looked at me as if I were demented.

Receive fax from Nachtmann whose glasses I am pleased, and paid, to sponsor. It confirms the etymology of the word Pennergluck. The penner constituent refers to a drunken tramp; Gluck or luck is something which makes you happy. The combined word has been coined in Germany for a 'very cheap and bad wine . . . sometimes with a screwcap.' Who was it who said our destinies lie in our names?

Cycle to Oxford Street for interview with Scott Chisholm of Talk Radio. Find myself sandwiched between Shirley Conran and Michael Portillo.

Visit St. James's Church Piccadilly to admire the Grinling Gibbons reredos (a useful therapy when feeling querulous). Acknowledge the memorial tablet of the Rev Edward Trotter who 'died of a lingering disorder' in 1777 at 48 years of age. Like Lear he went, one feels, without regret, hating 'him that would upon the rack of this rough world stretch him out longer.'

Friday 27th

It's World Duty Free Day! Curious few hours spent hosting a wine tasting at the new Duty Free Shop at Heathrow. Do it for the money. Spend most of my time discussing wine with Chelsea and Nicolette (who, so she tells me, recently graduated from Luton in Media Studies) who are amongst a bevy of hired ladies who are offering, on this special opening day, to accompany shoppers around the new emporium. Flights of fancy might be the term for certain of the wines on offer – like £800 for a bottle of Petrus – but others are bargains and those passengers I do get to talk to buy them. The Chileans especially.

Take the train back to Paddington. It is the so-called Heathrow Express. It is a lovely train staffed by intelligent and considerate people. This comment does not, however, apply to the person who over the loudspeaker constantly harangues her captive audience with news of special ticket offers on the service. This is an abuse of passenger privacy. It is also impossible, or very nearly, to escape the TV screen in every carriage. Only by finding a seat marked 'priority seating' did I manage to avoid the idiot box. (There are now, in the summer of 1999, special TV screen-free carriages.)

Have interesting dinner at the house of highly sophisticated cook who insists on serving his Chablis in Paris goblets – you know, those horrible mean pub glasses which look like freebies with a pack of eye lotion. Not only is this man a friend, he is a lovely chap who reads what I write – but he obviously turns the other cheek.

Chablis!? In Paris goblets!? Evening also enlivened by idiocy of one guest, immensely pretentious, whose throat is leapt down by alert woman on my left.

Saturday 28th

Dinner in Islington and the Pinochet affair is discussed with an extant British cabinet minister who sits opposite. This is immensely preferable to discussing the pinotage affair, or some such. Our clever host not only serves an unusual Australian red wine with the goose but, afterwards, supremely ripe English cheese. Goose perfectly cooked. Pinochet escapes similar fate, dialectically, due to sophistry of intricate legal argument I fail to refute. Takes me, deliciously, back to the sixties when we disputed over dinner tables about CND with old Moulin au Vent – then a great wine for 25 bob.

Monday 30th

Kindly Guardian food and drink editor takes me to The Square to discuss journalistic strategy. Drink the most marvellous old German wine which the wine waiter must only see once a year when German diplomats come in for a knees-up. I see no reason to elaborate on any of these points (or joints).

Tuesday 1st December

Bacchus Public Relations invites me to visit the cellars of the Cafe Royal to taste some Greek wines. Alas, I have to be in Manchester. Greece has scores of interesting wines and Oddbins is leading the field in importing the most sensational. But it is Retsina which so divides opinion where Greek wine is concerned. I am extremely fond of this wine as it happens but people often say 'surely, it's an acquired taste?' I respond by pointing out that no retsina offers more civilised an acquisition of taste than, for example, Sainsbury's specimen because it is so smooth and well-mannered. True, the worst wine I have ever drunk in my life is Cretan red retsina but Sainsbury's charming white is about as much a relative of that disgusting potion as is Norman Wisdom to William the Conqueror.

Visit the so-called first class lounge at Euston. It is a hubbub of banal mobile telephone conversation and piped music of the two-hands-in-sync piano style which is as monotonous as a road drill. Board 3pm Virgin to Manchester. One enters a Virgin with dread nowadays. There is no telling what the train will go down with.

Do a civilised book-signing at Dillons. No drunks or time wasters. Tesco wines a curate's egg: Reka Pinot Noir is aerated, ripe and raisiny; Ryland's Grove Chenin Blanc is sensational and considered plumper and more sensual than Luis Felipe Edwards' Chardonnay. Couple of good questions about breathing and South African whites. Staff give me Tom Wolfe's *A Man in Full* as a leaving present. Go to Nico for dinner afterwards. Memorable for successful gamble on red burgundy (Jean Pillot Chassagne Montrachet 1995) and immensely amusing mobile telephonist on next table who is desperate to impress the much younger woman he is with that he is a man of substance since he is an architect who lives in Derbyshire in a converted Wesleyan chapel. He shows an expanse of hairy chest and heaven knows what sort of brassy medallia lurk within.

Ask waiter for cheese at end of meal.

'Do you have any cheese?'

'Yes, we have cheese.'

'Can I see the board?'

'*%!! No board.'

'OK, then, what cheese do you have?'

'Er . . . goat's, English Stilton, er brie . . . goat's . . .'

'What is the goat's? Can I see it?'

'Too large to see. It's a big round.'

'OK. Hack me off a chunk.'

I get walnut shreds, celery sticks and several hard slices of chilled cheese. Nico: your name is on those bits of stale nut!

Wednesday 2nd

An invitation from the British Croatian Chamber of Commerce to go to the London Capital Club in Abchurch Lane EC4 to meet Mr Nadan Vidosevic, president of the Croatian chamber of commerce, and taste my way through a selection of Croatian wines. Alas, I must attend, by an interesting coincidence, a performance at my daughter's school of *Twelfth Night.* You will ask, as did my daughter, what has Shakespeare's most performed play got to do with Croatia? The answer is that the country in which old Will set this play, Illyria, is the old name for that section of the Adriatic coast in which modern Croatia is now situate. It is a pity I shall be unable to get to Abchurch Lane as not only might Croatian wine be an experience but I would also like to see inside the London Capital Club which is the former Gresham Club, which was, I think, erected during the First World War, and its interior is rumoured to make lavish use of mahogany in a very old-fashioned and compelling way. My daughter, however, has priority over carved wood.

Attend production of *Twelfth Night* (Feste's part particularly compellingly played) and the school outdoes all London theatres in which I have previously seen the play in one crucial respect: the interval wines are delicious. I have never been offered wine by the glass in a West End theatre that was not overpriced filth, but the school offers Wild Pig rouge and Foxwood blanc, both innovative, new-world influenced wines from the South of France made, respectively, by Thierry Frog-Boudinaud and Michael Kangaroo-Goundrey.

Thursday 3rd

Signing and auction at St Stephen's Church to raise money for asthma charity. It also involves dinner cooked by Caroline Bretherton and she has prepared artichoke soup, roast lamb, and lemon tart. Waitrose generously supplies the wines and they go down splendidly: Teroldego Rotalino 1997 (£4.79), La Palma Merlot 1997 (£4.49), Chateau des Combes Canon 1996 (£7.99), Deer Leap Sauvignon Blanc 1997 (£3.99), Redwood Trail Chardonnay 1996 (£5.49), and Las Lomas Moscatel (£3.75). Sign scores of books. Manage to auction a £25 butcher's shop gift voucher for £150 and get £260 for a case of Bordeaux I put together from my own coal hole stock and which I felt I would never drink. In with the case I throw in Robert Parker's latest book. I was sent, by mistake, two copies for review.

I sometimes think what an anti-social person I am. I leave the church pleased at having raised a few bob for a good cause and flogged a few books, but I am keen to return to the book I have begun reading and which I find difficult to put down. It is Jonathan Bate's *The Genius of Shakespeare* which clears up all sorts of mysteries including offering the most intelligent guess at the identity of W.H.

Friday 4th

Invited to Austrian neighbour's house for a festive glass of gluhwein. I find it undrinkable and find myself surreptitiously pouring it away and opening a Czech lager. Gluhwein, a warmed amalgam of wine, fruit juice, sometimes spirits and herbs, is more like a poultice than a beverage and though one can see its uses when the temperature is ten below and the snow needs clearing from the drive (and vicious elves pelt you with snowballs from adjacent trees), it is not a fitting concoction to draw out the spirit of Christmas from the glowing souls of temperate Notting Hill.

Saturday 5th

Ancient Italian artist (neo-classical with rococo tendencies), who refuses to speak English, comes to dinner. His American wife is an old friend. He is given risotto with Chilean merlot and pronounces the union extraordinary. 'Chile is where exactly?' he asks.

Monday 7th

Take twelve bottles of wine to local Sudanese restaurant for dinner. No resistance from staff or food.

Wednesday 9th

Visiting the laboratory of a wine chemist in Ockley, I encounter a 200-year-old bottle, alas empty, of Madeira. This is not a vintage which needs cut much ice in such an ancient Surrey village. It was called Ockley-on-Stone Street before the age of the internal combustion engine dictated the need for brevity on public signage and in the Saxon Chronicle it is referred to as Acla which is where the Danes met a bloody comeuppance at the hands of our own King Ethelwulf (839–858). A Roman camp, bits of, is adjacent and nearby Leith Hill is said to offer a view not only of London thirty-two miles distant but of the sea and fourteen counties. The only ancient remain on view, however, on this cold, damp morning is one quizzical wine writer.

Encounter somewhat newer wine in evening: Kanonkop Kadette from South Africa. It goes perfectly with spicy bangers & mash and that tough Spanish cheese, manchego, which is of the consistency of saddle soap. It is the only cheese in the world which is a mix of cow's, goat's, and ewe's milk – or used to be at any rate.

Thursday 10th

The *Guardian Weekend* team invites me to the Blue Print cafe for Christmas lunch and Michael & Delia invite me to the Sainsbury's Magazine Christmas party in the evening. But both delicious dates, however, must be sacrificed for the tube to King's Cross, dropping off flowers to Diane and a corrected manuscript to Laura on the way (which also includes undrinkable coffee at the British Library's cafe), in order to reach Newcastle and Dillons. I particularly like the city, the people, the bookshops, the food, and the questions here. These latter are, amongst other thorns, to do with the perennial problems of corks, why wine tasting techniques are so theatrical, and how long should wine breathe. Provide satisfactory exegesis. We drink, all thanks to the generosity of Morrisons, Lindeman's Bin 65 Chardonnay, Pinotage from Neil Foubert, the own-label Chilean Sauvignon Blanc and the own-label Rioja. These last two, both under four quid, perform splendidly. One book-signee, after the tasting, approaches and asks me about the Newcastle section in last year's *Superplonk* introduction. 'My husband,' she says anxiously, 'thinks I'm the old drunk referred to in the last book.' I confirm that this is absolutely not the case and inscribe the book accordingly.

Go off to dinner, as is my habit when in Newcastle, to No 21 Queen Street and consume (compensation for my loss of newspaper lunch and magazine party) ham hock terrine, pheasant choucroute, and sticky toffee pudding. Mr Bate is my companion and he is delightful, providing much insight. Of course Prospero's 'water with berries' is wine. Why had I not seen this before? My berried water, this evening, is Maximin Grunhaus Abtsberg Spatlese 1993 whose maker Doctor Carl Von Schubert – he once greeted me on the banks of the Moselle wearing knickerbocker trews and a feathered hat – is perfectly suited to maintain the peerless integrity of an estate with a Roman cellar and buildings erected in the Middle-Ages. The sheer delicacy of the fruit from this man's vineyards is incomparable and though some may consider a Spatlese, that is late-picked, as sweet, this is as crude a simplification as saying that the Theatre is about people standing around in funny clothes on a stage shouting at a sitting audience. It is the silken acidity of Grunhaus wines which provides sublime harmony with the subtle richness of the fruit and with the food this night the pairing was a triumph (the gross pud apart of course).

Friday 11th

The jocund day stands tiptoe on the misty mountain tops. The Malmaison hotel sends up a kipper. I walk it off along the quayside before BBC taxi arrives. Study visiting battleship (with side trimming of well-used helicopter). Whistle goes. Ensign goes up. Sailors, all with hair like jousting weaponry, disperse, pouring themselves into waiting minibuses. Invasion of town perhaps? Do radio interview with my favourite Novocastrienne: Julia Hankin. Wrote about her in last year's book. But her mother is disbelieving. 'My mum,' says Julia, 'doesn't think this bit in your book about your favourite radio interviewer refers to me.' That's mothers for you, Julia. Mrs Hankin, you should have more faith in your lovely, lively daughter. Return to Newcastle centre by taxi, but not before I learn from my driver that Cafe Chinois has closed down and the British Telecom building's egregious failure 'to blend in' must lead to demolition. Have ten minutes to spare for the Newcastle Bookshop, resolutely secondhand, where I find a gem: the tough hardback original of a lavatory-papered Aldous Huxley I've handled so often it is crumbling and spineless. Get the 11.30am train back to KX. Tannoy, triumphing over the melancholy norm, announces the forty-year wedding anniversary of a travelling couple. Durham Cathedral lurches into view in the mist, always an inspiring sight, and then it disappears – and one feels a loss.

I am now a connoisseur of Tannoy timbre. 'Ladees and genteelmen, I'm please to announce we are now approaching Darlin'ton', it offers. I'm not convinced. Without my glasses (my eyes are on a book – severe myopics swallow words better that way), the countryside could be anywhere in northern Europe in a mild winter. The man's voice is not reassuring – almost as if it should be in the conditional or offer the possibility of error. Viz: 'With luck, the next station will be Darlington.'

Finish Bate's book. Unlike when one is staring at a plate

emptied of foie gras, another extraordinarily rich delicacy, I want to have more Bate and start him all over again.

Tannoy again (apprising, I assume, Darlington embarquees of the form): '. . . and dose passengers wishin' to smooch durin' the journey may do so in the frent of coach A . . .' Did he really say this? I quickly don glasses to see if any fellow passengers have reacted with alarm. I'm the only one who has heard the snogging option; my fellows railers are all adhering to their mobile phones like executive comfort blankets. Later, passing through what must be Lincs, the woman opposite, as effortlessly as plucking an eyebrow, fingers hers and is instantly talking to friend Robin in Singapore – 'Just to give you a few dates for your diary'. You have to admire the technology but it gives you the unsettling feeling there's a parallel world to your own right beside you and you will never penetrate it.

Read the *Guardian* which came with kipper. Fascinated by the Genetic Code breakthrough whereby 'by taking a tiny worm to bits' scientists 'have taken a giant step towards understanding the very stuff of human life.' Would it not be more civilised to take mobile phones to bits?

'Almost too ridiculous for words' – so Wittgenstein on the science of Aesthetics. So any writer on the subject of wine (or worms).

Tuesday 15th

Tube to Euston Square, walk to station to catch 4 o'clock to Manchester (again). Aiming for Bury this time. Consider batch of readers' letters. Should I include any in wine guide? ('A mere wine guide?! Dear boy, I thought you attempted here a work of art.' – thanks for that kind thought, Marcus.) 'Whoever said a word must have a fixed meaning?' – thus Lichtenberg who chose his with fussy exactitude.

Dictate answers to readers' letters, many on Safeway's bizarre pricing policies, before telephonic ding-donging makes the job impossible.

Does it take so little to prick us? So blunt and public an

instrument as a mobile phone sends me crackers. In tandem with a Tannoy's blatherings it is enough to produce something the KGB might have used to send political prisoners barmy. I sit here trying to read amongst an idiotic and possibly poisonous babble. Can you catch dyslexia? Is it a virus? Of course, these people, unlike me, work in groups in open plan offices. Babbling wallpaper comes with the job. Silence and extended contemplative moments would probably freak them out.

'Good evening, my name is George. Fair enough, see you in the office. I am your senior conductor. Fair enough, Bob, see you in the office. Coach G,H,K are for first class tickets. Yeah, 'gree 'gree, we need to establish the right commercial criteria I 'gree yeah 'gree. Super savers are not valid on this service. Can I speak to Mr Henderson at some point? The Buffet is now ope . . .'

Then, most sublime torture of all, so lightly applied, the man opposite puts his coat on the overhead rack as the train departs, he stumbles slightly, and in so doing blows my sheets of note-book blotting paper on to the floor. He fails to apologise or, during the rest of our short acquaintanceship, to show any other signs of humanity.

Shall I punctuate letters rhetorically or syntactically? On the whole, I go for the former; this is because I have acquired a taste for this micro-recording lark.

Arrive in Manchester 6.40pm. Too late, I estimate, to stroll to the tram platform and catch one to Bury which was my plan. Elect taxi. Driver can't find Waterstone's when we arrive at Bury but I spot Hodder sales rep standing by actual venue, a link in the O'Neill's chain, and am soon in the bar confronting a rowdy crowd. Much shouting needs to be done to keep order.

Many authors have simply not turned up on previous occasions I am told by bookshop manager. 'How unforgivably rude,' I remark, 'What do you do with all the people who've turned up?' 'We offer them free books.'

Black pudding is the theme. Bury is famous for it. Why not change the name of the place to Bloody? Three women, sitting right by me, make me feel like Macbeth – 'by the pricking of my thumbs something unedible this way comes'. Someone lights a cheap stogie. This is a bar, remember. On these hearty, aromatic premises, the bookshop's no-smoking rule carries no weight.

Nor does, I'm pleased to report, the wine writer. Questions, many heretical, fly thick and fast as I attempt to describe the variety of melon to be found in M&S's Honey Tree Semillon/Chardonnay. M&S has also cheerfully supplied Orvieto, Gold Label Chardonnay, a fat '92 Rioja, and an Aussie shiraz/cab (sounds like some kind of Antipodean rickshaw rather than a blended wine). At one point in this proceeding, calling for order, I feel I am soliciting for votes not handing out wine. But then, in a way, maybe that's what I am doing.

Q: 'What a cushy job. How did you get it?'

A: 'Luck.'

Q: 'Why do you hate corks? What about all those Portuguese birds nesting in cork trees?'

A: 'Not a reason to maintain faulty corks in wine. It's an incentive for the cork industry to expand the alternative use of corks, as in floors and ceilings.'

Q: 'What does Vin de Pays mean?'

A: 'Invariably, bloody good value for money.'

Q: 'Is Beaujolais Nouveau as bad as you write it is?'

A: 'Worse. Far worse.'

Kiss three ladies goodnight – they promise to send black pud to *Guardian* – and get into cab for Elbut Lane, Birtle, just ten minutes away. Destination: Normandie Hotel et Restaurant. It's that et which gets me.

Order wild duck. Good wine list here: Guelbenzu Jardin, Thelema, solid Chileans. Gamble on Givry 1990. It's excellent (not all red burgundies are crap but I prefer to gamble on them with the publisher's expenses rather than my own money). No conversations worth eavesdropping on. Forced to read book on romantic poets.

After dinner discover 15-year-old Calvados in hotel bar. Sit and sip and listen to middle-aged son describe to his female companion his gloom at facing Christmas with his old dad. 'He'll sit and argue with TV all Christmas. It's not as if he's got nothing to talk about. He goes on coach trips seven or eight times a year.' Examine bar watercolours by local artist Bob Richardson on wall. His style is very polite (he has some of Turner's mistiness but Mr Richardson is firmly on the side of the meteorological kind not the spiritual).

Wed. 16th

I say good morning cheerily to a silent breakfast room – crunchings of toast apart – where four sales reps, each at his separate trough, contemplate plates. Not even an echo of a 'good morning' returns. I order kipper.

8.15 Taxi to Piccadilly station. Discuss the resident and non-resident charms of Rochdale as we pass through it: Gracie Fields, Lisa Stansfield, world's widest bridge, co-op movement. Reach Middleton, I think it is, where a comedian called Bernard Manning has a night club. I am vaguely aware of this man's reputation for fruity humour but mercifully the driver spares me examples of it.

Station full of security men. Is it a convention? Or an unconvention perhaps? Costa coffee revives.

Usual Virgin crap train – like something you might find carrying sheep in Bulgaria. Doesn't Branson realise the damage this does the image of all things Virgin? BA didn't have to resort to dirty tricks to discredit our Richard. They should have connived in buying him a railway. But they were spared even this expense. The silly blighter went out and bought one without being pushed. Another year of Virgin trains like this and even Italian olive oil producers will need to revise their language. No towel in loo (discovered after hands wet). 10% of lights in ceiling work. 90% simply crackle. Constant hum of dissatisfied, out-of-date, out-of-kilter electrics.

Functionaries arrive with pots. 'Tea?' 'No thank you.' 'Coffee?' 'Nope, thanks.'

Even at a Best Western hotel the staff show a bit more style, not to mention manners, than this.

Twenty minutes later same staff come round, no pots visible. They say, as curtly as they have been trained to do, that 'Tea and coffee no longer available. This is due to a defect in the boilers. We would like to take the opportunity to apologise for this.' I feel like responding that I'm glad they get some pleasure out of the opportunity to bring us uncongenial news but what we passengers would like is to never again have to board a train with Virgin on the side. How do you fulfil the role you have created for yourself when you work for such a hopeless outfit? And to think: the daft 'ap'orth who owns the company spends half his life in a balloon. Head in the clouds when it should be on the ground.

Maybe instead of asking celebrities what their Christmas reading will be, as papers do, they should enquire as to the nature of people's bookmarks. Tells you a lot about a person a bookmark. The lady opposite, telephonically bare, demonstrates her taste with a bookmark like a money clip. I discover this when she attaches it to her book before going off (I assume) to the loo. My bookmark is a freebie and not half so grand. It says Elgin Books, 6 Elgin Crescent, London W11 on one side (failing to mention that right next door is an Oddbins branch) and has a list of authors on the other in small, obliquely set type. Since Melly, Conran, du Cann, Blyton are amongst the names which appear here I am not hugely miffed that I do not. The name Burt also appears. He works in the shop now and then and gives the establishment authorial gravitas. It is quite scandalous that Faber say his stuff is out of print. I would buy his books if I could.

Train not late into Euston. This is seen as some kind of triumph. I see it as simply the terms of the ticket and timetable conditions fulfilled. Nobody from the *Guardian* would dream of going into ecstasies because my copy always appears on time. It is my job to deliver it thus.

Walk from station to lunch at the newly refurbished Sheekey's fish restaurant in St Martin's Court. Eat some terrific, if somewhat refined, jellied eels. My agent, who is treating me to our annual Christmas lunch, suspects, I think, that I must be slightly mad to order such prosaic fare when she would cheerfully stomp up the dosh to regale me with caviare and lobsters. But for true ichthyolatrists jellied eels are the bees knees. Afterwards, I walk to Jermyn Street and buy some cheese at Paxton & Whitfield. Alas, it is not the shop it was in the sixties. Neal's Yard is better by several streets.

Thursday 17th

My scheduled appearance at a James Thin bookshop in Portsmouth has been cancelled due to lack of interest. Only 2000 tickets were sold apparently. Sorry. Um, did I say 2000? I meant, er, only 20 were sold. Oh well, can't be helped. Can't say I will miss going to Waterloo though. It's quite my least favourite station amongst London termini apart, of course, from the in-the-belly-of-the-beast bit which admits passengers to the Paris-bound train. I think what I so dislike about it is that it makes me feel like a stranger. The people rushing off the trains all seem peculiarly and miserably intent upon a further destination (like a melancholic office) and the ones embarking are as pathetic to contemplate as doomed souls boarding a tumbril.

Thursday 24th

Many a writer on food and drink has traditionally begun his day with a large Scotch. Today, I begin mine with a large Scott. That is to say I have been invited back by Talk Radio's rugby-playing Kiwi Scott Chisholm. Peter Mandelson comes into the conversation. Then callers clog the lines with questions about low fat wines (!), screwcaps, what to eat with turkey, old champagnes, and one caller, who used to work as a wine salesman, reveals he is a childhood friend of my brother and surely I remember him forty years ago coming round my parents' house. This happens to me now and then. Bloke in

Cheshire once said to me 'Hello. Clifford. Used to sit behind you in Brooksy's class.' I look at him. Forty-two years have passed. I strain for the memory like a blocked turd. Nothing comes. Is there some kind of mnemonic enema for this sort of blockage? I do remember doodle-bugs and VE Day bonfires, but not young Cliff.

Thursday 31st

Last thought of 1999. How can I contrive to write a book entitled *The Seven Deadly Vins*?

Thursday 21st January 1999

Last signing of book tour is in Orpington, at a new Methvens branch (one of eight). Have wonderful evening drinking M&S dry. Lots of lively women, and some sentient men (one of whom brings his young son, Max, who declines wine in favour of orange juice). Curious experience of rep from other publisher helping me as I sign bookshop stock of wine guides. Answer questions about the time a wine takes to breathe, flying winemakers, grape varieties, stainless steel, cold fermentation, value for money, and why I never have a 20-point wine in my wine guides.

Able to answer as follows. Always let wine breathe by putting it into a large glass jug as this not only permits air to get to all the alcohol but also removes wine bottles from table and thus at a dinner party this means male guests don't spend valuable gossiping time studying wine labels etc. Flying winemakers are not making homogenous styles of wine worldwide but attempting to interpret local grapes in more modern ways. Stainless steel and cold fermentation aid the retention of fruit. Value for money does not have a set price level. And I rarely find a 20-point wine on a supermarket shelf because such a wine would almost certainly be mature and supermarkets don't sell old wines, they sell wines for immediate drinking (for the most part).

Bookshop is a gem and very generously gives me two books, which I ask the staff to sign. These are *The Floating Egg* by

Roger Osborne about geology and Seamus Heaney's *Opened Ground* which is of course poetry. The manager of the shop points out that the Heaney book carries the author's signature and that the addition of the staff's would devalue it. Jellied Eels I say to him. Now I have a rare tome indeed where Heaney's regal scrawl is joined by the signatures of Nina, Alex, Pascale, Nicky, Joan, Shirley, Jeremy, Martin, and, under the imperative NZ WINES RULE! ESPECIALLY HAWKES BAY, a name I cannot read but hereby acknowledge.

On the trip back to inner London where I live the driver, in a car thoughtfully provided by the publisher, takes me past the Millennium Dome, a neon belly-up arachnoid in the night, under the tunnel, past Canary Wharf and along the river and I think I have never seen London so beautiful or so eerily magnificent. I conclude that I must be amongst the happiest Londoners who have ever lived.

Health Warning!

Health Warning is an arresting phrase. I hope by employing it I may save you from working yourself up into a state. Let me explain.

I get a few letters a week from readers (both column and book) telling me that a wine which I have said is on sale in a certain supermarket is not there and that the wine has either sold out or the branch claims to have no knowledge of it; I get letters telling me that a wine is a bit dearer than I said it was; and I get the odd note revealing that the vintage of the 16-point wine I have enthused about and which my correspondent desperately wants to buy is different from the one listed.

First of all, let me say that no wine guide in the short and inglorious history of the genre is more exhaustively researched, checked, and double-checked than this one. I do not list a wine if I do not have assurances from its retailer that it will be widely on sale when the guide is published. Where a wine is on restricted distribution, or stocks are short and vulnerable to the assault of determined readers (i.e. virtually all high rating, very cheap bottles), I will always clearly say so. However, large retailers use computer systems which cannot anticipate uncommon demand and which often miss the odd branch off the anticipated stocking list. I cannot check every branch myself (though I do nose around them when I can) and so a wine in this book may well, infuriatingly, be missing at the odd branch of its retailer and may not even be heard of by the branch simply because of inhuman error. Conversely, the same technology often tells a retailer's head office that a wine is out of stock when it has merely been completely cleared out of the warehouse. It may still be on sale in certain branches. Then there is the fact that not every wine I write about is stocked by every single branch of its listed supermarket. Every store has what are called retail plans and there may be half-a-dozen of these and every wine is subject to a different stocking policy according to the dictates of these cold-hearted plans.

I accept a wine as being in healthy distribution if several hundred branches, all over the country not just in selected parts of it, stock the wine. Do not assume, however, that this means every single branch has the wine.

I cannot, equally, guarantee that every wine in this book will still be in the same price band as printed (these bands follow this introduction). The vast majority will be. But there will always be the odd bottle from a country suddenly subject to a vicious swing in currency rates, or subject to an unprecedented rise in production costs which the supermarket cannot or is not prepared to swallow, and so a few pennies will get added to the price. If it is pounds, then you have cause for legitimate grievance. Please write to me. But don't lose a night's sleep if a wine is twenty pence more than I said it is. If you must, write to the appropriate supermarket. The department and the address to write to are provided with each supermarket's entry.

Now the puzzle of differing vintages. When I list and rate a wine, I do so only for the vintage stated. Any other vintage is a different wine requiring a new rating. Where vintages do have little difference in fruit quality, and more than a single vintage is on sale, then I say this clearly. If two vintages are on sale, and vary in quality and/or style, then they will be separately rated. However, be aware of one thing.

Superplonk is the biggest selling wine guide in the Queendom. I say this not to brag but, importantly, to acquaint you with a reality which may cause you some irritation. When *Superplonk* appears on sale there will be lots of eager drinkers aiming straight for the highest rating wines as soon as possible after the book is published. Thus the supermarket wine buyer who assures me that she has masses of stock of Domaine Piddlewhatsit and the wine will withstand the most virulent of sieges may find her shelves emptying in a tenth of the time she banked on – not knowing, of course, how well I rate the wine until the book goes on sale. It is entirely possible, therefore, that the vintage of a highly rated wine may sell out so quickly that new stocks of the follow-on vintage may be urgently brought on to shelf before I have tasted them. This can happen in some instances. I offer a bunch of perishable pansies, not a wreath of immortelles. I can do nothing about this fact of wine writing life, except to give up writing about wine.

Lastly, one thing more:

'*Wine is a hostage to several fortunes (weather being even more uncertain and unpredictable than exchange rates) but the wine writer is hostage to just one: he cannot pour for his readers precisely the same wine as he poured for himself.*'

This holds true for every wine in this book and every wine I will write about in the years to come (for as long as my liver holds out). I am sent wines to taste regularly and I attend wine tastings all the time. If a wine is corked on these occasions, that is to say in poor condition because it has been tainted by the tree bark which is its seal, then it is not a problem for a bottle in decent condition to be quickly supplied for me to taste. This is not, alas, a luxury which can be extended to my readers.

So if you find a wine not to your taste because it seems pretty foul or 'off' in some way, then do not assume that my rating system is up the creek; you may take it that the wine is faulty and must be returned as soon as possible to its retailer. Every retailer in this book is pledged to provide an instant refund for any faulty wine returned – no questions asked. I am not asking readers to share all my tastes in wine, or to agree completely with every rating for every wine. But where a wine I have well rated is obviously and patently foul then it is a duff bottle and you should be compensated by getting a fresh bottle free or by being given a refund.

How I Rate a Wine

Value for money is my single unwavering focus. I drink with my readers' pockets in my mouth. I do not see the necessity of paying a lot for a bottle of everyday drinking wine and only rarely do I consider it worth paying a high price for, say, a wine for a special occasion or because you want to experience what a so-called 'grand' wine may be like. There is more codswallop talked and written about wine, especially the so-called 'grand' stuff, than any subject except sex. The stench of this gobbledegook regularly perfumes wine merchants' catalogues, spices the backs of bottles, and rancidises the writings of those infatuated by or in the pay of producers of a particular wine region. I do taste expensive wines regularly. I do not, regularly, find them worth the money. That said, there are some pricey bottles in these pages. They are here either because I wish to provide an accurate, but low, rating of its worth so that readers will be given pause for thought or because the wine is genuinely worth every penny. A wine of magnificent complexity, thrilling fruit, superb aroma, great depth and finesse is worth drinking. I would not expect it to be an inexpensive bottle. I will rate it highly. I wish all wines which commanded such high prices were so well deserving of an equally high rating. The thing is, of course, that many bottles of wine I taste do have finesse and depth but do not come attached to an absurdly high price tag. These are the bottles I prize most. As, I hope, you will.

20 Is outstanding and faultless in all departments: smell, taste and finish in the throat. Worth the price, even if you have to take out a second mortgage.

19 A superb wine. Almost perfect and well worth the expense (if it is an expensive bottle).

18 An excellent wine but lacking that ineffable sublimity of richness and complexity to achieve the very highest rating. But superb drinking and thundering good value.

17 An exciting, well-made wine at an affordable price which offers real glimpses of multi-layered richness.

16 Very good wine indeed. Good enough for any dinner party. Not expensive but terrifically drinkable, satisfying and multi-dimensional – properly balanced.

15 For the money, a good mouthful with real style. Good flavour and fruit without costing a packet.

14 The top end of the everyday drinking wine. Well-made and to be seriously recommended at the price.

13 Good wine, true to its grape(s). Not great, but very drinkable.

12 Everyday drinking wine at a sensible price. Not exciting, but worthy.

11 Drinkable, but not a wine to dwell on. You don't wed a

wine like this, though you might take it behind the bike shed with a bag of fish and chips.

10 Average wine (at a low price), yet still just about a passable mouthful. Also, wines which are terribly expensive and, though drinkable, cannot justify their high price.

9 Cheap plonk. Just about fit for parties in dustbin-sized dispensers.

8 On the rough side here.

7 Good for pickling onions or cleaning false teeth.

6 Hardly drinkable except on an icy night by a raging bonfire.

5 Wine with more defects than delights.

4 Not good at any price.

3 Barely drinkable.

2 Seriously – did this wine come from grapes?

1 The utter pits. The producer should be slung in prison.

The rating system above can be broken down into six broad sections.

Zero to 10: Avoid – unless entertaining stuffy wine writer.

10, 11: Nothing poisonous but, though drinkable, rather dull.

12, 13: Above average, interestingly made. Solid rather than sensational.

14, 15, 16: This is the exceptional, hugely drinkable stuff, from the very good to the brilliant.

17, 18: Really wonderful wine worth anyone's money: complex, rich, exciting.

19, 20: A toweringly brilliant world-class wine of self-evident style and individuality.

Prices

It is impossible to guarantee the price of any wine in this guide. This is why instead of printing the shop price, each wine is given a price band. This attempts to eliminate the problem of printing the wrong price for a wine. This can occur for all the usual boring but understandable reasons: inflation, economic conditions overseas, the narrow margins on some supermarket wines making it difficult to maintain consistent prices and, of course, the existence of those freebooters at the Exchequer who are liable to inflate taxes which the supermarkets cannot help but pass on. But even price banding is not foolproof. A wine listed in the book at, say, a B band price might be on sale at a C band price. How? Because a wine close to but under, say, £3.50 in spring when I tasted it might sneak across the border in summer. It happens, rarely enough not to concern me overmuch, but wine is an agricultural import, a sophisticated liquid food, and that makes it volatile where price is concerned. Frankly, I admire the way retailers have kept prices so stable for so many years. We drink cheaper (and healthier) wine now than we did thirty years ago. The price banding code assigned to each wine works as follows:

Price Band

A Under £2.50	B £2.50 to £3.50	C £3.50 to £5
D £5 to £7	E £7 to £10	F £10 to £13
G £13 to £20	H Over £20	

All wines costing under £5 (i.e. A–C) have their price band set against a black background.

ACKNOWLEDGEMENTS

I must doubly acknowledge the input of Ben Cooper in the preparation of this book. Last year, his name was left off these acknowledgements when it would be quite impossible for me to write an accurate word about some of the behind-the-scenes goings-on at retailers but for Mr Cooper's assiduous research. I thank him – doubly. Linda Peskin, whose unquenchable flame burns brightly into every crevice of this little book, is also to be acknowledged for it is she who assists me in running all the computer software systems necessary to compile, check, recheck, and list in sensible order all the wines I taste. Sheila Crowley, Karen Geary, Kate Lyall Grant, Jamie Hodder-Williams, Martin Neild, and Diane Rowley at my publisher are also to be thanked. Diane in particular does so much to make the running of my wine tasting and book signing life a smooth affair. I am, as ever, grateful that I fell into the arms of Felicity Rubinstein and Sarah Lutyens, literary agents.

ASDA

It's lost its virginity, but will it also lose its name?

Leaving Kingfisher at the altar, when innocents like me thought the couple had already been well-bedded and had said 'I DO!', Asda agreed a takeover by the US retailer, Wal-Mart, during the summer. This is far less interesting for you and me than the fact that Tesco wine buyer Sarah Marsay (using her married name of Brook) decided to quit and join Asda's wine-buying team which before her arrival resolutely consisted of men (Russell Burgess and Alastair Morrell).

It was the details of the takeover offer, however, which made the headlines. Wal-Mart went 20% higher than Kingfisher, a bid described as 'compelling' by Asda chairman Archie Norman who it was said stood personally to make several million pounds on his shares. It had been widely rumoured for some time that Wal-Mart, the world's biggest retailer which has some 3,600 stores in the US, was looking for an acquisition in the UK. It had previously been linked with both Asda and Safeway.

It is far too soon to comment further. Does it even interest me much? As long as the wines stay well-priced and well-formed, who cares who publishes Asda's balance sheet? Already, though, regular Asda tipplers will have noticed something different about the retailers' wines last year. They moved. Asda took the decision to rearrange its wine displays – to 're-merchandise' as the retailer jargon has it – displaying them by country of origin rather than by style. Nothing particularly radical about that, you may say, except for the fact that four years ago Asda had taken the bold step of displaying its wines by style – the white wines by sweetness, the reds by levels of fruitiness – rather than by country which is how every other retailer does it. The Asda way did not catch on. It was wine-guide unfriendly for one thing, since how else can I arrange wines in a book such as this except by country of origin?

Interestingly enough, an article in *Supermarketing* magazine which reported the change of policy back in May 1998, cast aspersions on the wine knowledgeability of Asda customers. The article suggested that the original decision four years ago was taken because Asda customers were not as *au fait* with countries of origin as other wine consumers. Wine-buying manager, Russell Burgess, who has now replaced the author of Asda's revolutionary displays, Mr Nick Dymoke-Marr, said that customers at Asda had become more knowledgeable about wine during the four years so it was time to go back to the merchandising by country. Mr Burgess is a polite man. I suspect he realised pretty quickly when he took the job that the idea of taxonomy by style is ill-advised. Asda likes being out of step in certain areas and can be admired for it. But where wines are concerned, simplicity and familiarity of display are more important than dubious innovations.

At about the same time, the world was becoming obsessed with the World Cup Finals. This encouraged a significant amount of Cup-themed marketing activity. It was reported that Asda's World Cup gimmick was to offer a replacement husband to World Cup widows. These are the lucky souls who were left to their own devices while their men were glued to the box or even schlepping around France hoping to prise a ticket from the French who seemed somehow to have acquired the lot. The replacement husbands, who were, alas, merely assigned to assist the women with their shopping, were reported to be Chippendale-style men. When I first heard this I admit to being sufficiently unhip immediately to imagine men made from carved pine and highly polished but it was explained to me it was a reference to an all-male dance troupe about whom I know little.

Another Asda football connection came to light during the year. I learned via *The Grocer* (a trade magazine with one eye, titularly at least, on the past) that Allan Leighton, Asda's chief executive, is also a non-executive director of Leeds United football club where the retailer has its head office. Some City analysts were apparently rather concerned that Asda's top men were spreading themselves a little thin. In December 1998, Mr Leighton took the decision to take on marketing responsibilities after the departure of marketing director, Steven Cain. Asda's chairman and spiritual driving force, Archie Norman MP, is also a non-executive director of Railtrack and is also in charge of a major reorganisation at Tory Central Office, a weekend sideline for so dynamic a character. He obviously enjoys being involved in arranged marriages and so one wonders if it was he who sorted out his leader's nuptials.

But Asda's boardroom is clearly not inhabited entirely by such corporate polymorphs. In fact, it was revealed in August 1998 that Asda finance director, Phil Cox, had quit his £380,000 a year job saying that he wanted time to think what to do next. I don't know what happened to Mr Cox. Perhaps he has indeed said farewell to the world of commerce and is working as a crofter in the Hebrides or as a lifeguard in Australia. Perhaps at 48, Mr Cox felt that he was getting on. Certainly being a board director at Asda appears to be a young man's game. In April 1999, the retailer named a 32-year-old, Andy Hornby, as a director of its management board.

While Mr Cox seemed to be bidding farewell to Mammon, Asda was inviting as many of its staff as it could to join the share-owning democracy. Back in July 1998, *The Times* reported that Asda was offering some 26,000 of its staff free shares worth an average of £900. The company reckoned that by the end of the month 82% of its staff would be part of the shares scheme.

Also showing Asda's labour relations in a positive light was a feature on race relations in the *FT* in March in which the Asda store in Hulme, Manchester was cited as a model for equal opportunities in practice by the Commission for Racial Equality. Applications, promotions and complaints were monitored for racial issues and the management tries 'to be sensitive to the particular needs of ethnic minorities' the article said. When the store opened in early-1998, 50.7% of its staff came from ethnic minorities.

Asda's shareowning employees were presumably all a little bit richer – though possibly concerned for their futures – when news broke in April that the company was to merge with the Kingfisher group to form a gargantuan retail giant with Europe-wide sales of more than £19 billion. The group would have been Europe's fifth largest retail concern with UK sales around £15 billion, about 8% of the country's total retail spend. Analysts apparently thought calling the deal a merger was pushing the definition of the term. Accountants would call it a takeover as, undoubtedly, is the scrapping of this marriage in favour of Wal-Mart.

Away from the boardroom, it seemed to be an active year for the retailer, breaking new ground in areas such as home shopping. Most of the major chains have taken a big step forward in this area in the past year and Asda is no exception. At the beginning of 1999, Asda extended its Asda@home initiative to more homes in south London. The service offers a range of 5,000 product lines with next day delivery.

In May 1999, Asda forecast in the *FT* that it will be able to deliver to two million London households by the beginning of 2000 when it opens three new depots at a cost of £20 million. It is little wonder that the major retailers have been stepping up their activities in this area. Andersen Consulting said it expected the grocery home delivery market to be worth £2 to £3 billion in the next three to five years.

Asda seems to have well and truly caught the technology bug. In May 1999, it launched a scheme in collaboration with the *Sun* offering a free internet service, known as the CurrantBun. The CD giving users access to the service was available free at Asda stores. Asda had some 3 million copies of the disc in its stores at the time of the launch. At that time Tesco had 300,000 users signed up to its internet scheme but with some 6 million people passing through Asda's stores each week, Asda reckoned they would pass Tesco within five days of the launch.

Not only that, Asda is now selling its own brand computer. In fact, the Asda Home Pro 300 budget computer, selling for £799 including software, was introduced back in September 1998, in time for the return to school. However, another new product launched with schoolchildren in mind ran into a snag. In April 1999, Asda was sued by Adidas over the supermarket's trainer which the sportswear company said infringed its trademark. Asda said it was very surprised to receive the writ as Adidas trainers have three stripes while the Asda George trainers have four.

Such litigation notwithstanding, Asda predicts that its George fashion brand will break through the £1 billion mark in the next three years. The brand already has sales of £500 million. Last year, the company signed up its fashion guru, George Davies, founder of the Next chain, for three more years at £1 million a year. And it seems to have been quite a good year for the Asda brand as a whole. Asda was reported to have taken over from Sainsbury's as the supermarket selling the highest percentage of own label products. In the eight weeks to October 1998, reported *The Grocer*, own label accounted for 46% of Asda's sales. All the more remarkable when one considers that prior to 1985, Asda had no own label range at all.

The own label is of course very strong in the wine market but it is also apparently strong in the loo paper sector, accounting for around half of the £1 billion market. Asda's loo paper activities hit the headlines (in the *FT* no less) back in September 1998 when it ended its 10-year own label deal with the US giant, Kimberley-Clark, who own Andrex, in favour of a British firm, AM Paper of Skelmersdale. (It was conjectured that this new deal was to be marketed under the slogan British Paper for British Bums! but I can find no evidence for this intriguing line of thought.)

Paper in other forms is becoming a more important feature in the Asda product range. Since the breakdown of the Net Book Agreement, something the publisher of this very book was the first to initiate, books have featured more prominently in the Asda range. The *Bookseller* revealed that Asda regularly carries some 200 bestsellers. Although Asda began discounting books before the collapse of the NBA, supermarkets today have free rein to offer tempting discounts on all kinds of titles. At one stage last year, Asda was offering discounts of up to 80% on 150 titles. That promotion promised to yield sales of £1.5 million if all the books were sold – the sort of turnover that could keep a small bookshop going for quite a few years, one imagines.

Meanwhile, the prospect of Euro-bother loomed for Asda earlier this year as it emerged that the retailer was flouting European legislation on food labelling. In this instance, the law appeared to be a Euro-ass. Asda was sensibly putting allergy warnings on its cosmetic and toiletry products in plain English rather than referring to the ingredients by their Latin names as a Euro directive requires. The retailer said nut allergy sufferers would otherwise have to look for arachis hypogaea rather than peanut oil. Under Euro law, only doctors and classics scholars are apparently safe from anaphylactic shock.

Finally, among the many other new products launched at Asda over the past year I was particularly intrigued by the instant tea bag. How much more instant can a tea bag really be? It turns out that Asda's Tea Total tea bag (tee hee!) also contains whitener, presumably so that your tea comes ready-ruined. Whitener, which has crept into common usage in recent years, is an interesting term. It is both extremely vague and very precise at the same time. By not telling us whether it is milk, cream, semi-skimmed, evaporated, condensed, or none of these it is extremely vague and evasive and yet by describing itself solely in terms of what it actually does do, namely whiten, it is being most accurate and precise. Whitener, as I recall, was the substance that one put on one's plimsoles – before the days of three or even four stripe trainers – prior to school Sports

Day. I had no idea you could put it in tea (does it make you run faster?).

From the point of view of the wine buyer, Asda continues to offer one of the strongest and best value ranges of wines around. This has not endeared the supermarket to many wine critics, snobby self-serving creatures in the main, who regard this sort of pandering to the likes of what you and I actually like in a wine, rather than what so-called superior palates dictate, as criminal. I admire the iconoclasm of Messrs Burgess and Morrell and – a rare fit this – the PR outfit it has appointed (after years of hiring totally inappropriate consultants). Mrs Brook is joining an exciting and dynamic wine retailer bubbling with ideas and, if absorption by Wal-Mart only strengthens this and provides even greater opportunities for expansion, it is wine drinkers who will benefit.

Asda Stores Limited
Asda House
Great Wilson Street
Leeds
LS11 5AD
Tel: 0113 243 5435
Fax: 0113 241 8146
web site: www.asda.co.uk

SEE STOP PRESS SECTION AT END OF BOOK FOR LAST-MINUTE ADDITIONS OR UPDATES TO THIS RETAILER'S RANGE.

ARGENTINIAN WINE RED

Argentinian Bonarda 1998, Asda 15.5 B

Juicy yet with a rich undertow of tannins, soft not earthy, and a hint of spice.

Argentinian Pinot Noir Oak Aged 1997, Asda 12 C

Possibly the least pinot-like pinot noir I've tasted in a coon's age. Makes a lovely savoury jelly to accompany salamis and cold cuts.

Argentinian Red 1998, Asda 15.5 B

Such softly gathered blackberries and plums, a warm coat of unaggressive tannins, and a hint of leather and cherries on the finish. Lovely stuff.

Argentinian Sangiovese 1998, Asda 14.5 B

Juicier than any Chianti, this is teasing tippling.

Argentinian Syrah 1998, Asda 14.5 C

Very dry and rich, hint of juicy freshness on the finish, but overall like a Rhone red in a zoot suit.

Argentinian Tempranillo 1998, Asda 15.5 C

Gorgeous juiciness and dry tannins towed in its wake. Lovely texture and ripely ready fruit.

ARGENTINIAN WINE WHITE

Argentinian Chardonnay 1998, Asda 15.5 C

Very quiet but not subdued. The dry melon/nut fruit is elegant, not overstretched, and handsomely demure.

Argentinian Chenin Blanc 1998, Asda 15.5 B

A deliciously well-priced welcome-home-from-the-coalface-darling white of energy, crispness, soft underlying fruitiness and immense modern charm.

Argentinian White NV, Asda 14 B

Excellent value for light fish suppers. A real sense of dryly purposeful fruit.

AUSTRALIAN WINE RED

Command Shiraz Elderton Estate 1993 15 H

Sweet and savoury broth.

Hardys Cabernet/Shiraz/Merlot 1995 14.5 D

Ribena School pay attention! This is your wine! You will love it! (So do I – a bit – but the sheer softness and sweet/dry fruit is very ripe and jammy.)

Hardys Nottage Hill Cabernet Sauvignon/ Shiraz 1997 14 D

Hardys Stamp Cabernet Shiraz Merlot 1996 

Yes, it's juicy but there are tannins and tenacity. So: you get backbone!

Karalta Oak Aged Red 1998, Asda 

Difficult to conceive how an Aussie red can be made so drinkable yet cost so little.

Karalta Shiraz/Cabernet 1998, Asda 

Dry, rich, lingering, full of pizzazz and personality.

Leasingham Clare Valley Grenache 1996 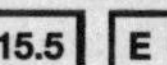

This is improving nicely in bottle. Terrific sweet/rich, soft/hard, juicy/dry grenache.

Mount Hurtle Cabernet/Merlot 1995 

Mount Hurtle Grenache Shiraz 1996 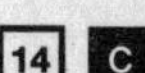

Oxford Landing Cabernet Sauvignon/Shiraz 1997  

Penfolds Clare Valley Cabernet Shiraz 1996 (organic)  

Very medicinal in feel.

Peter Lehmann Seven Surveys Mourvedre/Shiraz/Grenache 1997 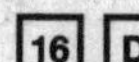

Seven quid well spent here for some glorious tannins, savoury and thick, married to ripe, dry fruit of great class and composure.

Peter Lehmann Vine Vale Grenache 1998 15.5 C

Hint of leather, spice and rich, very rich, damson fruit. Jam of a highly sophisticated kind.

Rosemount Estate Pinot Noir 1997 13.5 E

Takes nicely to chilling and drinking with seared salmon steaks.

Rosemount Estate Shiraz 1997 15 E

Rather raunchy and sensual in its aromatic richness and texture.

Rosemount Estate Shiraz Cabernet 1998 15.5 D

So deliciously sweet and fruity: soft and full yet delicate on the finish. Deliciously approachable and warm.

South Australia Cabernet Sauvignon 1996, Asda 14 C

AUSTRALIAN WINE WHITE

Cranswick Nine Pines Vineyard Marsanne 1998 16.5 C

Astonishing value here and surprising level of mature layers of rich, ripe fruit. Textured and taut.

Hardys Nottage Hill Chardonnay 1997 16.5 C

Ooh . . ! It oozes with controlled richness yet calm, insouciant, relaxed fruitiness of inexpressibly delicious firmness and flavour.

Hardys Stamp Riesling Traminer 1997 

Hardys Stamps of Australia Grenache Rosé 1997 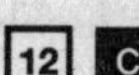

Karalta Oak Aged White 1998, Asda 14.5 B

Great value here: warmth, spice, good humour.

Karalta Semillon 1998, Asda 13.5 C

Under 14 points purely because, though drinkable, it's a pound more than it's worth.

Karalta South East Australian Semillon/ Chardonnay 1998 

Clash of styles with the blend of grapes and this results in a pleasing texture and good tension.

Oxford Landing Sauvignon Blanc 1997 

Penfolds Barossa Valley Semillon Chardonnay 1997 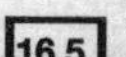

Love its richness and utter regality. It really lords it over other chardonnay blends.

Penfolds Organic Chardonnay/Sauvignon Blanc 1997 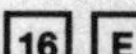

Quite superb level of fruit here: fresh, deep, dry, layered and lush without being remotely ungainly or blowsy.

Penfolds Rawson's Retreat Bin 21 Semillon Chardonnay Colombard 1997 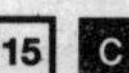

Peter Lehmann Eden Valley Riesling 1998 16 D

The youth of the wine is not as striking as its warmth and mature mineral complexity. Drink it now or cellar it for five years.

Peter Lehmann The Barossa Semillon, 1997 15.5 D

Delicious bouncy richness with a faint lemonic undertone.

Rosemount Estate Semillon/Chardonnay 1997 15 D

BULGARIAN WINE RED

Bulgarian Cabernet Sauvignon, Svichtov 1995, Asda 14 C

Bulgarian Country Red, Asda 14 B

Bulgarian Merlot 1996, Asda 13.5 B

Bulgarian Oak Aged Cabernet Sauvignon, Svichtov 1993, Asda 15 C

Svichtov Controlliran Cabernet Sauvignon 1993 13 C

BULGARIAN WINE WHITE

Bulgarian Chardonnay 1997, Asda 11 B

Bulgarian Oaked Chardonnay 1996, Asda 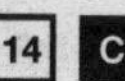

CHILEAN WINE — RED

35 Sur Cabernet Sauvignon 1998 16.5 C

Superb cabernet of wit, warmth, character, concentration, softness yet dryness, approachability yet seriousness and a great potency of flavour on the finish. A vivacious cabernet of punch and pertinacity.

Araucano Cabernet Sauvignon 1996 13.5 E

Chilean Cabernet Sauvignon 1997, Asda 15 C

Chilean Cabernet/Merlot 1997, Asda 15.5 C

Chilean Red 1997, Asda 14.5 B

Cono Sur Cabernet Reserve 1997 16 D

Concentrated and classy, it is in the class of the 35 Sur, which is a pound cheaper, and arguably has the more elegant tannins, but it doesn't deliver a pound more whack on the finish. But this is very compelling and high-rating wine.

Cono Sur Oaked Cabernet 1997 16 D

Superb dry edge gives the thrillingly soft, ripe fruit dignity and compelling richness.

Cono Sur Syrah Cabernet 1998 15.5 D

Good blend of personalities: has pepper and plumpness, complexity yet simplicity, finish and flavour.

Cono Sur Zinfandel 1998 16 D

Lovely nutty dryness gives the rampantly fresh and spiced plum fruit the drive it needs to be long and lush.

Gato Negro Chilean Merlot 1997 15 C

Pionero Chilean Merlot 1997 13.5 C

Rowan Brook Oak Aged Cabernet Sauvignon 1995 16 D

Deliciously minty and oaky yet very fresh and lively. Chile is effortlessly able to pull this trick off.

Urmeneta Merlot 1998 14.5 C

Balanced, bonny, easy drinking. Yet it has character and style – and the fruit lingers.

CHILEAN WINE WHITE

35 Sur Sauvignon Blanc 1998 16 C

Superb! The grassiness of the acidity and the richness of fruit, still classic dry sauvignon, makes for a wonderful crisp mouthful.

Araucano Chardonnay, Lurton 1997 16 E

Remarkably Californian style Chilean (i.e. elegant and very classy).

Canepa Oaked Semillon 1997 14 C

Very rich and dry with a disturbing sense of unaccomplished balance. Great with complex fish dishes and oriental food.

Chilean Sauvignon Blanc 1997, Asda 15.5 B

Chilean Sauvignon Blanc 1997, Asda 15.5 C

Chilean White 1997, Asda 14 B

Pionero Chardonnay 1997 15.5 C

Rowan Brook Chardonnay Oak Aged Reserve, Casablanca 1996 16 C

Rich, woody, elegant, stylish, balanced, flavoursome, drinkable, good with food – what more can one say?

Urmeneta Sauvignon Blanc 1998 16.5 C

Superb richness and thickly interwoven fresh grassiness. A remarkable sauvignon of great class.

ENGLISH WINE — WHITE

Three Choirs Coleridge Hill English White 1996 13.5 C

Three Choirs Madeleine Angevin 1997 11 D

FRENCH WINE — RED

Beaujolais Villages 1998, Asda 14 C

Good dry raspberry-cherry fruit at a sane price.

Beaune 1er Cru Clos Roy 1990 13 H

Pleasant bitter edge. £22, though. Something to chew on.

Buzet Cuvee 44 1997 

Chateau de Parenchere Bordeaux Superieure 1996 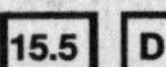

Marvellous claret for the money: violets, blackcurrants (crushed and chewily rich and stalky) and earthy tannins of bite and bravado. A real food wine – chops, steaks, stews, cheeses.

Chateau Haut Bages Liberal, Pauillac 1994 

Interesting, serious and dry. Like tasting a dead librarian.

Chateau Lahore Bergez, Fitou 1997 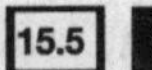

Lovely booster rocket of dry, earthy, herby fruit reveals fresh ripe cherries and goes into orbit.

Chateau Peybonhomme les Tours, Premieres Cotes de Blaye 1996 15.5 D

Chateau Vaugelas Cuvee Prestige Corbieres 1997 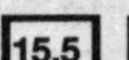

Most controlled performance, if a touch dry/jammy on the finish, and it motors well over the taste buds with purpose and smoothness.

Chateauneuf-du-Pape 1997, Asda 13.5 E

Chenas 1997, Asda 14 C

Claret NV, Asda 14.5 B

Comte de Gasparin, Cotes du Rhone 1997 16 D

Curiously cheeky Rhone red. It carries its herby tannins with vigour, youth and ripe intent.

Domaine de Picheral Bin 040 VdP d'Oc 1998 (organic) 14 C

Dry, faintly tobacco-edged, cherryish and very very cheering. Great chilled.

Domaine Pont Pinot Noir 1996 13 D

Gigondas Chateau du Trignon 1995 15 F

Hale Bopp Merlot 1997 13 C

La Domeq 'Vieilles Vignes' Syrah 1996 16 D

A most compellingly flavoursome and vibrant syrah, with sunny fruit and earthiness but an underlying richness of great elegance.

Merlot, Vin de Pays d'Oc 1996, Asda 15 B

Morgon Jambon 1997 13.5 D

Moulin a Vent Oak Aged 1997, Asda 13.5 D

Oak Aged Cotes du Rhone 1998, Asda 14 C

Earthy and full of life.

Pauillac Bellechasse 1995 13 F

Has some classic charm. But it's a bottle you want someone else to pay for.

Reserve du Mouton 1997 13.5 D

Tramontane Grenache VdP d'Oc 1997, Asda 15.5 C

Tramontane Merlot VdP d'Oc 1998, Asda 14 C

Good value merlot of a soft leathery tannic middle coated in ripe-ish fruit.

Tramontane Red VdP de l'Aude 1997, Asda 14.5 B

Tramontane Reserve Oak Aged Cabernet Sauvignon VdP d'Oc, Asda 14.5 C

Curiously dry on the finish when it is juicy and very un-cabernet-like as it makes its initial impact on the taste buds.

Tramontane Reserve Syrah VdP d'Oc 1996, Asda 16.5 D

Superb Aussie confidence shaker. From Aussies in the Languedoc this lovely rich, deep, aromatic, textured wine knocks many a homespun Aussie wine into a cocked hat.

Tramontane Syrah VdP d'Oc 1997, Asda 13.5 C

Tramontane Syrah/Merlot VdP d'Oc 1997, Asda 14.5 B

FRENCH WINE WHITE

Chablis 1996, Asda 13.5 E

Chablis Grand Cru Bougros 1996 13 G

Lemonically limpid but twenty quid is a lot of money.

Chablis Premier Cru Les Fourchaumes, 1995 14 F

Chardonnay, Jardin de la France 1997 14 B

Chateauneuf-du-Pape Blanc 1997 13 G

Hugely drinkable but fourteen quid? Difficult to fault as a well balanced, classy tipple but . . .

Chenin Blanc Loire 1998, Asda 12.5 B

Touch sweetish.

Hale Bopp Semillon/Sauvignon 1997 14 C

James Herrick Chardonnay VdP d'Oc 1996 14.5 C

La Domeq 'Tete de Cuvee' Blanc 1997 14 C

Muscadet 1998, Asda 12 B

Not so crisp and dry as is typical. It will suit light fish dishes but it lacks punch.

Oak Aged Cotes du Rhone Blanc 1997, Asda 14 C

Pouilly Fuisse Clos du Chapel 1995 12.5 E

Premieres Cotes de Bordeaux Blanc, Asda 14 C

Puligny-Montrachet 1995 13 G

Classic touches of vegetality and finely knit texture.

Rosé d'Anjou 1998, Asda

Sweet – too so.

Sancerre Domaine de Sarry 1997

St Veran Domaine des Deux Roches 1998

An exemplary white burgundy at a non-obscene price: vegetal, clean, balanced, classy and brilliant with food.

Tramontane Chardonnay VdP d'Oc 1997, Asda

Tramontane Chardonnay/Vermentino 1998, Asda

Delicious clash of lemony verm and melony chard.

Tramontane Reserve Oak Aged Chardonnay 1997, Asda

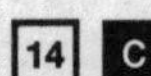

Tramontane Sauvignon Blanc 1998, Asda

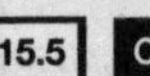

Delicious cleanness of gooseberry concentrated fruit. Real class here.

Tramontane Viognier 1998, Asda

Superbly cool performer: apricoty, fresh, balanced, very classic and finely wrought.

VdP du Jardin de la France Chardonnay 1997, Asda

Vouvray Denis Marchais 1997 14 C

Delicious sour/sweet aperitif. Will age with great style for some years and acquire more points.

GERMAN WINE — WHITE

Deidesheimer Hofstuck Riesling Kabinett 1997, Asda 11 C

Devil's Rock Riesling Kabinett 1997 14 C

Liebfraumilch Gold Seal 1997 13.5 B

Wild Boar Dry Riesling 1996 14 C

HUNGARIAN WINE — RED

Hungarian Cabernet Sauvignon NV, Asda 13 B

Hungarian Private Reserve Merlot 1997, Asda 15 C

Solid fruit of good texture, balance, ripeness yet not rowdiness, and a hint of depth from the rich tannins. Excellent glugging wine.

River Route Merlot/Pinot Noir 1997 14 B

HUNGARIAN WINE — WHITE

Hungarian Gewurztraminer 1998, Asda 14.5 C

The most authentic gewurztraminer Hungary has ever turned out: delicious.

Hungarian Irsai Oliver 1998, Asda 15 B

Wonderfully dry yet curiously floral aperitif. Delicious with fish.

Hungarian Medium Chardonnay 1998, Asda 13 B

Bit too sweet for a chardonnay.

Hungarian Pinot Noir Rosé 1997, Asda 12 C

Hungarian Private Reserve Sauvignon Blanc 1997, Asda 12 C

Private Reserve Hungarian Chardonnay 1997, Asda 12 C

ITALIAN WINE — RED

Allora Primitivo 1997 16 C

Wonderful strident complexity as the wine flexes its fruity muscles as it flows over the taste buds – it shows many sides of itself including herbs, hedgerows and gripping tannins.

Amarone della Valpolicella Sanroseda 1993 (50cl) 15 D

Barolo Veglio Angelo 1994 12 E

Curiously antique in colour and fruit. Over-mellow and under dry, it seems sere before its time.

D'Istinto Nero d'Avola Sangiovese 1997 14 C

La Vis Trentino Oak Aged Merlot 1997, Asda 14.5 C

A deliciously rich and vibrant merlot which will take terrifically well to chilling and consuming with food.

Montepulciano d'Abruzzo 1997, Asda 14 B

Montepulciano d'Abruzzo Cantine Tollo 1997 14 B

Piccini Chianti Reserva 1995 14.5 C

Old style Chianti at first sip, modern and juicy as it descends.

Puglia Toggia 1998, Asda 15 C

Interesting layers of flavour which go from dry herbiness to cherry/plumminess and back again. Good slow progress over the taste buds. Delicious in-form Italian red.

Sicilian Rosso NV, Asda 13.5 B

Valpolicella Classico San Ciriaco 1997 15 D

Very juicy and ripe with a hint of spiced cherry and summer pudding. Great chilled as a personality-packed alternative to rosé. Good with food.

Valpolicella NV, Asda 

ITALIAN WINE WHITE

Cantina Tollo Rosato 1996 14 B

D'Istinto Catarratto Chardonnay 1997 (Sicily) 14 C

Frascati Colli di Catone 1998 14 C

As agreeable as Frascati Superiore gets? Just about.

La Vis Pinot Grigio 1998, Asda 15.5 C

Simply one of the craggiest pinot grigios I've tasted. Intensely dry yet peachy.

La Vis Trentino Chardonnay 1997, Asda 15.5 C

Lambrusco Bianco NV, Asda 13.5 B

Wonderfully sweet but far from sickly.

Lambrusco dell'Emilia Bianco Goldseal NV 13 B

Lambrusco Rosato NV, Asda 13 A

A thirst quencher for light-palated guests.

Oaked Soave 1998, Asda 14 C

It is not the barrel which legitimises the word 'oaked' but oak staves placed in the steel vat. Frankly, I taste no wood whatsoever but I like the clean fruit nonetheless.

Orvieto Classico 1998, Asda 13.5 B

Good value if a touch reluctant on the finish.

Pinot Grigio Lis Neris 1997 14.5 E

Terrific tenner's worth of lemon and apricot fruitiness. Real class here.

Puglia Chardonnay 1997, Asda 14.5 C

Sicilian Bianco NV, Asda 14.5 B

Soave NV, Asda 14 B

MALTESE WINE RED

Maltese Red 1998 13.5 C

Juicy yet dry to finish. Odd ripeness to it.

Paradise Bay Delicata 1998 12.5 C

MALTESE WINE WHITE

Maltese White, Bill Hermitage 1998 13.5 C

Starts well, finishes a bit muddily – and it costs.

St Paul's Bay White 1997 13.5 C

MOROCCAN WINE RED

Cataplana Cabernet Syrah 1998

Immensely impressive freshness yet fatness of flavour: bright, plummy, developed tannins, good wallop on the finish. Very classy.

NEW ZEALAND WINE WHITE

Timara Sauvignon Blanc/Semillon, Marlborough 1997

PORTUGUESE WINE RED

Bright Brothers Baga 1997 14 C

Douro 1997 13 C

Duro Douro 1997 13.5 C

PORTUGUESE WINE — WHITE

Bright Brothers Atlantic Vines Fernao Pires/Chardonnay 1997 15.5 C

Vinho Verde 1998, Asda 10 B

SOUTH AFRICAN WINE — RED

Cape Cabernet Sauvignon/Merlot Reserve 1997, Asda 15 D

Ripe, compressed fruit you can spread on toast.

Cape Cabernet Sauvignon/Shiraz 1998, Asda 14 C

Juicy yet dry. A compelling case for matching it to rich food.

Cape Cinsault/Cabernet Franc 1997, Asda 15.5 C

Cape Cinsault/Ruby Cabernet 1997, Asda 14 C

Cape Merlot 1997, Asda 14.5 C

Cape Pinot Noir Reserve 1997, Asda 13.5 D

Cape Red NV, Asda 13.5 B

Capewater West Ruby Cabernet 1998 15.5 C

A wine for Indian food with its compressed dry/sweet fruit but also a great glugging red of some deep quaffing qualities.

Kumala Cabernet Sauvignon/Shiraz 1997 14 C

Landskroon Cabernet Franc/Merlot 1998 16 C

Delicious rampancy of characterful yet juicy, blowsy richness – yet it never gets too ripe or OTT.

South African Cabernet Sauvignon 1997, Asda 14 C

South African Pinotage 1997, Asda 14 C

SOUTH AFRICAN WINE WHITE

Cape Chardonnay 1998, Asda 13 D

Bit too cloying on the finish to rate higher.

Cape Muscat de Frontignan NV, Asda 14 C

Cape Reserve Chardonnay 1997, Asda 13 D

Cape Sauvignon Blanc 1997, Asda 14 C

Cape White 1997, Asda 12 B

Kumala Chenin/Chardonnay 1997 13 C

SPANISH WINE RED

Baron de Ley Reserva Rioja 1994 13 D

Don Darias Tinto NV 15 B

Terrific new-found polish and plumpness.

Hecula 1997 14.5 C

Curiously exotic edge to some fairly hefty tannins. Very pleasing individuality.

Jumilla Tempranillo 1997, Asda 14 B

Monastrell 1998, Asda 15.5 B

Lovely broth of wine combining herby dryness with fruity richness. It has a lovely baked edge of sunny warmth and the texture is outstanding for the money.

Oaked Tempranillo 1997, Asda 14.5 C

Rich, chillable fruit of lushness and litheness. Sure it's a touch ripe but it's never soppy or unrestrained. It has piles of flavour and style.

Rioja NV, Asda 14.5 C

Valdepenas Reserva 1993, Asda 15.5 C

Delicious, full, firm and fruity, it has hint of a louche earthiness well held by the richly textured hedgerow flavours. A classy yet democratic wine of savour and savvy.

Vina Albali Gran Reserva 1991 16 D

Terrific grilled meat wine – anything from boar to Toulouse sausage. It's ripe, vanilla-tinged, dry yet full, nicely textured, warmly tannin-undertoned and very friendly. Better than many Riojas.

SPANISH WINE WHITE

Airen Spanish White 1998, Asda 13 B

Good with grilled fish. Light and gently frilly on the finish.

Jumilla Airen 1997, Asda 14.5 B

La Vega Verdejo/Sauvignon Blanc 1998 14 C

Sprightly fresh, knife-edge keen.

Macabeo 1998, Asda 13 B

Moscatel de Valencia NV, Asda 16 B

Brilliant sweet wine for creme brulees, ice creams and fruit salad. Has a delicious undertone of marmalade.

USA WINE RED

Arius Carignane 1997, Asda 15.5 C

Arius Zinfandel NV 10 C

Growers who nurture zinfandel fruit and go pink instead of red should be spit-roasted over slow fires.

California Red 1997, Asda 14.5 B

California Syrah 1997, Asda 14.5 C

So thick and clinging you could apply it to the tongue with a paintbrush. It tastes of baked plums. It will chill. It will be a conversation piece over all manner of grilled food.

USA WINE WHITE

Arius Californian Chenin Blanc 1997, Asda 13 C

Arius Californian Oaked Colombard 1997, Asda 14.5 C

Arius Colombard/Chardonnay 1997, Asda 14.5 C

Californian White 1997, Asda 13 B

Chardonnay Ken Rasmussen, Napa Valley 1996 13.5 G

A lot of wood here. Hugely aromatic, and enticingly so, but the tempestuous vegetality of the finish seems awkward.

FORTIFIED WINE

Amontillado Sherry Medium Dry, Asda 14 C

Fine Ruby Port, Asda 14 D

Not so much sweet as vibrantly, all-embracingly fruity and rich. Terrific with sweetmeats and blue cheese.

Fino Sherry, Asda 14 C

LBV Port 1990, Asda 14 D

Tawny Port, Asda 15 D

Sweetish, yes, but the tea-leaf and nut edge relieves this impression and the finish is merely rich.

Vintage Character Port, Asda 14 D

SPARKLING WINE/CHAMPAGNE

Asti Spumante NV, Asda 11 C

For garrulous grannies only – it sticks dentures together.

Blue Lake Ridge Brut NV (Australia) 14 C

Blue Lake Ridge Rosé NV (Australia) 13 C

Blue Lake Ridge Sparkling Grenache NV 10 D

Cava Brut, Asda 16.5 C

Utterly superb. It's better than Krug at £100. More authentic value for money, unpretentious freshness and classic dryness.

Cava Medium Dry, Asda 13 C

Cava Rosada, Asda 15 C

Champagne Brut NV, Asda 13.5 F

Champagne Brut Rosé NV, Asda 13 F

Cremant de Bourgogne 1997 14 D

Light and lissom. Very charming aperitif.

Nicholas Feuillate Blanc de Blancs NV 13 G

Nicholas Feuillate Demi-sec Champagne 11 G

Nottage Hill Sparkling Chardonnay 1996 15 D

Three Choirs Cuvee Brut (England) 10 D

Veuve Clicquot Yellow Label Brut NV 11 H

Vintage Cava 1996, Asda 15.5 D

Touch more fruit than Asda's non-vintage Cava but not necessarily a pound's worth more of elegance.

Vintage Champagne 1993, Asda 14.5 G

Preferable to the '92 by virtue of its greater cleanness and purity of fruit.

BOOTHS

Sally, pride of our wine aisles, joins a Men's Club.

Booths is one of those private companies which likes to keep a low profile and maintain a gentle air of secrecy (as though making a noise about itself will bring an analyst hot-foot from Wal-Mart down on its head). Therefore, finding an in-depth interview with Edwin Booth, the company's chairman, in the supermarket magazine, *Checkout*, earlier this year came as something of a surprise and a most welcome one. Mr Booth, great-great-grandson of the company's founder, also called Edwin Booth, does not appear to have much time for journalists so *Checkout* is to be commended for pinning him down. 'We spend much more time on, and are much more excited about, romancing our customer base than talking to you guys', he told *Checkout*'s journalist interviewer. 'We haven't courted publicity from the supermarket press because we are not a public company and we don't have to impress institutions – but we do have to impress our customers.' I found myself warmly applauding these sentiments (and I think we can permanently squeeze the Wal-Mart analyst back in his box).

It is precisely because he feels Booths has succeeded in this that he decided it was time to become a bit more vocal. 'I've just been looking at Tesco and Somerfield,' he said, 'and all the other guys and thinking, hell, here we are with a like-for-like sales increase of 7.2% last Christmas – we had the best Christmas and January I think we've ever had, and that was compounding some very good previous years, while, accumulative to financial year end 1 April, we're looking at 7.5%.' Mr Booth was clearly warming to his task.

Mr Booth likes to describe the Preston-based company as the Waitrose of the North. It is not just because of the product mix and consumer base but also stems from the inclusive relationship the staff enjoy with the company. Just as Waitrose is part of the John Lewis Partnership with employee-shareholders, Edwin Booth is proud of the fact that some 300 Booths employees are shareholders in the company. The Booths stores range widely in size and are spread through Yorkshire, Cheshire, Cumbria and Lancashire with a customer base mainly composed of middle class forty-plus year olds. Mr Booth admits that with between 26,000 and 27,000 product lines, the company's eyes are probably a bit too big for its tummy but he is unrepentant. 'If I'm blatantly honest, I'd probably say it's a wee bit on the dense side. We are a bit hedonistic: we love what we buy.' (As I have personal cause to know. See below.)

In January 1999, the company's store refurbishment programme, which began back in 1996 and included renewal of fixtures and fittings in all its 24 stores, was completed. The company is set to expand its home delivery service Booths Door-to-Door to two more stores in Windermere and Ulverston. The service is currently only available from the Booths supermarket in Kendal. Booths has also developed a blueprint for a city centre format. Mr Booth says the company has no plans to move south but does say that it plans to double its turnover in the next ten years.

Checkout magazine seems to be having a blitz on Booths in 1999. The magazine also interviewed Chris Dee, IT and marketing director and one-time wine buyer at the company, earlier in the year. The magazine was not particularly interested in Mr Dee's views on EPOS-driven replenishment and internet shopping but rather on his passion for cooking. It also ascertained that his happiest moment came when York City beat Manchester United 3–0 in the FA Cup and that the question Mr Dee would most like to be asked is 'Will you become the chairman of York

City Football Club?' I am a fan of York city but only as an architectural achievement, so I cannot comment further.

Into this heady environment has stepped Sally Holloway, to take over from soccer-loving Chef Chris Dee as wine buyer. Year-into-the-job Sally has assembled some attractive wines – in particular two utterly scrumptious Spanish reds: Mas Donis Capcanes Tarragona 1997 and Mas Collet Capcanes Tarragona 1997. Donis is massively elegant yet richly characterful. It combines a medley of hedgerow fruits, deeply developed tannins and a compelling finish with a hint of spice. A wonderful wine of aplomb and presence, it rates 16.5 points and costs £4.29. Collet is a touch more dazzling and was quite simply the second best red at Booths. I'd rather drink it than the monstrously expensive bottle of Domaine de la Romanee Conti Edwin Booth once offered me at a tasting (replying, when I said he oughtn't to open such things for me, that 'I've not opened it for you. I've opened it for me'). Collet presents stunning complexity – deft, daring, gently fantastical – combining blackberries and plums, a hint of raspberry, with superb tannic incisiveness. Wonderful, soulful wine for the money, it rates 17 points, and costs £4.99 (Booths even managed to sell it cheaper than Majestic's £5.49). Of course, both wines at the vintages stated are probably history now but there may be the outside chance that the odd bottle lurks at the back of a Booths shelf.

E.H. Booth & Co. Ltd
4-6 Fishergate
Preston
Lancs PR1 3LJ
Tel: 01772 261701
Fax: 01772 204316

ARGENTINIAN WINE RED

Finca El Retiro Malbec 1997 13.5 D

Touch too sweet for glugging but with Indian dishes it would shine, shine, shine.

Libertad Sangiovese Malbec 1998 14 C

Fleshy and fat with a touch of welcome freshness on the finish.

Mission Peak Red 13 B

Valle de Vistalba Barbera 1997 14.5 C

Lovely soft textured fruit.

ARGENTINIAN WINE WHITE

Libertad Chenin Blanc 1998 16 C

Superbly fresh, peachy edge (plus pear) to a wine of texture and tautness. Dry, decisive, fantastic value.

AUSTRALIAN WINE RED

Australian Red, South Eastern Australia NV, Booths 11 B

Brown Brothers Tarrango 1998 13 C

They should put it on a lolly stick.

CV Shiraz, Western Australia 1996 13.5 E

---

d'Arenberg 28 Road Mourvedre, McLaren Vale 1996 16.5 E

Brilliant subtle spices and soft textured rich fruit with emphatic but gentle tannins.

---

d'Arenberg d'Arrys Original Shiraz/ Grenache 1998

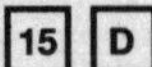

Health restorer for tired tongues. Will revitalise cuisine, too, with which it must be drunk.

---

d'Arenberg The Custodian Grenache 1996

Yep, Indian cooks could build dishes round it.

Mount Barker Pinot Noir 1997

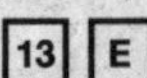

Touch sweet on the finish to some otherwise pleasant pinot touches.

Penfolds Bin 407 Cabernet Sauvignon 1996 13 F

Seems a bit much for so modestly fruity, if impressively tannic, a wine.

Riddoch Cabernet Shiraz 1997 16 E

Lovely hints of spice, mint and blueberries and blackcurrants. An Aussie red you can sip.

Rosemount Estate Shiraz/Cabernet Sauvignon 1998 15.5 D

The jamminess is extraordinarily toothsome and charming.

Stonyfell Metala 1996 12 E

Bit too juicy and cough-mixture-curious for any but lovers of oddities.

Tim Knappstein Cabernet Franc 1997 15.5 E

Lovely tannins, savoury and dazzling, make this an unusually complex Aussie.

Wakefield Estate Cabernet Sauvignon 1997 15.5 D

Linctus flavoured and textured, this big softie needs food – lots of it, and fast.

Yaldara Grenache 1998 13.5 D

Very juicy and thickly textured. The Ribena school will love it.

AUSTRALIAN WINE WHITE

Barramundi Semillon/Colombard/ Chardonnay NV 15 C

Capel Vale Unwooded Chardonnay 1998 16 E

Better, in its steely yet rich fruit, that so many vaunted Chablis.

Capel Vale Verdelho 1998 16.5 E

This is a lovely, softly textured, gently spicy artefact of immense charm.

Chateau Tahbilk Marsanne 1997 16 D

Apricots, peaches, strawberries, lemons – marvellously rewarding bottle, this.

Cranswick Botrytis Semillon, Zirilli Vineyard, Riverina 1995 (half bottle) 15.5 F

---

d'Arenberg The Olive Grove Chardonnay 1997 16.5 D

Very fleshy yet plump and muscular with it. Terrific oily texture to the body, too. Yummy.

---

d'Arenberg White Ochre 1998 14 C

Very perfumed and ornate.

Deakin Estate Chardonnay 1998 15 C

The rampant richness is tightly controlled yet satisfyingly well-developed on the finish. Splendid price for such class.

Hardys Stamp Riesling/Gewurztraminer 1998 15.5 C

The perfect Thai dish wine. It has spice and freshness, pace and plump, roseate fruit.

Ironstone Semillon Chardonnay 1998 16 D

Really handsome, quality quaffing. Has pizzazz, personality, dryness yet richness. Also suits loads of fish dishes.

Ninth Island Chardonnay 1998 16 E

An expensive treat with its creamy depth and complex finish. Has a suggestion of old world vegetality but it is a triumph of cold fermentation and full fruit-retaining winemaking techniques.

Penfolds Clare Valley Organic Chardonnay/ Sauvignon Blanc 1997 14 E

Curious overripe touches here. Great with rich fish dishes.

Rawsons Retreat Bin 21 Semillon/ Chardonnay/Colombard 1998 15 C

Fat and full of fun. Great striding style of behaviour over the taste buds.

Riddoch Chardonnay 1998 15.5 D

Curious richness to the finish, like overripe gooseberries and some soft red fruit. But what a wonderful food wine!

Shaw & Smith Sauvignon Blanc 1997 13.5 E

BULGARIAN WINE RED

Domaine Boyar Cabernet Sauvignon & Merlot NV 15.5 B

Quite brilliant: tannins, hedgerow, buckets of flavour and fruit – but also class.

Stambolovo Merlot Reserve 1993 15 B

Deliciously rampant fruit.

CHILEAN WINE RED

Carmen Grande Vidure Cabernet Sauvignon 1998

Rousingly perfumed, nobly leathery and cassis fruit, with piles of fruity texture. A lovely wine.

Cono Sur Pinot Noir 1998

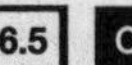

Very rich and ripe, not classic, but feral raspberries and truffles are detectable and the texture is superdeep. But it elevates itself over ten thousand red burgundies asking five times more.

Vina Linderos Cabernet Sauvignon 1998

Typical Chilean cabernet approachability and active fruit attack. Lovely tannins.

CHILEAN WINE WHITE

Isla Negra Chardonnay, Casablanca Valley 1997

Tocornal White NV

Via Vina Chardonnay 1998

Curiously dry chardonnay for Chile.

FRENCH WINE RED

Biovinum Cotes du Rhone 1998 (organic) 15.5 C

One of the best organic reds I've tasted. Lovely purity of fruit, typical Rhone earthiness, and soft finishing touches.

Bourgogne Pinot Noir, Joillot 1996 13 D

Interesting raw-edged burgundy. Has rampant tannins and a tetchy personality. But I like it (well, almost).

Bourgueil Domaine Pierre Gautier 1995 15 C

Crushed wild strawberry and shattered slate roof tiles. What a delicious mish-mash!

Cahors Cotes d'Olt 1997 15 C

Real country richness and nerve here. D'Artagnan bottled! Has buckle, swash, and some swish.

Chateau Ducla, Bordeaux 1997 15 D

Real claret at a lovely price.

Chateau l'Euziere Pic St Loup 1997 14.5 D

Rich, tobacco-edged, very soft and instantly likeable. Not, though, as concentrated as previous vintages.

Chateau Mayne-Vieil, Fronsac 1996 16.5 C

What wonderful claret! Lovely cheroot undertoned richness, great dryness, yet a compelling fruity finish. Sophisticated and svelte.

Chateau Pierrail Bordeaux Superieur 1996

One of the most elegant and warmly textured clarets I've tasted for some time. Lovely tannins.

Chateau Pouchaud-Larquey, Bordeaux 1996 15.5 D

Delicious, organically formed claret of richness and depth. Very dry but really concentrated and textured.

Cotes de Luberon Grenache/Syrah 1998

Touch of spice, herbs, hint of the earthy scrub of obscure Provence. Terrific quaffing here.

Cotes du Rhone Villages 'Epilogue', G. Darriaud 1995 13.5 C

Cuvee Aristide Haut Medoc 1996

A richly textured claret of unusual plumpness of fruit. Lovely stuff.

Domaine Abbaye St-Hilaire Coteaux Varois 1998

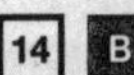

Dry, characterful, richly earthy and energetic.

Domaine de l'Auris Syrah, Cotes de Roussillon Villages 1996

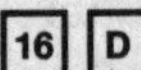

The ultimate communion wine label, in one sense, and the wine inside, far from sacerdotal, presents itself erect, very dry, earthy and most rudely rustic.

Domaine du Trillol Corbieres 1996 15.5 C

Has soft chewy edges of tobacco and some very accomplished fruit which finishes deliciously.

Domaine Pailleres et Pied Gu, Gigondas 1997 16 D

Has what new world winemakers die to achieve: fruit with soul! Lovely richness and raunchiness here. Cool, elegant, characterful and deeply, decisively delicious.

Faugeres Gilbert Alquier 1997 15 E

Has a sense of ruggedness but the smoothness of the earthy fruit is so polished it stays a delicious hint only.

Fitou Mme Parmentier 1997 13 C

Julienas, Paul Boutinot 1997 11 D

Pretty dull for the money.

La Ciboise Coteaux de Tricastin, Chapoutier 1997 15 C

Very fruity and approachable. The tannins attack way after the fruit has descended.

La Reserve du Reverand Corbieres 1997 14 C

Approachable, fresh, not especially dry. Good with food.

Lirac, Domaine du Seigneur 1997 15 C

The essence of deliciously earthy and herby Cotes du Rhone – lovely texture.

Marcillac 1997 15 D

Very vegetal and herby; dry and decisive. Great food wine.

Merlot Cabernet VdP d'Aigues 1998 15.5 B

Superb value for money. Has a lovely touch of characterful dryness undercutting the plummy fruit.

Oak-aged Claret Bordeaux Superieur 1996, Booths 14 C

Pernands Vergelesses, Cornu 1997 10 E

Rasteau Domaine des Coteaux des Travers, Cotes du Rhone Villages 1997 15.5 D

Delightful soft and gooey Rasteau – hint of floral herbiness.

Vin Rouge, Booths 14 B

FRENCH WINE WHITE

Bergerac Blanc NV, Booths 14.5 B

Bergerac Rouge, Booths 13 B

Bordeaux Blanc Sec NV, Booths 13.5 B

Chablis Domaine de l'Eglantiere 1996 11 E

Chardonnay, Domaine Maurel VdP d'Oc 1998 14.5 C

Lovely dusky edge, quite rich and ripe, but stays dry to the finish which has some class to it.

Chateau d'Angludet Rosé 1997 13 D

Chateau Lamothe Vincent, Bordeaux 1998 13.5 C

Chateau Pierrail Blanc Prestige 1996 15.5 D

Very elegant and civilised.

Chateau Pique-Segue, Montravel 1998 14.5 C

Haughty, posh, very dry and crisply elegant.

Dom Casteillas Rosé, Cotes de Roussillon 1996 14 D

Edelzwicker Aimé Stentz 1998 14.5 C

A lovely individual aperitif.

Gewurztraminer d'Alsace Turckheim 1998 16.5 D

Not the perfect wine for oriental food but a wonderful pre-prandial tantaliser. Gorgeous concentration of rose-rich fruit.

James Herrick Chardonnay 1998 16.5 C

Cracking performer: elegant toasty fruit, firm balance of fresh acid (lemon-edged) and an overall politeness of manner and form. Has well-established credentials which the '98 vintage only amplifies.

Joannis Rosé, VdP de Vaucluse 1998 13 C

Le Pecher Viognier VdP Vaucluse 1998 14.5 C

Apricot fruited, good viogniers always are, and perhaps it's a touch fat but it isn't blowsy and it would be great with Thai food.

Louis Chatel Sur Lie VdP d'Oc 1998 15.5 B

Amazing price for such rich balanced fruit. Very fresh and bouncy, yet not without elegance.

Muscadet Sur Lie La Roche Renard 1998 13.5 C

Pouilly Fume les Cornets, Cailbourdin 1997 10 E

Oh, what!

Riesling d'Alsace Amie Stentz 1997 13 D

Sancerre Domaine du Petit Roy, Dezat 1998 14.5 E

A great vintage for Sancerre!

Vermentino Les Yeuses VdP d'Oc 1998 16 B

What a fabulous bargain! Crisp, concentrated, cool, classy – for a song.

Vin de Table Blanc NV, Booths 13 B

GERMAN WINE WHITE

Liebfraumilch NV, Booths 13 B

Niersteiner Speigelberg Spatlese 1997 12 C

Piesporter Michelsberg NV, Booths 13.5 C

HUNGARIAN WINE WHITE

Chapel Hill Oaked Chardonnay, Balaton Boglar NV 15.5 B

ITALIAN WINE RED

Amarone Classico Brigaldara 1994 15 G

A great big soppy broth of a wine. Super-ripe grapes (cherries and spiced damsons) and rich tannin. A wonderful food wine.

Barocco Rosso del Salento 1998 

Has a cute bruised fruit edge making it a terrific food wine. Raisiny and ripe.

Col-di-Sasso Sangiovese & Cabernet 1997 

Superb savoury richness here: full, polished, deep, complex and dry. Classy and sophisticated.

La Piazza Nero d'Avola 1998 

Curious amalgam of fat fruit and thin acidity, with a hint of muscularity from the tannins.

La Prendina Cabernet Sauvignon 1996 13 F

Bit over the top for me.

Le Vigne Sicilian Nero d'Avola 1998 15.5 C

An edge of fruit cake to some well-developed tannic richness makes this a quaffable food wine of substance and class.

Valpolicella Classico, Viviani 1997 12 D

Valpolicella Ripasso Viviani 1994 14 E

Gorgeously scrumptious fruit.

Vigna Flaminio Brindisi Vallone 1995

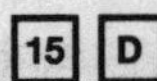

Rampant richness and ripeness here. Wonderful vibrant fruit.

ITALIAN WINE WHITE

La Piazza Trebbiano 1998

Good vegetal touches to clean fruit which only pales a touch on the finish.

Le Rime Pinot Grigio/Chardonnay 1998

Le Vigne Sicilian Chardonnay 1998

The idea that Sicily could turn out so rich and elegant a chardonnay would have been laughable a few years ago.

Soave Classico Pra 1997

Expensive, if highly drinkable.

LEBANESE WINE RED

Hochar Red 1995

Raisiny and ripe, touch old hat.

NEW ZEALAND WINE — WHITE

Jackson Estate Riesling 1998 13.5 D

Don't like the finish for seven quid.

Lincoln Chardonnay 1998 13.5 D

Fails on the finish, a touch, at this price.

Vavasour Sauvignon Blanc 1997 14 E

Old-style herbaceous Kiwi fruit.

PORTUGUESE WINE — RED

Alfrocheiro Preto Dao 1996 10 F

Sally, a word: twelve quid is too much for sweet fruit juice like this (okay, so that's eleven words – that's what a bargain is).

Alta Mesa Red 1998 15 B

A deliciously fresh and cherry-ripe glugging wine.

Bela Fonte Baga 1998 16 C

From the great '98 vintage; drink it before spring 2000. The wine has lovely immediacy and rapid, fine tannins. It's immensely food friendly.

Dao Dom Ferraz 1997 16.5 C

Fabulous tufted texture and soft, ripe, curvaceous fruit. It really wraps itself round the taste buds. Quite gorgeously quaffable and delicious.

Espiga 1998 15.5 C

Very ripe but controlled. Then the exuberance of the fruit is not OTT but, in the end, tantalising.

Foral Douro Tinto 1996 13 B

Jose Neiva Oak Aged Red, Estremadura 1996 13.5 B

Portada Red 1997 15 B

Ripe cherries, crisp apple, mature plums – about do for you? (Does for me.)

Quinta da Villa Freire Douro 1996 15 D

Very robust and firm – good tannins (beefy and bullish) – good rich finish. A rousing food wine.

Quinta das Setencostas 1998 16.5 C

From the great '98 vintage comes such texture, such richness, such satin-sided aplomb. Very elegant stuff.

Vinha Nova Vinho de Mesa 13.5 B

PORTUGUESE WINE WHITE

Bical Bela Fonte 1997 15 C

Delicious steely specimen. Hard as nails. Oysters will love it – they'll go down singing.

Portada Estremadura White 1997  

SOUTH AFRICAN WINE RED

Heldeberg Shiraz 1996 

Needs a robust lamb casserole to set it off. Or ripe cheeses.

Robertson Wide River Pinotage 1998 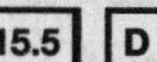

Very pinot in character – very little age. A fresh, aromatic, cherry/truffle wine of class and clout.

Spice Route Andrew's Hope Merlot/ Cabernet 1998 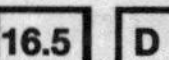

Quite superbly aromatic, textured and sunnily dispositioned fruit. Huge class and quaffability here.

Stormy Cape Cinsault/Shiraz 1998 

Wonderfully offensive stuff: dog-eared, cheroot-stained, rubber-necked, spicy fruit, utterly quaffable and food friendly. A storm in a glass.

SOUTH AFRICAN WINE WHITE

Altus Sauvignon Blanc 1998 

Nicely dry and fresh.

Jordan Chardonnay, Stellenbosch 1997 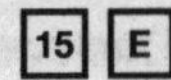

Big chewy white burgundy taste-alike. Great wine for chicken and posh seafood dishes.

Landema Falls 1998 

Spice Route Abbotsdale Colombard/ Chenin 1998 

A superb marriage of grapes. The result is restrained apricots and gooseberries allied to complex acids.

Welmoed Sauvignon Blanc 1998 

A terrific fish wine. Has grass and gaiety to its crisp, concentrated fruit.

SPANISH WINE — RED

Amezola de la Mora Rioja Crianza 1995 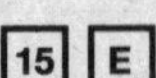

Creamy and super-rich. Needs food and candles, soft music and wily conversation.

Casa de la Vina Tempranillo, Valdepenas 1998 13 C

Casa Morena, Valdepenas NV 

Cries out for rich food. Curries will make it.

Glorieta Bodegas Piqueras 1998 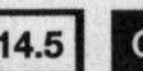

Very smoothly put together, rich plum fruit with a hint of pear and apple.

Guelbenzu Jardin Garnacha, Navarra 1996 15.5 D

Marius Reserva Bodegas Piqueras 1993

A mature, rich, sweet-edged but dry, raisiny wine for rich, spicy food.

Mas Collet, Capcanes Tarragona 1997

The best red at Booths. Stunning complexity – deft, daring, delicious – combining blackberries and plums, hint of raspberry, with superb tannic incisiveness. Wonderful wine for the money.

Mas Donis Tarragona 1998

Concentrated, full, complex, deep, thought-provoking fruit of style and vim. Great price for such wit.

Ochoa Tempranillo/Garnacha, Navarra 1997

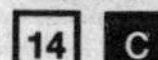

So dry and daintily finished.

Scraping the Barrel Tempranillo, Utiel-Requena NV 14.5 B

Simply Spanish Soft Red NV 9 A

Quite revolting.

Vina Alarba, Calatayud 1998

Brilliantly constructed of sympathetic boots, plums, celery, herbs, cherries and a hint of dry earth to the tannins. Robust, soft, rich. Terrific with food.

SPANISH WINE — WHITE

Castillo de Almansa 1998 16 C

Huge presence and charisma here: crisp, clean, collected, consummately dry and delicate.

Estrella Moscatel de Valencia 16 C

Either as a dessert wine or as a sweet, floral aperitif, this wine is brilliant. It is sunshine itself, packed into a bottle.

Santa Lucia Viura, Vino de la Tierra Manchuela 1998 14 B

Has a good form finish and crisp fruity attack.

Simply Spanish White NV 12 A

Rather flat on the finish. Needs to be blended with more rich fruit to give it extra wallop.

Vinos Sanz Rueda 1998 15.5 C

Gooseberries (ripe and ready), great acidity, firm, rich, dry finish.

USA WINE — RED

Redwood Trail Pinot Noir 1997 14 D

Cherries and soft raspberry-edged fruit with a hint of tannin. Better than a thousand Nuits St Georges.

Stonybrook Merlot 1997 16 D

Massively gluggable, gorgeous, textured, ripe, stylish and beautifully tailored, soft, leather fruit.

USA WINE

WHITE

Redwood Trail Chardonnay 1996 15.5 D

Stonybrook Chardonnay 1997 16 C

Beautifully tailored for a fiver. Has substance yet delicacy, style and gentility, finesse yet fullness. Terrific value.

FORTIFIED WINE

Amontillado, Booths 14 C

Amontillado del Puerto, Lustau 16 E

Sure, it smells mouldy and too ripe for comfort but imagine a glass, well chilled, with a bowl of almonds and an absorbing book. Great combination.

Banyuls Chapoutier 1996 (50cl) 16 E

A red wine of wonderful sweet richness. It's like liquid Christmas cake.

Churchill's White Port 13 E

Crusted Port Churchill, Bottled 1988, Booths 16 F

Lush, rich, utterly extravagant in its commitment to sheer pleasure.

Finest Reserve Port, Booths 14 E

Fino, Booths 14 C

Henriques & Henriques 5 year Old Madeira 15 F

Manzanilla, Booths 14.5 C

Niepoort LBV 1994 13 F

Sweet, and you can taste the alcohol.

Niepoort Ruby Port 13 E

Old East India Sherry, Lustau 16 E

Terrific molasses-rich fruit, gorgeous and sweet. Great with cakes and sweet biscuits.

Taylors Quinta de Vargellas Port 1986 15.5 G

SPARKLING WINE/CHAMPAGNE

Bollinger Grande Annee 1990 11 H

Bruno Paillard Champagne NV 15 G

Very accomplished example of the champagne blender's art.

Champagne Brossault Rosé 11.5 F

Champagne Fleury NV (organic) 17 G

A bio-dynamic masterpiece.

Champagne Gemillet NV 14 G

Very elegant and classically styled.

Champagne Paul Nivelle NV 14 E

Chapelle de Cray Brut Rosé 1993 (France) 13 C

Good spritzer base.

Cremant d'Alsace Cuvee Prestige (France) 13 E

Deutz Marlborough Cuvee (New Zealand) 13.5 F

Has a faintly fleshy finish.

Hunter's Miru Miru 1996 (New Zealand) 15 F

More elegant than a thousand Champagnes. More gentility in the fruit department, more style in the acid.

Palau Brut Cava NV 10 C

The first cava in some time I don't much care for.

Petillant de Listel, Traditional 12 A

Piper Heidsieck Brut Champagne 12 G

Seaview Rosé Brut 15 D

BUDGENS

Learning a new language.

The review of the Budgens' year used not to be a particularly time-consuming affair either to write or read. Nothing much seemed to happen at dear old Budgens. Not so any longer. I still wouldn't characterise Budgens as a boiling cauldron of capitalist enterprise but the retailer is on the move and has been for some time. The days when you could rely on little changing at Budgens from one year to the next have well and truly passed – it is having some successes.

But one innovation at Budgens which does not seem to have been a glittering triumph is its dabbling in the discount market. The retailer decided in 1998 to shut down its Freshsave operation and convert the eight stores to the Budgens name and format. The company's convenience store operation appears to have fared rather better.

Last December, Budgens unveiled the new look, created by the design consultancy, Made by Man, for its b2 convenience store. The company planned to roll out the new look throughout its chain of 56 convenience stores which were re-badged as b2 shortly after being acquired from 7-Eleven. Budgens is also going full steam ahead with its petrol station forecourt stores. In January, *Retail Week* magazine announced that the company was keen to expand its forecourt stores business. It then had 32 petrol station stores and hoped to reach its target of 40 stores by the end of the year. It was also reported that the company intended to launch at least 10 co-branded forecourt outlets in collaboration with Total during the next two years.

Co-branded? Re-badged? I didn't realise Budgens could feel at home with such hi-falutin' marketing terminology. Next will come the revelation that Budgens has become a predatory corporate raider to boot. (In fact the company was reportedly out to acquire the food distribution group, Booker, last year but decided to pull out.)

Being what retail analysts probably call a multi-format retailer actually has some interesting implications for the people behind the wine range at a company like Budgens. The company now has around 480 wines in its range, but obviously the smaller stores can only carry a small proportion of these. Wine buyer Tony Finnerty said earlier this year that the company was developing ranges specifically tailored to the different types of outlets. Mr Finnerty also reported in *The Grocer* magazine that wine sales were 23% up on last year largely thanks to merchandising developments, like the colour-coding of countries of origin, and promotional work.

Not that you will necessarily have to step inside a Budgens store to sample of the fruits of Mr Finnerty's labours. In July 1998, it was reported that Budgens was quietly conducting trials for a home shopping service and it was later reported that it planned to launch Budgens Direct in 1999. The company signalled its move into this business with the acquisition of Teleshop in September 1998. The scheme will be available via phone, fax and internet.

I suppose one should have expected that the pace of life was changing at Budgens when it was announced in *Marketing* just over a year ago that it had appointed a marketing director. Nothing remarkable in that you may say. But the promotion of marketing controller, Stephanie Rice, to the newly created position of marketing director means that there is a marketing post on the board at the retailer for the first time in its history. The retailer has more to shout about than it used to and now it has someone to do the shouting. The fact that it is a woman in the job cheers me immensely also. I have for a long time thought that in a business in which the aim is to sell things to women it makes sense to have a woman at the marketing helm – if I had my way I'd extend this feminine franchise to include many other controlling jobs but that's another story – and so Budgens, perhaps for the first time, is taking a lead. Certain other supermarkets still have a lot to learn where women are concerned.

Budgens Stores Limited
P O Box 9
Stonefield Way
Ruislip
Middlesex HA4 OJR
Tel: 0181 422 9511
Fax: 0181 422 1596

ARGENTINIAN WINE RED

Etchart Rio de Plata Tempranillo/Malbec 1998 13.5 C

Very dry and a touch mean . . . but with food?

ARGENTINIAN WINE WHITE

Etchart Rio de Plata Torrontes/Chardonnay 1998 12 C

Bit cosmetic.

La Fortuna Sauvignon Blanc 1998 13 C

Odd sauvignon which seems bitter and a little twisted. Rotten childhood, perhaps.

AUSTRALIAN WINE RED

Australian Red NV, Budgens 10 C

They laid the fruit out in the sun and the vultures pecked it dry.

Haselgrove Grenache 1997 12 D

Toffeed fruit of no delicacy and little tact. Good for marinating beef, I suppose, but any living tongue needs to be well insulated with rich food.

Penfolds Bin 389 Cabernet Shiraz 1995 15 F

Expensive muscle here. It's a bouncer of a wine: you don't get in without a hassle. Highly drinkable with food – spicy, rich, deep.

Tarvin Ridge Mataro/Grenache 1997 11 C

Wynns Coonawarra Shiraz 1996 16.5 D

Superbly classy and rich. Hints of mint cling to the deeply textured (denim and corduroy) fruit (plums, cherries and blackcurrants) and the sheer cheek of the fruit, its bounce yet gravitas, is terrific – the finish is syrup of figs.

AUSTRALIAN WINE WHITE

Australian White NV, Budgens 11 C

Oh dear. Budgens' first own-label Aussie and it's struggling, at a middle-weight price, to punch its weight.

Brown Brothers Dry Muscat 1997 15.5 C

Superb thirst-quencher and aperitif. It is genuinely dry and classy and richly refreshing.

Haselgrove Semillon 1998

Bit fat and frowsty.

Loxton Lunchtime Light (4%)

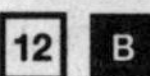

Very light for a miserable lunchtime.

Rawsons Retreat Bin 202 Riesling 1997

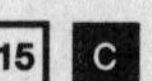

Richmond Grove Cowra Vineyard Chardonnay 1997

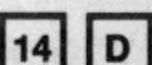

Fat and full of itself but has an edge of green fruit (touch woody in the background) which suggests useful food-matching opportunities.

Rosemount Estate Hunter Valley Chardonnay 1997

It's the lushly controlled fruit, that hint of creamy, woody vanilla on the finish, that establishes its silky class.

Rosemount Estate Semillon/Chardonnay 1997

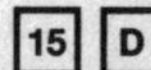

Tarvin Ridge Trebbiano 1996/1997

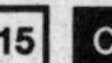

An utter curiosity, the 1996. Essential to have with food (anything from fish and chips to a monkfish casserole). It takes the dullest grape in Europe, lets it age (four years is late middle-age) yet provides sticky, dry fruit which will cling like liquid tentacles. The '97 is closely following on its heels.

White Pointer NV

A lot of labellous hooha about an indecisive wine.

CHILEAN WINE RED

Antu Mapu Merlot Reserva 1998 14 D

Plump, rounded, good polish to the leather and some dry riches on the finish.

Millaman Cabernet Malbec 1997 13 C

Millaman Merlot 1997 12 C

CHILEAN WINE WHITE

Antu Mapu Sauvignon Blanc 1998 12 C

Touch stick-in-the-throat.

Vina Tarapaca Chardonnay 1997 16 C

A dry, wry wine of some substance and serious-minded demeanour – but the final fruity flourish is firm yet light-hearted. A classy wine.

CYPRIOT WINE RED

Keo Othello NV 10 C

FRENCH WINE RED

Abbaye St-Hilaire Coteaux Varois 1998 15 C

Soft, fruity, rich-edged, highly quaffable, lovely price. A great Budgens bargain.

Bourgogne Rouge Vienot 1996 12 D

Chateau Belvise Minervois 1997 14 C

Rich, hint of earth, cherry/plum finish. Needs food.

Chateau Belvize Minervois 1996 14 C

Classy, austere, touch posh, very good value red for roast meats, cheese and vegetables.

Chateau de Malijay Cotes du Rhones 1996 13.5 C

Bit austere and ragged on the finish.

Chateau Graulet Cotes de Blaye Bordeaux 1996 14 D

Claret, Budgens 13 B

Corbieres Chateau Saint-Louis 1997 13 C

Cotes du Rhones Villages Cuvee Reserve 1997 14 C

A rich and very dry roast meat wine.

Cotes Marmandais, Beaupuy 1996 13.5 C

Crozes-Hermitage Quinson 1997 

The wine inside the bottle seems almost as big a mess as the label outside.

Domaine Jean Fontaine Cairanne, Cotes du Rhone Villages 1995 

Superb balance and richness here: soft yet deep and dry, herby, scent of the hillsides, touch of earth – but overall terrific warm fruit.

Domaine Marguerite Cotes de Beaune Villages 1997 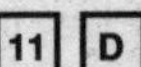

Not up to much for seven quid.

Domaine St Roch VdP de l'Aude 

Faugeres 1997 

Gargantua Cotes du Rhone 1997 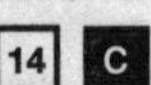

Not hugely Rabelaisian but drinkable, dry, hints of richness and a sound, firm finish.

Labretonie VdP de l'Agenais NV 

Brilliant value: has dryness and earthiness and thus immense food friendliness.

Le Haut Colombier VdP de la Drome NV 

Listel Cabernet Franc, VdP d'Oc 1998 

Terrific savoury fruit. Has spiced black cherries as its fruit. Brilliant stuff which goes with a range of foods and a variety of moods.

Pontet Saint-Bris St Emilion 1996 13.5 D

Premium Oaked Cabernet Franc/Syrah, Devereux NV 14 C

Very dry and rich hints of leather pepper. Needs food (a casserole).

Rouge de France Special Cuvee NV 10 B

FRENCH WINE WHITE

Blanc de Blancs Special Cuvee 13.5 B

Bordeaux Blanc Sec 1998 15 B

Bargain crisp – lettuce crisp, indeed – fruit.

Chablis Delaroche 1998 13.5 D

An oddly sunny Chablis, none of the steely typicity of the breed, but highly drinkable – if expensive.

Chardonnay VdP de l'Isle de Beaute 1997, Budgens 13.5 B

Chateau Lacroix Bordeaux 1997 13 C

Cotes du Marmandais Beaupuy NV 13 C

Domaine Argentier Cotes de Thau 1998 15 B

Deliciously subtle: hints of ripeness nicely subsumed under fresh, firm fruit.

Domaine Villeroy-Castellas Sauvignon 1998

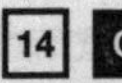

Hints of green gooseberry to a fresh clean finish. Good food wine.

James Herrick Chardonnay 1998

Cracking performer: elegant toasty fruit, firm balance of fresh acid (lemon-edged) and an overall politeness of manner and form. Has well-established credentials which the '98 vintage only amplifies.

Laroche Grande Cuvee Chardonnay VdP d'Oc 1997

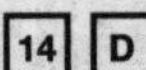

Macon-Ige les Cachettes 1997

Dry but very refreshing. The desert is dry, true, but it too is refreshing – as a break from routine. So is this wine.

Premium Oaked Chardonnay VdP d'Oc, Devereux NV

Warm, sunny fruit, hint of ripe, spicy melon. Delicious with food.

Rosaline Cotes du Marmandais Rosé 1998

GERMAN WINE WHITE

Flonheimer Adelberg Auslese 1997

Like licking a sugar-coated woolly jumper.

GREEK WINE — RED

Kourtaki Vin de Crete Red 1997

C

GREEK WINE — WHITE

Kourtaki Vin de Crete White 1997 14 C

Something dry for Greek food that isn't Retsina? This deliciously nutty, dry wine is it. Suits all fish dishes.

Orino Spiropoulos Greek Dry White 1996 (organic) 14.5 C

Samos Vin Doux NV (half bottle) 16 B

Brilliant value here. A rich, oily, waxy, almost biscuity, honey drenched pudding wine for the solo hedonist (in the useful half bottle) to get stuck into – and stuck is the carefully chosen word – as he or she attacks a block of foie gras, a creme brulee with fresh blueberries, or simply a goat's cheese with a bunch of fresh grapes.

HUNGARIAN WINE — RED

Petofi's Castle Kekfrancos 1998 10 B

Uses the castle's stones rather than the grapes.

Spice Trail Zweigelt 1997 10 C 

Bit like stale soup.

HUNGARIAN WINE — WHITE

Spice Trail Irsai Oliver/Pinot Grigio 1998 13.5 C

Makes a not unpleasing aperitif.

ITALIAN WINE — RED

Avignonesi Vino Nobile de Montepulciano 1993 12 E

Merlot del Veneto Rocca NV 9 C

So spineless it can't walk.

Nexus Grave del Friuli San Simeone 1996 14 E

Primitivo Puglia Torrevento 1996 15.5 B

ITALIAN WINE — WHITE

Canaletto Chardonnay 1998 14 C

A lemon-rich wine of great appeal to mollusc eaters.

Colombara Soave Classico, Zenato 1997 16 C

Superbly cool class and sophistication here. Strikes the palate with huge style.

Frascati Superiore Casale del Grillo 1998 12 C

Marc Xero Chardonnay, Salento 1997 13 C

Has a screwcap! Delicious innovation. The fruit is somewhat less innovative.

Verdicchio dei Castelli di Jesi 1997 13 C

NEW ZEALAND WINE RED

Montana Cabernet Sauvignon/Merlot 1997 

Deliciously combative stuff. Really works its way across the taste buds with unstoppable tannins and rich leathery/blackcurrant fruit.

Waimanu Premium Dry Red 1996 12 C

NEW ZEALAND WINE WHITE

Waimanu Muller-Thurgau & Sauvignon Blanc 1998 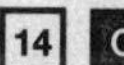

Getting better, this wine, with this vintage. More defined and refined.

PORTUGUESE WINE RED

Alta Mesa Red 1998 15 B

A deliciously fresh and cherry-ripe glugging wine.

Dao Dom Ferraz 1997 16.5 C

Fabulous tufted texture and soft, ripe, curvaceous fruit. It really wraps itself round the taste buds. Quite gorgeously quaffable and delicious.

SOUTH AFRICAN WINE RED

Cape Medium Fruity Red NV, Budgens 11 B

Like a very rich, undiluted soft drink with alcohol added.

Helderberg Cinsaut Shiraz 1996 13 C

SOUTH AFRICAN WINE WHITE

Cape White NV, Budgens 11 B

On the dull, uncertain-whether-to-be-dry-or-sweet side.

Clear Mountain Chenin Blanc NV 13.5 C

Helderberg Sauvignon Blanc 1997  

SPANISH WINE RED

Casa la Teja La Mancha Tempranillo 1998 14 B

Simple fruity (yet dry) slurping.

Castillo de Olleria NV 12 B

Fat and ear-clangingly raucous with fruit. Could be set as a savoury jelly to accompany game dishes.

Diego de Almagro Valdepenas 1995 

Very dry and arthritic – might be OK with a robust camel stew.

Don Ramon Campo de Borja 1996 

Brilliant with spicy food (curries etc).

Marques de Caro Merlot 1995 11 C

Palacio de la Vega Cabernet Sauvignon/ Tempranillo 1996 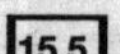 C

Mature, aromatic, very dry yet rich and deep, spicy (vegetal and a hint of pepper), and a lush yet controlled finish. A bargain Christmas lunch tipple.

Rioja Don Marino NV 10 C

Senorio de Sarria Crianza 1995 

Dry yet has rounded corners and finishes with some rich intent.

SPANISH WINE — WHITE

Cavas Hill Barrel Fermented Chardonnay NV 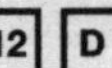

Very rich – unrelieved by enough acidity. Might go with fish curries, though.

Moscatel de Valencia Vittore 14.5 B

SWISS WINE — WHITE

Chasselas Romand 1996 10 C

UKRANIAN WINE — RED

Potemkin Bay Odessa Black NV 3 B

URUGUAYAN WINE — RED

Irurtia Nebbiolo 1997 12 C

URUGUAYAN WINE — WHITE

Irurtia Pinot Blanc 1997 12 C

USA WINE — RED

Angelo d'Angelo Rustica Sangiovese 1995 12 E

California Red NV, Budgens 13 C

Has some tannins and a little oomph. Bit stingy on the finish.

Glen Ellen Cabernet Sauvignon 1997 13 D

Strong and very cloying. To get involved with it is to experience a swathe of clotted fruit.

Stonegate Merlot 1995 10 F

Sutter Home Zinfandel 1995 13.5 C

USA WINE — WHITE

California White NV, Budgens 10 C

Immensely dull and meanly fruity. This is California? Tastes like Iceland.

Stonegate Chardonnay 1997 13.5 E

Very rich, tough nutty on the finish, very plump and chewily textured. Great with Thai fish cakes – but nine quid? Tough price, soft fruit.

FORTIFIED WINE

Amontillado Sherry, Budgens 14 C

Blandy's Dry Special Madeira NV 13 E

Manzanilla La Guita 13 C

Marsala Cremovo Vino Aromatizzato all'Uovo, Filipetti NV 15 C

Rozes LBV Port 1992 13.5 E

Rozes Ruby Port NV 13 D

Rozes Special Reserve Port NV 14 D

Warre's Warrior Port NV 13 E

SPARKLING WINE/CHAMPAGNE

Blanquette de Limoux Blanc de Blancs Divinaude 14 E

Brossault Rosé Champagne 11.5 F

Champagne Husson Rosé NV 11 G

Champagne Pierre Callot Blanc de Blancs Grand Cru Avize 12 G

Cremant de Bordeaux NV 13 D

Germain Brut Reserve Champagne 13 G

Lindauer Sparkling (New Zealand) 14.5 E

Expressive of nothing but great value for money and utterly charming sipping.

Mauler Sparkling Red Wine, Methode Champenoise NV (Switzerland) 10 E

They should really stick to yodelling.

Reservas Oro Cavas Hill Blanc de Blancs NV 11 D

Too sweet for me but any goodly soul who has received the Queen's telegram (are there such things any more – or does HM use Elizabeth-Mail?) might find it scrumptious.

Seppelt Salinger 1992 (Australia) 13 E

CO-OP (CWS & CRS)

All under one happy roof?

The idea that the appearance on TV of the spawn of Peter Stringfellow and someone who regularly sleeps with Jeremy Beadle should promote the family values of a retailer is a strange notion. But this was the thinking behind one of the year's most bizarre marketing innovations. The Co-operative Wholesale Society (CWS) in its first TV ad campaign for 20 years, decided rather than hire the celebrities themselves, they would feature their close relatives, namely Scott Stringfellow, Sue Beadle, wife of Jeremy, and Claire Rayner's daughter Amanda. I suppose the relatives came cheaper too, but then the last thing the Co-op needs to worry about is the suggestion that it sometimes does things on the cheap.

The Co-op also has something of a democratic ethos to foster and CWS had to act when its own consumer jury criticised misleading labelling on a number of its products last year. Among the products criticised was the Strawberry Cheesecake which was described as providing six to eight portions; it will now say six average portions. These consumer juries are clearly not to be messed with.

On the subject of labelling, the Co-op's wine range came under scrutiny. *Supermarketing* magazine reported in October 1998 that CWS was set to escape punishment for putting ingredients labelling on its own label wines even though this, amazingly, contravenes EU regulations. The 1997 Co-op Barrelaia Italian Red went on-shelf with ingredients such as potassium metabisulphate antioxidant, citric acid and acacia gum on its label.

The former Co-op wine buyer, Dr. Arabella Woodrow (now defected to Scottish merchant and importer Forth Wines), said at the time: 'We are trying very hard to look across all food and drink to provide honest labelling and acknowledge that the consumer has the right to know.' The Co-op consumer panel had supported extending this to wines and spirits. EU wine regulations are specific about what can be included on a wine label and no mention is made of ingredients. Neither is mention made of units of alcohol which have been included on Co-op labelling for years.

The departure of marathon running Arabella in December wasn't the only change to the Co-op wine buying team over the past year. In April, *Off Licence News* revealed the new CWS team. Paul Bastard, wine buyer, now heads up the department, Tara Fisher and Angus Clark completing the team. The new boss said at the time that beers, wines and spirits sales were up 22% in November/December 1998 in comparison with the previous year. Wine sales had risen by 11% compared with the 1997 festive period. Indeed, the CWS and CRS wine buying operations have now merged, so there will be no need for separate wine entries for each. This will make buying wine a simpler concept at Co-ops in the future since the majority of them will, I guess, be stockist of the same lines. We will see how this develops, as the two co-op movements get closer and closer together.

In March, the CWS wine department was clearly feeling like celebrating when it cut the price of Lanson Champagne after obtaining supplies via the grey market in the EU. Lanson Black Label was to be available in more than 800 Co-op stores at a third off the usual price, £13.32 versus £19.99. The retailer had previously made a similar move with Moet & Chandon which it said prompted the champagne house to reduce its wholesale price by £1.

For the legal eagles, this move did not contravene the 1998 European Court ruling on grey market-sourced branded goods which prevented retailers from sourcing products via the grey market outside the European Union. The Co-op considered this to be quite a coup because of the rumours (totally untrue and a fiction created by the French to stimulate demand) that champagne is in drastically short supply in advance of Millennium celebrations.

However, there appeared to be little cause for the popping of champagne corks at Co-operative Retail Services, by some measure the largest retailer in the Co-op movement. It has clearly been a difficult year for CRS which appears to be looking after neither pennies nor pounds with particular prudence. In April, *The Times* reported that CRS chairman, Peter Rowbotham, was to step down in recognition of a need for a change of direction at the co-operative high street operation. Later that month, *The Times* further reported that 3,000 jobs were to go at CRS as it merged its buying operation with the CWS-run Co-operative Retail Trading Group (CRTG) buying alliance and closed its 46 Living department stores and 10 Homeworld furniture stores.

By May, *The Grocer* trade magazine was suggesting that a CWS-CRS merger was once again on the cards. The last serious merger attempt had been in 1994 but news that CRS had joined the CRTG had fuelled rumours of a rapprochement. The merger was thought to be one way of fending off possible takeover bids by third parties for CWS. City pundits believed the US finance house, Babcock & Brown, was lining up a £2 billion move for CWS.

Also in the same issue, *The Grocer* examined the implications of CRS joining the CRTG. Its £1.2 billion sales brought the CRTGs buying power to £4.5 billion but it was the death knell for the CRS buying team in Rochdale and the CRS own label. Managers there were being given the chance to apply for jobs at the CRTG which is co-ordinated by the CWS in Manchester. I once tasted wine at the CRS's extravagant head office in Rochdale, marvelling at the OTTness of the interior design, and I believe the cost of this building contributed to the retailer's financial troubles.

Any merger would of course inevitably result in the formation of yet another set of initials for us to grapple with. The proliferation of these corporate monograms is one of the immutable laws of nature within the co-operative movement. In fact, co-operative groups are thought to be discussing the formation of the Co-operative Acronym Creation Consortium (CACC) to oversee future mergers.

The contrasting fortunes of the CWS and CRS were brought into focus in May 1999. The CWS reported that like-for-like sales rose by 4.2% in 1998 and in the year to date were up by 4.4%. Food operating profits in 1998 were £34 million, £1 million ahead of the previous year. A week later, the CRS revealed that its trading losses had doubled to £57.7 million. The results were attributed to poor trading in non-food. Food operating profits were said to have improved while food turnover was static at £1.2 billion. The CRS sold some stores to competitors to make ends meet (and doubtless caused fury at the CWS since they were presumably prime site locations from which the merged company would be considerably strengthened).

How could I conclude on such a downbeat note? I search for a good news item, Trevor Macdonald-style, and the trusty Co-op does not disappoint. I was pleased to learn that the Co-op had this year prevailed on the football pitch. The United Norwest Co-op football team won the final of the 1999 Reed Retail Cup against Waitrose Chichester (last year's winners) in a tense penalty shoot-out. The tournament is sponsored by Reed Retail which publishes the popular supermarket trade papers, *Supermarketing* and *Checkout.* Among those taking part were Budgens, Sainsbury's, Tesco and a team which Co-op Norwest was surely particularly glad not to be facing in that penalty shoot-out, Kwik Save.

On the more serious wine front, though I was initially appalled to be compelled to wear a jacket and tie (never the most congenial habiliments on a bicycle on a torrid July morning) in order to sample Mr Bastard's latest wines at the Lansdowne Club by Berkeley Square in London, it quickly became apparent that this venue was a congenial one (and one twentieth, so Mr Bastard revealed, of the cost of hiring a West End hotel room for a day's tasting). I do now and then wear a jacket and tie – a funeral five years ago, dinner at the German ambassador's this spring (all those old rieslings!) – but to be asked to tolerate this get-up to taste Co-op wines revealed to me the inverted snob *au fond* that I must be. In the event, I quickly divested myself of the strangulatory uniform once I had passed the Club reception's interrogatory gaze; and once a tasting glass found its way into my hand and I tasted Mr Bastard's latest offerings, I was a happy man indeed. As the entries which follow, many being the fruits of that tasting, will confirm.

Co-operative Wholesale Society Limited
PO Box 53
New Century House
Manchester M60 4ES
Tel: 0161 834 1212
Fax: 0161 834 4507

SEE STOP PRESS SECTION AT END OF BOOK FOR LAST-MINUTE ADDITIONS OR UPDATES TO THIS RETAILER'S RANGE.

ARGENTINIAN WINE RED

Argentine Malbec/Bonarda 1997, Co-op 15.5 B

Balbi Malbec 1998 13 C

Juicy.

Bright Brothers San Juan Reserve Shiraz 1997 15.5 D

Very jammy up-front but the tannins keep knocking at the door and, finally, as the wine quits the throat, they are admitted.

Elsa Barbera 1996 13 C

Marques de Grinon Diminio de Agrelo Malbec 1997 15.5 D

Lovely squashed fruit of richness with polished tannins.

Marques de Grinon Tempranillo 1997 16 C

The sheer elegance and restrained richness of this wine are superb.

Martins Merlot 1996 12 C

Mission Peak Argentine Red NV 5 B

The sample I tasted was horrible. Like licking a boot after a twenty mile forced march.

Weinert Malbec 1994 13 E

Very fleshy and maturely developed (middle-age spread) and dutifully serious on the taste buds, deep and rich. Touch too old? Perhaps. And nine quid is too much.

ARGENTINIAN WINE WHITE

Argentine Sauvignon/Chenin Blanc 1998 15 B

Scrumptious melon/lemon/pineapple and soft pear fruit salad which manages, incredibly, to be deeply refreshing and striking.

Elsa Chardonnay/Semillon 1996 14 C

Etchart Rio de Plata Torrontes 1997 13 C

Martins Chardonnay 1997 14.5 C

AUSTRALIAN WINE RED

Australian Cabernet Sauvignon 1997, Co-op 14 C

Juicy and ripe.

Barramundi Shiraz/Merlot 14 C

Hardys Cabernet Shiraz Merlot 1995 14.5 D

Jacaranda Hill Shiraz 1997, Co-op 13 C

Leasingham Cabernet Sauvignon/Malbec 1994 16 E

This is what the Field-Marshal's boots smell of: gravy, leather, rich polish etc. The fruit is not so militarily correct but it is organised, bold and full of ideas. It's soft rather than firm, deep, developed and deft on the finish, and immensely drinkable with food.

Oxford Landing Cabernet Sauvignon/Shiraz 1997 15.5 D

Delicious tobacco-scented fruit which though dry has a flowing, juicy finish to it. Well-behaved but has a hint of a dark past.

Oz Premium Australian Red NV  C

Fun bouncy fruit. Not at Co-op Convenience stores.

Rosemount Estate Grenache/Shiraz 1998  D

Yes, it's immensely juicy but fine tannins interrupt the flood – well in time.

AUSTRALIAN WINE WHITE

Bright Brothers Viognier Reserve 1998 16.5 C

Magnificent richness and texture here of depth and dainty-finishing acid/fruit. A plump, deftly-integrated apricot-fruited wine of style and wit. Fantastic price for such class. Co-op Superstores only.

Hardys Chardonnay Sauvignon Blanc 1997 16 D

Hardys Chardonnay Sauvignon Blanc 1998 14.5 D

Nutty, soft, rich, deftly double-whammied and most unhesitant to please.

Jacaranda Hill Semillon 1997 15 C

Fun slurping here with an immediacy of lushness which deceives the taste buds as it suddenly switches tack and becomes fresh and lithe.

Lindemans Bin 65 Chardonnay 1998 16 C

Supremely sure of itself, this well-established brand showing, in its '98 manifestation, what a great year this is for Aussie whites from the region (Hunter Valley). This has great hints of warm fruit balanced by complex crispness and acidity. A lovely under-a-fiver bobby dazzler.

Wildflower Ridge Chardonnay 1998 16 D

An unusual chardonnay with its peachiness and supple acidity of citricity and lychee freshness, and purists will find it eccentric, but it's lovely stuff. Co-op Superstores only.

BULGARIAN WINE RED

Plovdiv Cabernet Sauvignon Rubin 1996 15.5 B

Sliven Merlot/Pinot Noir NV 13.5 B

Good chilled.

BULGARIAN WINE — WHITE

Lyaskovets Chardonnay Reserve 1996 — 15 B

A keen, fresh chardonnay of lemonisity which manages to strike up a beautiful affinity with shellfish. Terrific price.

CHILEAN WINE — RED

Antares Merlot 1998 — 16 C

Touch of spice to the leather but it's the grip of the wine, the sheer effrontery of the texture, which wins it. Not at Convenience Stores.

Casa Lapostolle Merlot Cuvee Alexandre 1997 — 17.5 F

One of the world's most delicious merlots, it is also stonking good value and unusually health-giving. A remarkable performer (for heart and soul).

Chilean Cabernet Sauvignon, Curico Valley, Co-op — 15.5 C

Four Rivers Cabernet Sauvignon 1997 — 15.5 C

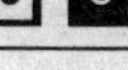

La Palma Cabernet Sauvignon 1997 — 17 C

Love it for its meaty richness, gently ruffled texture, hint of jam and captivating full-flow of elegant fruit as it finishes. Superb character of a wine. Not at Convenience Stores.

La Palma Merlot Gran Reserva 1997 16 E

Materially it's silk and velvet. Spiritually, it has the feel of midnight berries lightly crushed. A gorgeous wine for fireside conversation.

Old Vines Carignan 1998 14 C

Hint of spiciness to the jammy fruit. Not at Co-op Convenience stores.

Terramater Zinfandel Shiraz 1997 15.5 C

Unusual marriage and the partners fight a bit but this makes for some interesting breadth as well as depth to the fruit. Needs food.

Tierra del Rey Chilean Red NV 15 B

Vina Gracia Merlot 1998 16 C

Open, hearty, welcoming, rich, soft and leathery, this is an utterly luscious merlot of consummate quaffability.

Vina Gracia Relativo Pinot Noir 1997 16.5 E

More satisfyingly pinot in character – truffley, wild raspberryish and spicy – than a thousand Volnays. Great treat in store for pinot freaks here (and the rest of humanity). Superstores only.

CHILEAN WINE WHITE

Antares Sauvignon Blanc 1998 16 C

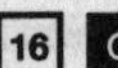

Fabulous value. Like an old-fashioned Sancerre (at one third of the price). Has impressive silky texture and mineralised undertones. Co-op Superstores only.

Four Rivers Chardonnay 1998

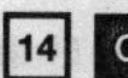

Frolics on the taste buds. Not a serious wine, but goes down well and winningly.

Tierra del Rey Chilean White NV

Vina Casablanca Chardonnay Sauvignon Blanc 1997

Has zip and vigour, serious depth, rich lingering fruit, a beautiful turn of litheness as it slides down the throat, and its overall confidence is world class. Available at Co-op Superstores.

Vina Gracia Temporal Chardonnay Reserva 1996

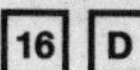

Delicious sherbert-lime fruit of vim and vigour. Has class, style, immense refreshing qualities and a hint of hay and wood as it descends. Subtle touches, perhaps, but it's a very good wine. Co-op Superstores only.

CYPRIOT WINE — RED

Island Vines 1998

Wonderfully juicy and lush yet has real quality tannins which give it a Gothic splendour.

Mountain Vines Reserve Cabernet Sauvignon & Maratheftiko 1997

C

Eagerness saved from a begging posture by the alert, savoury tannins. Very classy and individual. Superstores only.

CYPRIOT WINE WHITE

Island Vines White Wine 1998, Co-op 15.5 B

Goodness, from where did Cyprus conjure this up? It's got marvellous melon/lemon richness, a touch of apple and pineapple with the acidity, and the whole construct is balanced and bouncing with style.

ENGLISH WINE WHITE

Dart Valley Madeleine Angevine, Oak Aged, 1996, Co-op 11 C

FRENCH WINE RED

Bad Tempered Cyril Tempranillo/Syrah NV 14 C

Beaujolais Villages, Domaine Granjean 1996 12 C

Bergerac Rouge, Co-op 12 B

Bourgogne Pinot Noir, Cave de Buxy 1996 15 D

Terrific earthy tannins and characterful fruit. Great stuff here, really gripping. Not at Convenience Stores.

Bridge over the River Barrique 1997 13.5 D

A river of fruit in full flow which finishes sweetly. Not at Convenience Stores.

Chateau Fonfroide 1997 15.5 C

Tobacco to the fruit gives it charm, and the gentility of the tannin surprises, but it's the svelte texture which gets top billing.

Claret Bordeaux, Co-op 15 C

Corbieres Rouge NV 15 B

Real earth, herbs, hedgerow fruit and neatly rolled up and packed with personality. Terrific value.

Cotes du Luberon, Co-op 11 B

Cotes du Rhone, Co-op 13 B

Domaine des Salices Merlot VdP d'Oc 1996 14 C

Domaine les Combelles Minervois 1996 15.5 C

Hints of raspberry and plum to the gently ripe fruit which finishes with a surge of juicy richness. Superstores only.

Fitou, Co-op 13.5 C

Fleurie Pierre Leduc 1998 13.5 E

Highly drinkable, but too highly priced.

James Herrick Cuvee Simone 1997 16.5 C

Gorgeous, tobacco and plum aroma, invigoratingly rich, dry

fruit as the palate is struck, and a fine fulfilling finish. Classy and full of wit, this wine. Fantastic price, too.

La Baume Syrah 1997 15.5 C

Spiced plums to the lovely jam-ripe fruit which is saved from sloppy spreadability by the firm tannins. Not at Convenience Stores.

Louis Mousset Crozes Hermitage 1997 15 D

Excellent value for a usually more expensive wine. It has character, bite, balance and that hint of charcoal richness on the finish which marks the breed. Superstores only.

Minervois, Co-op 13 B

Morgon Domaine Brisson 1996 

Goodness, I really like it! Juicy, yes, but it has mature, soft tannins and a hint of cigar. Touch of wildness, too. Superstores only.

Oak Aged Claret NV 14 C

Oak? A touch, I guess. But it's the juice and the tannins. The Co-op is in the juice. Not at Convenience Stores.

Rivers Meet Cabernet Merlot, Bordeaux 1996 13.5 C

Vin de Pays d'Oc Cabernet Merlot NV 15 C

Lovely texture to the wine, rich and deep and persistent, and the fruit levels off nicely on the finish to provide a hint of herbs and earth. But it's fruity and soft overall. Grand little glugger.

Vin de Pays d'Oc Merlot NV 14.5 B

Not the classic leather sofa, this specimen – more the cat's whiskers. A feline wine of jammy freshness and furry flavour.

Vin de Pays d'Oc Syrah NV 14 B

Juicy with a hint of tobacco and wood.

Vin de Pays d'Oc Syrah/Malbec, Co-op (vegetarian) 13.5 C

Vin de Pays d'Oc Syrah/Malbec, Co-op (vegetarian) 14 C

Juicy yet characterful. Ripe yet not OTT, full yet with some delicacy of purpose.

Vin de Table Red, Co-op (1 litre) 13 C

FRENCH WINE WHITE

Alsace Gewurztraminer Producteurs A. Eguisheim 1997 16.5 D

What a delicious, rich, unpretentious, calm and collected gewurz we have here! Wonderful fruit (hints of lime, mango, lychees, rowanberry, papaya, guava – okay, only kidding) but it is faintly spicy and rosy rich. Superstores only.

Angels View Gros Marseng/Chardonnay, VdP des Cotes de Gascogne 1997 16 C

Terrific marriage of the uncouth gros marseng with the hip international chardonnay. It's an elegant, individual wine of substance and wit combining the raw, almost spicy gooseberry of one grape and the rich melon of the other.

Blanc de Blancs Dry White, Co-op 8 B

Bordeaux Sauvignon Blanc, Co-op 13 B

Bourgogne Chardonnay Cave de Buxy 1996 14 D

Just about rates 14, even at six quid, because it has burgundian touches and makes a tasty change from the New World fatness of fruit and vegetal poverty. Superstores only.

Chardonnay VdP du Jardin Pierre Guery 1998 

Lemony and lightly lush, lilting and largely lovely. An L of a wine? Almost. Superstores only.

Chardonnay-Chenin Vegetarian NV, Co-op 

This wine is not made from grapes. It employs carrot tops, potatoes, kohlrabi and runner bean – or is it just my fancy? Not at Convenience Stores.

Chateau Pierrousselle Entre Deux Mers 1997 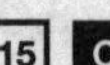

Clean and pebble-fresh, this is a marvellous fish wine of sterling texture and sappy fruit. Not at Convenience Stores.

Domaine des Perruches Vouvray 1997 

Vineyard of the budgies? Or the blabbermouths? Perruche translates either way depending which side of the street you stand. I stand firm at 14 points and the comment: 'Let it age three or four more years!'

James Herrick Chardonnay 1997 16 C

One of southern France's most accomplished, classically styled, bargain chardonnays.

La Baume Chardonnay VdP d'Oc 1997 15.5 C

Monbazillac Domaine du Haut-Rauly 1995 (half bottle) 14.5 C

Rose d'Anjou, Co-op 13.5 B

Sancerre Domaine Raimbault 1998 13 E

Alas, at eight quid this represents arguable value. If you must have Sancerre on your dinner table then I pity you, but, surely, taste the Co-op's Antares Chilean Sauvignon Blanc (qv) first. Not at Convenience Stores.

VdP d'Oc Sauvignon Blanc NV, Co-op 14 C

Vin de Pays d'Oc Chardonnay Chenin Blanc NV, Co-op 14.5 C

Modern, fresh, gently fruity, clean and excellent value. Boring testimonial? Perhaps, but chardonnay sometimes gets me that way.

Vin de Pays d'Oc Chardonnay NV, Co-op 13.5 C

Vin de Pays de l'Herault Blush 10 C

Vin de Pays des Cotes de Gascogne, Co-op 14.5 B

Limey fruit of considerable charm. £2.99 is still in there, fighting!

Vin de Pays des Cotes des Pyrenees Orientales, Co-op 14 B

Vin de Pays Sauvignon Blanc, Co-op 12 C

Wild Trout VdP d'Oc 1997 15.5 C

GERMAN WINE WHITE

Four Rs Rivaner/Riesling 1997, Co-op 12 C

Bit of a confused blend, it seems to me.

Hock Deutscher Tafelwein, Co-op 8 B

Kirchheimer Schwarzerde Beerenauslese 1998 (half bottle) 14 C

More like an auslese than a beerenauslese (for those to whom such distinctions matter – and they do), this wine has some decent honeyed fruit and sweet, unrotted character but it's too young yet for rich puddings. A light fruit flan would be the ideal partner. Superstores only.

Liebfraumilch, Co-op 10 B

Mosel Deutscher Tafelwein, Co-op 10 B

Ockfener Bockstein Riesling von Kesselstatt 1996 14 D

Reichsgraf von Kesselstatt Ockfener Bockstein Riesling 1996 17 D

Terrific price for a fully-charged, raring-to-go riesling of lively mineral acids, not a touch of honey or discernible sweetness, and rich length of persistence. A wine of studied charm, complexity and concentration. Not at Convenience Stores.

HUNGARIAN WINE RED

Chapel Hill Cabernet Sauvignon 1996 13.5 C

Hungarian Country Wine NV 13 B

Bit juicy for me.

HUNGARIAN WINE WHITE

Chapel Hill Irsai Oliver 1997 13.5 B

Hungarian Chardonnay 1998, Co-op 15 B

A lemon-scented and -fruited bargain. Great fun to quaff, good with salads and fish dishes. Not at Convenience Stores.

Hungarian White NV, Co-op 13.5 B

Rustic freshness and rawness. Good with fish and chips, though.

Hungaroo Pinot Gris 1996 13.5 C

ITALIAN WINE RED

Barrelaia Toscano 1997

Hints of sullen, bruised plums undertone the flavours of this curious wine. Needs a plate of rocket salad with parmesan shavings. Not at Convenience Stores.

Merlot Veneto NV

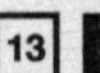

Though Puccini gets top billing on the label there is nothing Bohemian about the fruit. Not at Convenience Stores.

Puglia Primitivo-Sangiovese 1998

Unusually jammy for a Puglia wine, but the tannins, thank Bacchus, are there and warm the cockles.

Sicilian Red, Co-op

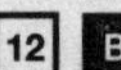

Trulli Primitivo 1997

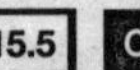

Spicy, warm, herbal, rich, yet has a stealth-of-foot deftness as it quits the throat. Generous quaffing here and food-friendliness.

Valpolicella, Co-op

ITALIAN WINE WHITE

Bianco di Custoza Vignagrande 1997 13.5 C

Chardonnay delle Venezie NV 13.5 C

Ornate in label, not quite in life.

Orvieto Secco 1998 15 C

As charming a food wine as this region produces: delicate yet chewy, fresh and fruity, balanced and effortlessly well-mannered.

Sicilian White, Co-op 13 B

Soave, Co-op 12 B

Trulli Chardonnay Salento 1998 16 C

Delicate progression of richness yet delicacy courses over the taste buds here, leaving one refreshed and panting for more. It would be easy to quaff this wine too quickly and miss its abundant charms as it trips, with variegated steps, down the throat.

MEXICAN WINE RED

Casa Madero 400 Cabernet Merlot 1997 14.5 C

Juicy and ripe initially, then it spreads like an oily puddle over the tongue, revealing some character.

MEXICAN WINE WHITE

Casa Madero 400 Chardonnay 1997 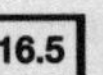 

A wine to startle your dinner guests as they grapple with the smoky, spicy depths and warmth of the fruit here. A cuddly, endearingly enveloping wine of immense versatility with food – from mint-scented lamb kebab to lobster thermidor. Not at Convenience Stores.

NEW ZEALAND WINE RED

Terrace View Cabernet Merlot 1996  

Juice with attitude. A nice touch of bristle shows through the baby soft fruit.

NEW ZEALAND WINE WHITE

Explorer's Vineyard Sauvignon Blanc 1998 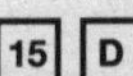

In a rich vein, this individualistic Kiwi. The clotted texture is full of interest. The fruit is full yet fresh to finish.

PORTUGUESE WINE RED

Portada Vinho Regional Estremadura 1996 15 C

Layers of fresh jam interleaved with tannins and pert acidity. Integrated, fresh, firm – a lot going for it. Not at Convenience Stores.

Portuguese Dao 1996, Co-op 13.5 C

Ramada Vinho Regional Estremadura 1998 13 B

Very juicy.

PORTUGUESE WINE WHITE

Portuguese Rose, Co-op 10 B

Ramada Vinho Regional Estremadura 1998 15.5 B

What amazingly good value this wine is. It has such classy acids and gentle fruit, you imagine it costs much more.

Vinho Verde, Co-op 12 B

ROMANIAN WINE RED

Romanian Prairie Merlot 1997, Co-op 14 B

Sahateni Barrel Matured Merlot 1995 14 C

SOUTH AFRICAN WINE RED

Arniston Bay Ruby Cabernet-Merlot 1998

Naked, unashamed juiciness with an echo of character.

Birdfield Shiraz 1998

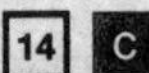

Hugely prolonged juiciness – the tannins take 20 seconds to impinge on the molars. Needs to be drunk with smoked warthog. Superstores only.

Cape Indaba Pinotage 1998

Touch too juicy for me, though I like the cheroot edge to the perfume. Superstores only.

Cape Ruby Cabernet, Oak Aged 1998

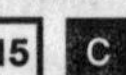

Richness here and some backbone and personality. Very well textured and warm.

Elephant Trail Cinsault/Merlot NV

Curious amalgam of tobacco, soft fruits, and some kind of exotic nut.

Fairview Cabernet Franc 1997

The grape in this manifestation is not like the Loire version, it being friendlier, no less spicy, but with fewer tannins, more polish to the texture, and a lovely, richly amalgamated flood of flavour on the finish. Superstores only.

Jacana Cabernet Sauvignon 1996 16 C

Rich, perfumed, gorgeously textured, rampant but not wild, elegant yet not simpering or reluctant. A terrific, forward wine of great class.

Jacana Merlot 1995 16.5 D

SOUTH AFRICAN WINE WHITE

Arniston Bay Chenin Chardonnay 1998  C

Extremely forward but not flashy. Has warmth and piles of soft fruit but manages to stay refreshing and engagingly plump without being obscenely Rubenesque.

Cape Chenin Blanc, Oak Aged 1998 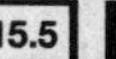 C

Lovely texture and lip-smacking richness of fruit which continues to finish with aplomb. The style is forward, yes, but it's not over-eager.

Cape French Oak Chardonnay 1999 15 C

This has more immediate grip than the '98.

Cape White, Co-op 12.5 B

Fairview Chardonnay 1996 15 D

Oak Village Sauvignon Blanc 1998 15 C

Delicious persistence of gentle melon and nutty fruit. Will go well with loads of fish dishes. Superstores only.

SPANISH WINE RED

Baron de Ley Rioja Reserva 1991 11 D

Like dilute port, raisiny and over the hill. Superstores only.

Berberana Rioja Tempranillo 1997 15.5 C

Classic vanilla edge (American wood) but it's not too dry or sulky but silken and fresh.

Campo Rojo, Carinena 14 B

Chestnut Gully Monastrell-Merlot 1997 14 C

Odd medley of flavours, and it is indeed nutty, but the tannins get there in the end after waiting for the ripe plums to shut up. Not at Convenience Stores.

Marino Tinto NV 14 B

Spanish Red NV, Co-op 10 B

Tempranillo Oak Aged NV 13 B

Bit like a cough syrup in taste if not in texture.

SPANISH WINE WHITE

Albacora Verdejo/Chardonnay 1996 13 C

Berberana Carta de Oro 1995 13 C

Berberana Carta de Oro Rioja Blanco 1994 13 C

Sticky, woody, musky and grouchy. Superstores only.

Spanish Dry NV, Co-op 10 B

Torres Vina Sol 1998 13 C

USA WINE RED

Blossom Hill Cabernet Sauvignon 1997 11 C

Not at Convenience Stores.

California Red, Co-op 13.5 B

Fetzer Valley Oaks Cabernet Sauvignon 1996 16.5 D

Warm, all-embracing, deep, broad, and most charmingly well-textured and ripe on the finish. Superstores only.

USA WINE WHITE

California Colombard, Co-op 13 B

Garnet Point Chardonnay-Chenin 1997 15.5 C

Oodles of flavour to open with, a touch of plump butter, then the fruit gets up steam and undefinable acids and blossoms get a look in, and then the whole construct, sighingly, descends with a leap of freshness. Superstores only.

SPARKLING WINE/CHAMPAGNE

Freixenet Cordon Negro NV (Spain) 13 D

Australian Quality Sparkling Wine 14 C

Light and delicate.

Blossom Hill NV (USA) 13 D

Not at Convenience Stores.

Brown Bros Pinot Noir/Chardonnay NV 14.5 E

Brut Sparkling Chardonnay NV (France) 13.5 C

De Bracieux Champagne NV 11 F

Not up to much. Bony and a touch raw.

Jacob's Creek Sparkling Chardonnay/Pinot Noir NV (Australia) 15 D

Great value.

Moscato Spumante, Co-op 14.5 C

Silver Ridge Sparkling Chardonnay Riesling NV 13.5 D

KWIK SAVE STORES LIMITED

Please refer to Somerfield/Kwik Save introduction on page 355.

ARGENTINIAN WINE RED

Maranon Malbec NV 13 B

AUSTRALIAN WINE RED

Australian Cabernet Shiraz 1998, Somerfield 14.5 C

Rollingly rich and frolicsome.

Australian Dry Red, Somerfield 15.5 C

Delicious! Delicious! Delicious! Did you get that? I said . . . oh, never mind.

AUSTRALIAN WINE WHITE

Australian Chardonnay 1998, Somerfield 16.5 C

Rich, smoky, developed, full and rich – hints of nut. Ripe but not too rampant. A lovely wine of great flavour.

Australian Dry White 1998, Somerfield 16 B

Superb value for money here, indeed astonishing: rich, fresh, classy, plump yet lissom, this is lovely wine of style and decisiveness.

Lindemans Bin 65 Chardonnay 1998 16 C

Supremely sure of itself, this well-established brand showing, in its '98 manifestation, what a great year this is for Aussie whites from the region (Hunter Valley). This has great hints of warm fruit balanced by complex crispness and acidity. A lovely under-a-fiver bobby dazzler.

Pelican Bay Medium Dry White 14 

BULGARIAN WINE RED

Bulgarian Cabernet Sauvignon 1996, Somerfield 13.5 B

Basic dry blackcurrant.

Domaine Boyar Lovico Suhindol Cabernet Sauvignon/Merlot 14.5 B

Domaine Boyar Reserve Gamza 1993 12 

BULGARIAN WINE WHITE

Bulgarian Country White, Somerfield 14 B

Fresh and lemony, simply appealing. Great with smoked fish.

Domaine Boyar Preslav Chardonnay/ Sauvignon Blanc 1996 16 B

Khan Krum Riesling-Dimiat NV 12 B

Suhindol Aligote Chardonnay Country White, Somerfield 14 B

Bit fresh: but fish will love its bony features.

CHILEAN WINE RED

Chilean Cabernet Sauvignon Vina La Rosa 1997, Somerfield  

A gorgeous bargain of not only consummate drinkability but also food matching possibilities. It is not only chocolate-rich with prime fruit but has a judicious dusting of fine tannins. The best red wine under a fiver in the UK? Well, I've not tasted anything better.

CHILEAN WINE WHITE

Chilean Chardonnay 1998, Somerfield 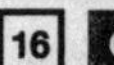 C

Woody complexity, hint of vegetality, persistence of rich fruit and clean acids – is this a bargain or what?

Chilean White 1998, Somerfield 15.5 B

Thunderingly tasty bargain on all fronts: fruit, balance with acidity, class and fresh finish.

FRENCH WINE — RED

Brouilly Les Celliers de Bellevue 1998 

Dull for the money. Beaujolais mostly is.

Cabernet Malbec VdP d'Oc 1997 

Hints at sweetness then turns deliciously dry and a touch cheroot-edged.

Cabernet Sauvignon VdP d'Oc NV, Somerfield 

Wonderful classy clods of earth, herbs, hedgerow fruits and all wrapped in a texture of crumpled velvet. Terrific character and class here.

Claret 1998, Somerfield 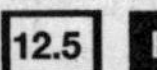

Very austere.

Corbieres Reserve Gravade 1996 

It is the savouriness, the dryness, the sheer texture of the humid fruit. It's gripping and very stylish indeed.

Corbieres Rouge Val d'Orbieu, Somerfield 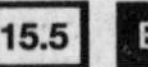

Terrific! Tasty, taut, tangy, tantalising! (Price suits to a T, too.)

Cotes du Rhone 1997 13 B

Cotes du Rhone Villages Lucien de Nobleus 1998 16 C

Terrific ripeness yet herby dryness here. Savoury, plump, layered, good rich tannins, this has lovely lingering texture and depth.

Les Oliviers VdT Francais Red NV 12 A

Bit like an anodyne cough-drop. I might marinate beef in it (or a pair of tired feet).

March Hare VdP d'Oc 1997 15.5 C

Lovely rich, dry fruit, herby, ripe and forward. Has developed richness and good tannin. Classy and civilised.

Merlot VdP d'Oc 1998, Somerfield 14.5 B

Most accomplished sense of balance between acid/fruit/tannins. Boring description? Yes, sorry.

Minervois Chateau la Reze 1996 16 B

Wonderful teeth-embracing tongue-curling, throat-charming fruit of style and wit. Fantastic value.

Morgon 1998 12.5 C

Rivers Meet Merlot/Cabernet, Bordeaux 1997 14 C

Very austere and proper – not pompous though.

Rouge de France, Selection Cuvee V E 13 B

Skylark Hill Merlot, VdP d'Oc 1997 15.5 B

Not a lot of leather, but a lot of love – terrific fruit here, soft yet dry, full yet elegant.

Skylark Hill Syrah VdP d'Oc 1997 15.5 B

Superb Cotes du Rhone taste-alike.

Skylark Hill Very Special Red VdP d'Oc 1997 14 B

St Didier VdP du Tarn 1997 15.5 B

Vin de Pays de l'Ardeche Red 1998, Somerfield 13 B

Dry and rustic.

FRENCH WINE WHITE

Blanc de France Vin de Table NV 15.5 B

What cheerful crispness and class! Astonishing . . .

Bordeaux Sauvignon Cuvee V E 1997 13.5 B

Chablis Domaine de Bouchots Cuvee Boissonneuse 1998 12.5 D

Has some clean-cut elegance.

Chardonnay en sol Oxfordien, Bourgogne 1998 14 D

Genuine white Burgundy. Hints of woodsmoke, vegetables, vineyard.

Chardonnay VdP du Jardin de la France 1998 14 C

Very fresh and knife-edge keen to finish. A wine for shellfish.

Chenin Blanc VdP du Jardin de la France 1997 15.5 A

Wonderfully crisp and cheerful. Delicious lemon edge. May have been replaced by the '98 vintage by the time this book appears (not tasted as yet).

Les Oliviers du Jardin Vin de Table NV 15.5 A

The best value white wine in the UK? Terrific, refreshing, delightfully refreshing edge.

Rivers Meet Sauvignon/Semillon, Bordeaux 1998 13 C

Very grassy undertone.

Rosé de France Selection Cuvee V E 12 B

Wild Trout VdP d'Oc 1997 15.5 C

Gorgeous ring-a-ding fruit combining freshness and fullness. Has elegance and bite.

GERMAN WINE — WHITE

Hock, Somerfield 12 B

Mix with Perrier and ice for a lovely summer spritzer (15.5 points).

St Ursula Devils Rock Riesling 1998 14 C

Go on – give it a try. Won't kill you. Though the Germans are killing themselves trying to make more dry, modern wines like this.

St Ursula Dry Riesling 1997 12 C

GREEK WINE RED

Mavrodaphne of Patras NV 14.5 C

As always, a real sweetie! Great with cakes and sweetmeats (and superb with Greek pastries).

GREEK WINE WHITE

Kourtakis Retsina NV 14 B

Brilliant value if you like, as I do, the musty tang of cricket bats.

HUNGARIAN WINE RED

Chapel Hill Merlot 1997 15.5 B

Stunning value for money – smells like a vintage Singer Le Mans tourer (back seats only).

HUNGARIAN WINE — WHITE

Hungarian Pinot Grigio, Tolna Region 1998

Utterly delicious back-garden thirst-quencher. Crisp in feel if not in finish, it has a delightful, subtle apricot edginess.

Rhine Riesling, Mor Region 1997

A light floral edge to dryish wine of no blemishes or huge complexity but simple sipping pleasure.

ITALIAN WINE — RED

Conti Serristori Chianti 1997

Lovely rich fruit, not typically Chianti-like (very hard baked) at first, but then the tannins cruise in. Excellent texture.

Gabbia d'Oro VdT Rosso 11 B

Merlot Venezie 1997 14 B

Montepulciano d'Abruzzo 1998, Somerfield 13 C

Montepulciano d'Abruzzo, Venier NV 14 B

Solicella, VdT Umbria NV 15 B

Terra Rossa Sangiovese 1997 16 B

Fantastic ripeness, clammy plums sweating richly all over the tannins, and the result is a gorgeous dry wine of great class.

Valpolicella Venier NV 13 B

ITALIAN WINE WHITE

Bianco di Puglia 1998, Somerfield 13.5 B

Gabbia d'Oro VdT Bianco 13 B

Pinot Grigio/Chardonnay Venezie 1997 15 B

Sicilian White 1998, Somerfield 14 B

Richly flavoured and thickly knitted in texture. A barbecued fish wine.

Soave 1998, Somerfield 14 B

Pity about the sad label but the fruit's in fine form. A dry wine of balance and food friendliness.

Soave Venier NV 13 B

Terra Bianca Trebbiano 1997 14 B

Villa Pani Frascati Superiore 1997 13 B

PORTUGUESE WINE RED

Alta Mesa Vinho Regional Estremadura 1998 13 B

Begins like cough syrup, ends sweetly. Some throats will love it.

Portuguese Red 1998, Somerfield 14 B

A light, tobacco-tinged cherry wine – best chilled.

Vila Regia 1995 15 B

PORTUGUESE WINE WHITE

Falua 1998 13.5 B

Pretty basic. Touch anodyne on the finish.

Portuguese White 1998, Somerfield 15 B

A proud fish and chips wine.

SOUTH AFRICAN WINE RED

Cape Red 1998, Somerfield 15 B

What a wonderful house red! It may bring the house down but you will be protected. This wine is an elixir – it wards off evil.

South African Cinsault Ruby Cabernet 1998, Somerfield 14 C

Very soft and juicy but hugely quaffable (chilled, too).

SOUTH AFRICAN WINE WHITE

South African Colombard 1998, Somerfield 14 C

Ripe melon and green lemon. A great fish wine is the result.

South African Dry White 1998, Somerfield 14 B

SPANISH WINE RED

d'Avalos Tempranillo 1997 15 B

Flamenco Red NV 11 B

Los Molinos Tempranillo, Valdepenas/Oak Aged 1993 15.5 B

Very ripe and tarry and delivers a lava-flow of warm, incandescent fruit.

Modernista Tempranillo 1997 16 B

Brilliant summer bargain for the barbecue! Has rich fluid fruit, developed and deep, and terrific tannins. Modern indeed!

Pergola Tempranillo, Manchuela 1998, Somerfield 15 C

Lovely dryness to what are some layers of savoury, rich fruit. Great pasta plonk.

Teja Tempranillo Cabernet 1997 14.5 B

SPANISH WINE WHITE

Muscatel de Valencia, Somerfield 

B

Hint of marmalade, lashings of honey and hint of strawberry jam. What a bargain pud wine this is. And its screwcap ensures it stays fresh and frisky.

USA WINE RED

E & J Gallo Cabernet Sauvignon 1997 13 C

Very juicy and a touch sweet.

E & J Gallo Ruby Cabernet 1997 11 C

USA WINE WHITE

E & J Gallo Chardonnay 1997 

C

Dull, dull, dull – and it's dull (overpriced, over-hyped, over-engineered and, worse, over here).

FORTIFIED WINE

Fino Luis Caballero, Somerfield 16.5 C

Gorgeous bone-dry fruit: saline, almondy, tea-leafy – it's sheer classic Spanish tippling. Great with grilled prawns fresh from the barbecue.

SPARKLING WINE/CHAMPAGNE

Cava Brut 1996 15 D

Has extra weight and concentration and the finish is enhanced as a result. Certainly bears comparison with much pricier bubblies.

Cava Brut NV, Somerfield 16 D

Elegant, not coarse, taut, wimpish or blowsy, but has hints of ripe fruit and a restrained edge. Fantastic value.

MARKS & SPENCER

As board directors get the chop, a new category of employee is invented: The Wine Developer.

Whatever tasty news I may be able to bring you about the wines at M&S is going to be of scant consolation to the men and women of this retailer's Baker Street London West End headquarters for whom this last year has been something of an annus horribilis. Anyone picking up the *FT* on 4th November 1998 and reading the headline 'M&S hit by clothing bloodbath' may have imagined some Tarantino-esque episode had taken place in women's hosiery. The actual truth was worse for the nation's most cherished retailer. Interim profits were down by 23% to £384 million and there was much worse to come six months later.

The negative press comment which M&S's boardroom shenanigans and clodhopping trading performance was eliciting at this time beggared belief. In fact, according to a PressWatch survey published later, M&S had more negative press coverage than any other UK company in the last three months of 1998. This was all the more staggering when one considers PressWatch's findings for 1997 when the media monitoring service said that M&S had received the largest number of positive articles.

The financial press were having a field-day over the succession of Sir Richard Greenbury, at that time both M&S's chairman and chief executive. A report in *The Times* in November suggested that Lord MacLaurin, the man who had put Tesco on the top of the heap but now having rather less success with English cricket, had been approached by a headhunter to take over as M&S chairman, but he was not interested in the job.

In the same month, there was an attempted boardroom coup with deputy chairman, Keith Oates, making a bid to wrest control from Sir Richard Greenbury. On 26th November, *The Thunderer* reported that Sir Richard had fought off an attempt to oust him, winning the backing of the board at a crisis meeting. Mr Oates' fate at that stage was not clear. The next day the retailer announced a boardroom re-shuffle naming Peter Salsbury as the new chief executive and revealing that Sir Richard was to retire as chairman earlier than previously expected. Mr Salsbury was apparently Greenbury's preferred successor. Keith Oates, quite possibly off Sir Richard's Christmas card list, was to take early retirement, the retailer said. Some analysts viewed the changes as not going far enough and M&S shares fell 6% on the news. The *Guardian*, not exactly sitting on the fence, described the new chief as shy, anonymous and unlikely to be the breath of fresh air that the company needs.

But it just would not be Marks & Spark's style (or should that now be Marks & DampSquib's style?) to appoint a whizzkid from outside. This is the company that promotes from within and rewards loyalty. What concerns the analysts, one supposes, is that when things start to go wrong – and they clearly have been going wrong – one is less likely to find that the answers lie with tried and trusted retainers for whom the M&S way has become a religion. I'm no management guru but I think they might have a point.

The M&S approach was questioned again in February when *Marketing* magazine revealed that the retailer had appointed James Benfield as its first marketing director for UK Retail. This was considered by many to be the appointment designed to rescue the beleaguered chain. Once again the man charged with taking the company out of the doldrums was no radical reformer but an M&S veteran through and through who had joined the company as a trainee in 1970. In the retailer's defence, the *Marketing* article quoted retail analyst Richard Hyman of Verdict Research saying that Mr Benfield was open-minded and very responsive to new marketing ideas. The article also said that M&S was looking to recruit other marketers from outside the company.

A few days later *The Times* revealed that M&S was cutting 31 top jobs, a cull implemented by the new chief executive. Among the casualties was John Sacher, the great grandson of M&S founder, Michael Marks, and the last member of the founding family to have been an executive director. David Sieff, another member of the family, remained in place as a non-executive director.

Just as M&S thought that things could get no worse it was reported in the *FT* that all five of M&S's stores in Istanbul were closed on 26th February after their merchandise was seized by a creditor of the company's Turkish franchise holder, Turk Petrol Holding. This seemed unconnected with the strife in the UK but was further evidence of that black cloud shadowing M&S wherever it went.

While enduring such a torrent of negative media coverage, M&S became embroiled in another somewhat bizarre battle over the press cuttings themselves. It was reported in *The Times* in November 1998 that the Newspaper Licensing Agency (NLA) was trying to make the retailer pay a licence fee for the photocopies of press cuttings which it distributes internally and had issued M&S with a writ to that effect.

Part of M&S's rebuttal in the article was the sentence 'We have never paid it' which doesn't sound like the most watertight of defences. I can't imagine the DVLA or TV Licensing being too impressed with that one. The M&S spokeswoman also said that the retailer challenged the NLA's right to charge a fee when the company only distributed the cuttings to senior management and said it planned a vigorous defence. In the light of the nature of press cuttings at that time, it was perhaps surprising that M&S had not already discontinued the practice on grounds of depressing staff morale.

As M&S grappled with its problems a number of reports emerged about how the retailer intended to drag itself out of its current difficulties. According to *The Sunday Times* in December 1998, the retailer had put the establishment of a loyalty scheme at the top of the agenda during a far-reaching review. In spite of the fact that there are 5 million M&S card accounts, they are used just for payment and not as loyalty cards, a rather baffling fact given the huge success of loyalty cards with other major retailers and their increasing importance to the likes of Tesco and Sainsbury's.

It was also revealed in *Supermarketing* in February that M&S was taking its first tentative steps towards internet shopping and had chosen wine as the product with which to pioneer cyber-shopping. The Winedirect scheme was launched in collaboration with BT.

The three-month trial was said to be a very tentative step by the retailer which has been more circumspect than most on the internet and home shopping fronts. Both home shopping and loyalty cards were areas where other retailers seemed to be stealing a march on the overly conservative M&S but a report in *The Sunday Times* in February suggested that the retailer was willing to be more radical than many had imagined. The paper revealed that M&S was considering carrying products under brands other than St Michael. The most likely scenario, according to the report, was that designer names, many of which are already featured anonymously in the St Michael range, would be incorporated with the St Michael brand such as Paul Smith at St Michael. Analysts said that they were encouraged that M&S was looking at everything at this difficult time, even such a sacred cow as the Saint.

Having issued a profit warning in January which had wiped £1.5 billion off the value of M&S shares, more bad financial news hit the retailer in March when it was informed that the credit rating agency, Moody's, had downgraded the retailer's credit rating from Triple A to Double A following a similar adjustment by Standard & Poors in January. In March, M&S

announced that it was doubling its advertising and marketing spend in the light of recent profit forecasts. Some £20 million would be spent on marketing and advertising in the next 12 months.

M&S again seemed to be considering initiatives which it had previously eschewed in order to respond to its manifest difficulties. In April, *Marketing* reported that M&S was to divide its 291-store chain into different formats, possibly with different names, in an attempt to reverse the slide in its trading performance. The retailer said it was too early to say whether they would take different names along the lines of Tesco Metro and the like but from next spring it would be aiming to differentiate different formats, such as city centre sites.

Most controversially of all, M&S turned its attention to its smalls. And the most established purveyor of lingerie in the country was not just thinking about changing its undies. In underwear terms, the retailer was supping with the devil. In May, *Retail Week* reported that the retailer had brought in lingerie designer, Agent Provocateur, in a bid to re-vamp its women's underwear range. The provocative company's founder, Joseph Corre, son of Vivienne Westwood, has courted controversy with criticism of the sterile environments of some retailers' lingerie departments. Famously, during London Fashion Week in 1995, Agent Provocateur models had paraded outside the show with banners bearing slogans including 'More S&M, Less M&S'.

In May, it was being predicted that M&S's profits for the year would fall to between £625 million and £675 million, compared to £1.3 billion the year before. This prediction turned out to be correct, prompting further negative media comment. However, to this less-than-qualified observer, by the later summer of '99 M&S seemed to be hitting back. The fashion show which heralded the new 1999/2000 clothing collection was considered a great success and Laura Craik, fashion editor of my own newspaper (yep, I know it seems surprising that the *Guardian* has such an individual but the newspaper, years ago now, made deeper and faster changes than any retailer) reported that 'recent charges of frumpiness could soon be a distant memory' and that the menswear collection 'should be a hit'. As I write this, I note that I can look down on a £20 pair of M&S green sneakers, a £10 pair of M&S blue shorts, and a tee-shirt bought in a M&S sale for £8. Hopefully, my fashion budget will not now require upwards revision in order to remain a M&S customer.

The wine department, run by Chris Murphy and Jane Kay, also ended the summer on a high note when a huge redesign programme was announced for the top 200 branches. A spokesman, quoted in the new trade magazine *Harpers Retail*, said 'Although supermarkets have done a lot to demystify wine, people are still intimidated and confused as to what wine to buy. We want to make the process of choosing wine as easy as possible but still keep it a special and exciting experience.' Tasting counters will be introduced, easy-to-read guides will be made available, and M&S will recruit so-called 'Wine Sales Developers' who will be on hand to provide advice. The spokesman, commenting on the nature of these non-wine experts, continued 'The new recruits will be very good at assessing people – to quickly understand what sort of service they need.' Think about that statement. Does it make any sense? How can a non-expert help somebody except to point where the red wines are and where the white wines hang out? *Superplonk* will investigate further and report back.

We could be in for some amusing times amongst M&S wine shelves which have long been, in design and layout terms, the dullest and most perfunctorily organised of any supermarket's. I have never considered that the organisation of these shelves remotely matched the flair and expertise which lies behind the wines.

Perhaps Chris and Jane will now get the public arena for their wares that their buying, blending, and tasting skills deserve (try the Chilean Casa Leona Merlot and taste what I mean). Strengths are certainly the Chilean range, pricey but superb Chablis, inexpensive southern French reds and whites (including a marvellous viognier), some terrific screw-capped Italian wines, excellent Aussie whites (less consistency with the reds), touch dull New Zealand wines (one chardonnay apart), and some largely uninteresting South Africans and Californians where more work, and softer pricing, is necessary. It is not a vast range of wines compared to the monster range at Tesco, say, but even so the coverage is broad considering there are only two buyers – perhaps the range weaknesses cited above are due to this stretching of resources. On the whole, one is tempted to remark that the nearer to Baker Street Chris and Jane can source a wine, the more accomplished it seems to be (Chile, disproof of this temptation, being the notable exception). Both of them are never happier, it seems to me, as when they are in France chattering away in a language they are at home in. With their fluency of fruit, many of those southern French reds are ample proof of this linguistic fluency.

Marks & Spencer
Michael House
57 Baker Street
London W1A 1DN
Tel: 0171 935 4422
Fax: 0171 487 2679

Bin 201 Shiraz Cabernet 1998 13.5 C

Very juicy.

Bin 252 Shiraz Malbec 1998 14 C

Nicely tarry and dry with a jammy undertone.

Bin 312 Shiraz Merlot Ruby Cabernet 1998 13.5 C

Very sweet and juicy.

HoneyTree Reserve Pinot Noir 1998 13 E

Has some good tannins and I'd rate it higher if it was £3.99 and merely said it was Oz Red.

HoneyTree Shiraz Cabernet 1999 15.5 D

Touches of jam to what is, in the final showdown in the throat, a delicate wine of layered complications: blackcurrants, plums, touch of spice, tannins etc.

HoneyTree Shiraz Reserve 1998 14 E

Some tightness to the fruit here. It doesn't slop all over the place – like blackberries in a bucket.

South East Australian Cabernet Shiraz 1999 13.5 C

Very blackcurrant-jammy.

South East Australian Merlot 1999 13.5 C

Very juicy and, lovely oxymoron!, on the finish it's positively anodyne.

South East Australian Shiraz 1999

I don't admire overmuch the fruit pie, baked and warm, of this urgent-to-please wine.

Vasarelli McLaren Vale Cabernet Sauvignon 1994

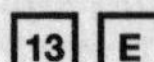

Absurd price.

Vine Vale Cabernet Shiraz 1995

AUSTRALIAN WINE WHITE

Australian Chardonnay 1998

Unusually elegant Aussie under four quid. It's dry, plump, rich, very friendly and rather demure but it's such remarkable value.

Australian Dry White 1998

Not white and not especially dry.

Bin 109 South Eastern Australian Chardonnay 1998

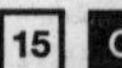

Unusual Aussie richness tempered by some exotic acids to which I cannot put a name. Delicious texture and tension.

Bin 266 Semillon Chardonnay 1998 16 C

Superb blend of grapes presenting ripeness with freshness and dryness. Impressive concentration of fruit. Has ambition and accuracy. It seems to know exactly what it is doing.

Bin 381 Semillon 1998  C

I see no reason not to declare this a masterpiece – when smoked salmon is on the plate.

Haan Barossa Valley Semillon 1997 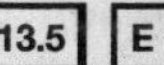

HoneyTree Reserve Chardonnay 1998 

Expensive for its hard-nose of freshness.

HoneyTree Semillon Chardonnay 1999 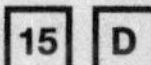

Delicious yet incisive. Has lemon scented and fruited flavours, excellent balance, and the finish strides out – no fading.

Lindemans Bin 65 Chardonnay 1998  

Supremely sure of itself, this well-established brand showing, in its '98 manifestation, what a great year this is for Aussie whites from the region (Hunter Valley). This has great hints of warm fruit balanced by complex crispness and acidity. A lovely under-a-fiver bobby dazzler.

Unoaked Chardonnay 1998  C

So plump and purposeful. It's delightfully uncluttered and beautifully, fleshily fruity.

Vasarelli McLaren Vale Chardonnay 1997 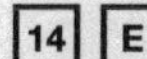

Lot of money.

Vine Vale Chardonnay, Barossa Valley 1996 

CHILEAN WINE RED

Casa Leona Cabernet Sauvignon 1999 16.5 C

Immensely delicious and richly classy savoury tannins swirling around with blackcurrants and plums and all things nice. Massively quaffable.

Casa Leona Merlot La Rosa 1999 

Goodness, it slips down like a trout across a fast-running stream. However, unlike the fish, the angler for sensations catches a lot: soft rich fruit, a hint of strawberry to the blackberries, and warm yet soft tannins.

Sierra Los Andes Merlot Cabernet 1998 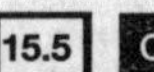

Chewy and accommodating, touch spicy, very richly textured and layered, and though a little restrained on the finish there is no mistaking the quality of the fruit.

Sierra Los Andes Merlot Cabernet Reserve 1998 

Rates the same as the non-reserve though there is a mite more substance to it. But two pounds' worth? Not quite.

CHILEAN WINE WHITE

Carmen Winemaker's Reserve Chardonnay, Casablanca Valley 1997 15 E

Rich and Aussie in style with a hint of California. Confused? Think how the wine feels.

Casa Leona Chardonnay 1999 15 C

Has some fine lingering flavours of lemon and melon, a very faint suggestion of spice, nicely wrought texture and a lingering finish.

Casa Leona Sauvignon Blanc La Rosa 1999 15.5 C

Utterly delicious, classically-styled sauvignon with clear, fresh fruit of concentration and lovely freshness. Beautiful texture.

Sierra Los Andes Chardonnay 1999 16 C

Superb warmth yet freshness in what is a very elegant, subtle wine. Has perfume, punch, prettiness and delicacy of fruit – yet the finish demands to be taken seriously (and further glasses).

Sierra Los Andes Chardonnay Reserve 1999 16 D

It has some woody chewiness to add to the smooth fruit and thus the vegetality of burgundy is an undertone. However, the richness of the fruit is pure Chilean on the finish which develops as it fades.

Sierra Los Andes Gewurztraminer 1999 16 C

Rich rose-petal perfume, sublimely well controlled rosy/melon/raspberry fruit and an excellent finish of substance and style. A worry for Alsace, this wine.

FRENCH WINE RED

Bin 80 Cotes de Malepere 1996 16 C

French country wine dragged deliriously into the late twentieth century! Fabulous quaffing wine, characterful, dry, rich, sunny, gently herby, which is also a terrific food wine.

Bordeaux Cordier 1998 15.5 C

Great value for claret lovers. Has real charcoal and pepper hints, good soft tannins and a classic finish. Like toasting the toes before a real coal fire, this wine brings back memories.

Cafe Red VdP de l'Herault 1998 14.5 C

Yes, it's juicy but the tannins help it get attractively past the finishing post. Middle-distance fruit, too.

Celebration Claret (Chateau Vigier Boise) 1998 13 D

Smooth and mildly characterful.

Chateau du Parc, Coteaux du Languedoc NV (organic) 14 C

Waitrose (qv) buy an excellent organic wine from the same estate (between Carcassonne and Narbonne). In its M&S manifestation it seems more controlled, sedate and even softer. But it's still a good, worthy wine.

Chateau Gressina 1998 12.5 C

Touch spineless, I felt.

Chateau les Aublines 1998 14.5 D

Very smooth and controlled. Not remotely austere for so young a claret – indeed, it's in fine, gluggable fettle and full of soft flavoured fruit.

Chateau Mathereau 1998 13 E

Highly drinkable but not at nigh on eight quid. It lacks a touch of class – and substance.

Classic Claret Chateau Cazeau 1998 13.5 C

Has a nice jammy overture but the climax seems a touch wan and wimpish.

Domaine Jeune Counoise 1998 13 C

Not as compelling as previous vintages.

Domaine St Pierre VdP de l'Herault 1998 13.5 B

Another juicy glugger but here there is a hint of tannin.

Gold Label Cabernet Sauvignon VdP d'Oc 1997 16 C

Superb jammy herbiness coated in thick rich tannin. Superb little cabernet which shames many a fancy claret.

Gold Label Cabernet Sauvignon/Merlot Barrique 1997 15.5 D

You think it's going to be another M&S sweetie whereupon a nice, tarry dollop of tannins saves the day.

Gold Label Merlot VdP d'Oc 1997 14 C

Nice chewy duskiness to the fruit.

Gold Label Pinot Noir, Domaines Virginies 1998 13.5 C

Curiously un-pinot like in its fruit, though the perfume has some subtle raspberry edging. Very gushing on the finish.

Gold Label Reserve Syrah Barrique 1997 13 D

Very ripe and juicy.

Gold Label Syrah 1998 13 C

Too rich and soppily sweet for me.

House Red VdP du Comte Tolosan 1998 12 B

Juicy!

La Tour du Prevot Cotes de Ventoux 1997 13 C

Getting too soft and juicy.

La Tour du Prevot Cuvee Speciale 1997 16 D

Very youthful, its character and depth have to be searched for. And time will help. It is ripe and responsive now, with classic Hermitage-like plumminess, but I think given a couple of years cellaring an 18-point wine might emerge. It has charm already and is rated thus, but the patient drinker (or, more accurately, non-drinker) may acquire an even greater treasure.

Margaux 1996 12 F

Merlot Cave de Rauzan 1998 14 C

Very unusual and juicy Bordeaux merlot with lingering tannins and cherries on the finish.

Millennium Margaux, Baron de Brane Cantenac 1995 12 G

Ho, hum . . .

Oak Aged Cave de Rauzan 1997 12 D

Not hugely taken with the raw woodiness which bookends the fruit – i.e. the smell and the finish overpower the volume in the middle.

Red Burgundy, Caves de Buxy 1997

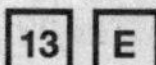

Goes a bit flat on the finish.

FRENCH WINE WHITE

Bourgogne Prestige Selection 1997

Calm, gently buttery and nutty, classic vegetal hints.

Cafe White VdP du Comte Tolosan 1998

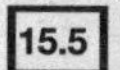

Superbly nutty edge to some faintly exotic fruiting. Utterly delicious controlled richness and fresh, pineapple acidity. Terrific modern winemaking.

Celebration Pudding Wine 1998 (half bottle)

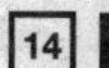

Delicious sipped with fresh fruit.

Celebration White Burgundy, Cave de Buxy 1997

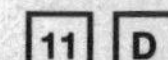

Lot of lemon, not a lot else.

Chablis 1996 14.5 E

Hints of asparagus and hay here – but finely wrought and balanced. A very clean, decent Chablis.

Chablis Grand Cru Grenouille 1993 17 G

Yes, well, twenty quid's a lot of loot but this is a very fine wine of perfect maturity, subtlety, complexity and class. This is chardonnay in its utterly remorseless, clean, classic mode.

Chablis Premier Cru 1994 15 F

Wonderful sourpuss! Classic wine. Really sharply focused and concentrated chardonnay fruit of great finesse.

Chardonnay Merlot Rosé 1998 13 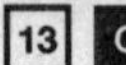

Odd specimen to find at M&S.

Cuvee de la Chapelle Muscadet Sevre et Maine 1998 16 

Brilliant! Muscadet as it should be: utterly sushi-knife sharp (not tart), crisp, clean, mineral edged and demurely fruity. The best Muscadet I've tasted in ten years.

Domaine Mandeville Chardonnay VdP d'Oc 1998 15.5 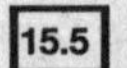

Starts fresh and clean – it's the new M&S white wine trademark – then it goes gently oily and smoothly rich. Delightful, dainty, delicious.

Domaine Mandeville Viognier VdP d'Oc 1998 16 

I've tasted Condrieus with less decisive gentility. A well-mannered apricot edge of fruit. Lovely stuff.

Gold Label Chardonnay Barrique 1998 15.5 D

Lovely controlled woodiness, subtle vegetality and calm, under-ripe melon fruit. Lovely burgundian style chardonnay.

Gold Label Chardonnay VdP d'Oc 1998 15.5 C

Superb haughtiness and high-minded fruit: it thinks it's a classic white burgundy.

Gold Label Rosé Syrah VdP d'Oc 1998 13 C

Very pear-drop fruity and adolescent.

Gold Label Sauvignon VdP d'Oc 1998 14 C

Very pert and properly po-faced sauvignon – that is to say, it's dry and very crisply turned out.

Millennium Chablis, La Chablisienne 1995 10 G

Absurd price for such ordinary fruit. Okay, there is an echo of decency to the texture, but . . .

Montbazillac Chateau Les Charens de Saint Mayne 1990 15 E

Lovely perfume of honeyed fruit (indefinable), gorgeous sticky texture and a rolling finish. Leaves behind the impression of baked pear tart.

Muscat de Rivesaltes 1974 (half bottle) 16 E

Delightful maturity here for a reasonable sum. The aroma is of Christmas pudding, the fruit is like creme brulee with honey, and the finish hints at toffeed melon. Great with pastry desserts (especially Greek or Lebanese sweetmeats).

Pouilly Fume 1998 15 E

Clean and fresh with a hint of fresh melon.

Vin de Pays du Gers 1998 14 B

Utterly flawlessly fresh and simply stainless.

ITALIAN WINE RED

Canfera 1996 16 E

Superb earthy balance here. Real class and complexity with marvellous warm tannins. A very accomplished wine indeed.

Chianti Classico 1997 13 E

Very jammy and super-ripe yet gently earthy underneath.

Ponte d'Oro Merlot del Veneto 1998 14.5 C

Pleasant, dry, cherry glugging. Delicious chilled with fish. Superb taint-free screwcap.

Ponte d'Oro Montepulciano d'Abruzzo 1998 16 C

Superb Italianate richness and dryness. And it's screwcapped. The wine's plummy and cherried, gently tannic and very taut. Lovely stuff.

Ponte d'Oro Sangiovese di Puglia 1998 15.5 C

Superbly fresh and bouncy yet fit and fleshy. Lovely texture and balance. A hugely gluggable wine of great charm. And it's screwcapped.

Reggiano Rosso Single Estate 1998 12 C

Very sweet and bubble-gum chewy.

Valpolicella Classico Single Estate 1998 13 C

Bit too juicy for me.

Vino Nobile di Montepulciano 1995 13.5 E

Supercharged dry ripeness.

ITALIAN WINE WHITE

Frascati Superiore Single Estate 1998 14.5 C

One of the most classy Frascatis I've tasted.

Orvieto Single Estate 1998 15 C

Delicious dryness yet gluggability here. Very accomplished sense of itself.

Ponte d'Oro Chardonnay du Puglia 1998 14.5 C

Delicious screw-cap here – so no nasty cork taint. A terrific fresh-edged chardonnay of easy drinkability and versatile food matchability. Brilliant with smoked fish.

Sauvignon Isonzo del Friuli Single Estate 1998 14.5 C

Curiously effective sauvignon with sticky rich fruit. Very good companion for rich fish dishes.

NEW ZEALAND WINE RED

Kaituna Hills Cabernet Merlot 1998 13 D

Kaituna Hills Reserve Cabernet/Merlot 1997 15.5 E

Nicely peppery and leathery as the nose enters the glass, the fruit quickly develops gently spicy cherry and plum undertones. The texture is fine (polished leather) and the fruit is firm and full.

NEW ZEALAND WINE WHITE

Kaituna Hills Gisborne Chardonnay 1998 14 D

Kaituna Hills Reserve Chardonnay 1998 15.5 E

Very delicate complexity presenting smoky melon fruit with a hint of nut and a suggestion of minerality. Impressively well cut and stitched together.

Kaituna Hills Sauvignon Blanc 1998 14 D

SOUTH AFRICAN WINE RED

Bellevue Estate 1996 16 D

This has improved magnificently in bottle since I first tasted it and is now a refined, fruity treat, offering vigour and flamboyance, style and elegance, well-tailored but very very gently raffish.

Bin 121 Merlot Ruby Cabernet 1998 15.5 C

Cape Reflections Cabernet Sauvignon Merlot 1995 12 E

Cheek! To ask a tenner for fruity juice!

Oaked Ruby Cabernet 1997 15 C

Rock Ridge Cabernet Sauvignon 1998 16.5 C

Magnificent bargain here. The tannins and fruit offer smelliness (tobacco-edged), savouriness and a hint of spice, and that luxurious texture of ruffled corduroy. A smashing wine – good enough to grace the poshest and most highly polished of dinner tables.

SOUTH AFRICAN WINE WHITE

Cape Reflections Chardonnay 1998 13.5 E

Finishes a touch ho-hum.

Perdeberg Sauvignon Blanc 1998 15.5 C

Rock Ridge Chardonnay 1998 14 C

USA WINE RED

Santa Monica Classic Red 1998 11 C

Like Ribena – without attitude.

Santa Monica Zinfandel 1998 10 C

Too much sulphur in the bottle I tasted. The fruit was overmuch juicy too.

USA WINE WHITE

Santa Monica Classic White 1998 

This is Californian? Well, well – or, rather . . .

Santa Monica Reserve Chardonnay 1998 

Bit reluctant to curtsey as it exits.

FORTIFIED WINE

Pale Dry Fino Sherry 

One of the best finos around, blended specifically to M&S's instructions, in which the bone dry salinity of classic fino has a background echo of gentle fruit so the result is a lingering pleasure, still very dry, of residual richness. A fino of exceptional style – and still a great wine for grilled prawns.

Vintage Character Port 15 D

SPARKLING WINE/CHAMPAGNE

Veuve Truffeau Colombard/Chardonnay Brut 13.5 C

Bluff Hill Sparkling Wine (New Zealand) 13 D

Cava Brut NV (Spain) 13.5 D

Cava Medium Dry NV (Spain) 12 D

Champagne de St Gall Blanc de Blancs NV 15 G

Classic.

Champagne de St Gall Brut NV 15 G

Best Champagne at M&S for the money.

Champagne de St Gall Vintage 1993 13 G

Champagne Desroches Non Vintage 13.5 G

Some dry, classic touches.

Champagne Orpale 1988 12 H

Silly price.

Champagne Oudinot Grand Cru 1993 13 G

Lot of money. Too much.

Gold Label Sparkling Chardonnay 1998 15 D

Delicious crispness and classic sparkling wine dryness. An excellent alternative to many champagnes.

Millennium Champagne Premier Cru 1990 15 G

A very finely ordered bubbly of class and distinction. It has a lovely biscuit aroma and a classic dry yet subtly rich finish.

Oudinot Brut Champagne 13 F

Sparkling Chardonnay Vin Mousseux de France NV 14 D

Vintage Cava 1994 15 E

More incisive than many a so-called great Champagne.

WM MORRISONS

Morrisons enters Banbury (and the 21st century).

My muckers in the north, Morrisons, claimed a couple of firsts during the past 12 months. The company's store in Bradford claimed to be the first supermarket to hold an art exhibition. 'Dreams and Promises' was an exhibition by local photographer, Ian Beesley, and included a seven-foot-tall portrait of Scunthorpe United's world famous striker, Ian Ormondroyd (said to be on Barcelona's shopping list at around £25 million, but frankly I think this is a fairy story). The other more significant first for Morrisons was the opening of its first store in the south-east (that funny part of Britain which was the only one, I'm proud to say, to elect Green Party MEPs). The retailer had been trumpeting its plans to move southwards for some time and the last 12 months have seen those plans come to fruition. Retail analysts in the City of London can no longer, sniffily, categorise this retailer as a northern supermarket chain.

But I have the sneaking suspicion that this is the last thing Morrisons really wants. Morrisons wants it to be acknowledged that it is expanding into new regions but it never wants analysts and critics to forget that it is the quintessential northern retailer, boasting solid merits of value for money, integrity and look-you-straight-in-the-eye honesty.

Last year was the company's centenary and auspiciously also saw the opening of its 100th store. But it was the location of the new stores which was receiving most attention. In October 1998, the *Independent* recorded the opening of Morrisons' new flagship 92,000 sq ft superstore in Erith with the headline 'Morrisons sails into the southern supermarket battle'. Morrisons had also opened a store in Banbury, a town which I believe is geographically at the very centre of England, in July.

In fact, in August to September 1998, there was a significant amount of noise in the press about Morrisons' moves south. The retailer has made much of its down-to-earth northern philosophy which it is now trying to bring to southerners. All it needs now is for some publication to reveal that Ken ay-by-gum I'll-go-to-the-bottom-of-my-stairs Morrison was in fact educated at Eton, Oxford and Sandhurst and is a member of the Garrick. No news on this as yet but he is, I notice, a CBE (which, if it doesn't stand for Chief British Entrepreneur, ought to). Incidentally, *The Grocer* magazine in October reported that the re-opening of the former CRS Pioneer store in Chingford in late September under the Morrisons fascia following its acquisition by the company had been a low-key affair accompanied by a leaflet drop in the area. Since the store had re-opened as a Morrisons, takings and customer numbers were up, store general manager Jim Toohey remarked in a low-key way.

This meant that the Chingford outlet was technically the retailer's first store in the south-east, opening just ahead of the much-trumpeted store in Erith. Still, I suppose the brand-spanking new store in Kent was a more sexy story than an old co-op in Chingford. Fancy that, somewhere within Morrisons' Wakefield HQ a spin doctor is at work. Chingford did eventually get a spin though. It was announced in March that the former co-op was to be the subject of a £3.5 million re-vamp.

Whether it was due to skilful spinning or simply sound commercial progress, Morrisons certainly seemed to be the darlings of the professional and financial media. In January, *The Grocer* ran the headline 'Morrisons' cheers; M&S tears' above an article reviewing Christmas performance. Food sales at Morrisons for the Christmas period jumped 12.5%. Like for like food sales were up 3.4% in the five weeks to January 3rd, while food sales in the five weeks to January 2nd at M&S had fallen by 1.6%.

And there was an added glow put on the company's drinks halo when Gary Cooper, manager of the beers, wines and spirits department at the Morrisons store in Hillsborough, won the 1998 Off Licence of the Year Award. *Off Licence News*, which sponsors the award, reported that the judging panel had been impressed by the high quality of the display at the branch and Gary's enthusiasm and commitment to customer service. He won a holiday of a lifetime courtesy of sponsors, Carlsberg, accompanied by Jilly Goolden (sorry, couldn't resist that last fabrication, though the holiday's genuine enough).

Having secured plaudits from *Off Licence News*, a couple of months later Morrisons was getting the thumbs up from the *Investors Chronicle* which commented positively on strong like-for-like sales growth. The magazine thought Morrisons was an attractive story with a bit of bid speculation built into the price. Back in September, *Supermarketing* had published other strong endorsements from City analysts about Morrisons.

Apart from the bit about bid speculation, that will have been music to the ears of Ken Morrison CBE (why isn't he made a Lord for heaven's sake? Maybe, like me, he considers the upper house as merely a place for fatuous fart-catchers and tedious time-servers). According to *The Grocer* in May, Morrisons claims to be the fastest growing supermarket chain in the country, with like-for-like sales growth running at 7.2% above last year. In the same article, Ken Morrison said that its market share had risen from 3.8% to 4.8% over the previous 12 months and scotched talk of any takeover.

On the wine front, Morrisons' buying department, represented by the addition of Fiona Smith to the established stalwart Stuart Purdie, continued to spread its wings and develop wines of the very latest kind. I refer to the new style own-label revolution. Tesco was the first to begin this with its own-label sherry back in 1969 but today we have moved into a more subtle own-label arena. We household wine buyers have retained our recessionary attitudes when buying wine, and bargains are widely hunted out, but we don't wish to be patronised by supermarkets to the extent of seeing their names on every bottle. Morrisons Cotes-du-Rhone for a casual midweek supper is fine but for the weekend, with more time to prepare food and experiment, or for entertaining, we want bottles which don't patronise us.

Hence, over the past year, a proliferation of wine ranges at supermarkets which though created specifically for the supermarket do not have the Name significantly emblazoned. Morrisons is the latest supermarket to join in this exciting new game. Earlier this year it introduced its own range of seven wines called Falcon Ridge – all Vin de Pays d'Ocs made by Australian Michael Goundrey at his Carcassone hideaway – and each offers fantastic value at £3.49.

In the *Guardian* in late spring I was able to report on these wines with enthusiasm. Chardonnay 1998 (15.5 points) is buttery with melon soft ripeness of fruit. Sauvignon Blanc 1997 (15.5 points) is more satisfying at this money than many a Sancerre at twice the price. Marsanne 1997 (14.5 points) is rich and hints at food-friendly stickiness. The reds are equally impressive. Cabernet Sauvignon 1997 (16.5 points) is quaffable yet complex, combining cassis richness with marvellous tannins. Syrah 1998 (16 points) presents strawberries, raspberries and damsons – well baked and warm plus meaty tannins. Merlot 1998 (16 points) has hints of ripe cherry and summer pudding but the tannins are so good and gorgeously rich that the overall effect is of dry, serious, high class fruit. And there is even a highly drinkable Rosé 1997 (14 points) which has cherry-fruited dryness and great versatility with food.

I include these wines in this introduction conscious that much of this range may not be alive once January 2000 itself comes round and that the '99 vintages will take until spring 2000 and onwards to arrive. At time of writing, however, the wines of the vintages above are selling like hotcakes but then it's late summer when I write this introduction whereas for the Morrisons wine entries themselves I am still sniffing, slurping and spitting in mid-September. But then that, if you will permit me a modest though factual gasconade, is what makes

Superplonk more up-to-date than any other published wine guide on earth.

Wm Morrison Supermarkets
Wakefield 41 Industrial Estate
Wakefield
W Yorks WF1 OXF
Tel: 01924 870000
Fax: 01934 921250

ALGERIAN WINE — RED

Coteaux de Tlemcen 1994 14.5 B

ARGENTINIAN WINE — RED

Balbi Barbaro 1997 16 E

A treat for rich game dishes. The fruit is packed with flavour – from raspberries to spiced prunes – and the tannins are electric.

Balbi Malbec 1998 13 C

Juicy.

Balbi Shiraz, Mendoza 1997 16 C

Starts babyish (and soft and lip-smackingly fruity) then goes dry, earthy and serious. Impactful stuff of charismatic charms.

Santa Julia Bonarda/Sangiovese 1998 13 C

Very juicy/savoury fruit. Might be okay chilled with rich fish dishes.

ARGENTINIAN WINE — WHITE

Rafael Estate Trebbiano 1998 10 B

Dullsville.

Rio de Plate Chardonnay 1997 13.5 C

AUSTRALIAN WINE RED

Barramundi Shiraz/Merlot NV 15.5 C

Unusually tobacco-edged fruit here, very savoury and ripe, and there's a hint of woodsmoke to the plummy depths of what is a hugely entertaining wine.

Castle Ridge Bin CR1 Red 1996 13 C

Corinda Ridge Cabernet/Merlot 1997 13.5 D

Hanging Rock Cabernet Merlot 1997 13 D

Hanging Rock Shiraz 1996 12.5 D

Bit ordinary on the fruit (though I like the tannins) for seven quid.

Hardys Cabernet Shiraz Merlot 1997 16 D

Bargain Aussie brew of bounce and flavour.

Lindemans Bin 45 Cabernet Sauvignon 1997 14.5 D

More correct than exciting but well formed and rich to finish. Good with food.

Rosemount Estate Shiraz 1998 14.5 E

In the Rosemount tradition of juice with an adult attitude. Totally quaffable.

AUSTRALIAN WINE WHITE

Banrock Station Chardonnay 1998 12 C

Like a boiled sweet without the sugar.

Barramundi Semillon/Chardonnay NV 16 C

Lovely oily fruit, hint of bellpepper and mango, and the whole thing is altogether more serious than the playful label suggests. A great wine to quaff or to match with oriental, European or South American meat and fish dishes.

Brown Brothers Chenin Blanc 1997 15 C

Delicious oriental food wine. Most individual and crisply rich.

Castle Ridge Bin CR4 Colombard Chardonnay 1997 13.5 C

Corinda Ridge Sauvignon/Semillon 1998 14 D

Cranswick Kidman Way Chardonnay 1998 15.5 C

Big, fat, rich, loads of warm personality and cracking with food.

Deakin Estate Chardonnay 1998 15 C

The rampant richness is tightly controlled yet satisfyingly well-developed on the finish. Splendid price for such class.

Deakin Estate Sauvignon Blanc 1998 14 C

Mineral tinge to the richness.

Hanging Rock Sauvignon Blanc 1998 13 D

Hardys Banrock Station Chenin Blanc/Chardonnay 1998 12.5 C

Very blowsy, fat and sticky rich. Odd fruit. Is it wine? Or jam?

Jacobs Creek Semillon/Chardonnay 1998 14 C

Old warhorse still good value and richly fruity (but balanced).

Lindemans Bin 65 Chardonnay 1998 16 C

Supremely sure of itself, this well-established brand showing, in its '98 manifestation, what a great year this is for Aussie whites from the region (Hunter Valley). This has great hints of warm fruit balanced by complex crispness and acidity. A lovely under-a-fiver bobby dazzler.

Penfolds Koonunga Hill Chardonnay 1998 16.5 D

What a great brand! Stunning richness and balanced, classy finish. If only white burgundians at three times the price could be this good.

Rosemount Estate Chardonnay 1997 16 D

Rich yet restrained, deep yet fathomable, turbulent yet affordable. This wine is packed with civilised incident.

BULGARIAN WINE RED

Boyar Bulgarian Gamza 1998 14 B

A bargain everyday glugger. Good with food, too.

Boyar Iambol Cabernet Sauvignon 1998 15 B

Brilliant dryness and wryness here. It seems so mature and serious yet it has great quaffability. However, it is a food wine.

Boyar Premium Oak Merlot 1997 13.5 C

Very juicy.

Bulgarian Reserve Merlot 1992 14 C

Hidden Valley Reserve Cabernet Sauvignon 1993 14 C

BULGARIAN WINE WHITE

Bulgarian Reserve Chardonnay 1995 15 C

Bulgarian Sauvignon Blanc 1996 14.5 B

CHILEAN WINE RED

Antares Merlot 1998

Touch of spice to the leather but it's the grip of the wine, the sheer effrontery of the texture, which wins it.

Castillo de Molina Reserve Cabernet Sauvignon 1996

A stunning cabernet with piles of rich tannic fruit and cassis/chocolate undertones. A marvellously fluent yet dry wine of massive charm, depth, complexity and lingering fruit.

Chilean Cabernet Sauvignon 1998, Morrisons

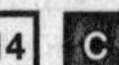

Bargain cab which takes you from nasal charm to full-throated cosy fruitiness.

Stowells Chilean Cabernet Merlot NV (3-litre box)

Brilliant wine box fruit! Has depth, tannicity, richness, balance and bite. Great stuff. Price bracket has been adjusted to the 75cl equivalent.

Undurraga Merlot 1998

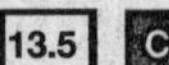

Villa Montes Cabernet Sauvignon 1998

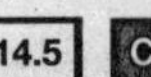

Hint of pepper to some ripe, rich vegetal fruit with gentle tannins.

Vina Gracia Cabernet Sauvignon 1997

As with the merlot, Vina Gracia makes beautifully soft and aromatically satisfying wines of huge drinkability.

Vina Gracia Merlot 1998 

Open, hearty, welcoming, rich, soft and leathery, this is an utterly luscious merlot of consummate quaffability.

CHILEAN WINE WHITE

35 Sur Sauvignon Blanc 1998 

Superb! The grassiness of the acidity and the richness of fruit, still classic dry sauvignon, makes for a wonderful crisp mouthful.

Antares Santa Carolina Chardonnay 1998 

Tingling rich fruit which remains balanced, sane, elegant and hugely slurpable.

Antu Mapu Reserva Rosé 1997 

Antu Mapu Sauvignon Blanc Reserve 1998 

Combines a sauvy NZ-style freshness with an Aussie-style hint of rich opulence. Lovely food wine.

Castillo de Molina Reserve Chardonnay 1997 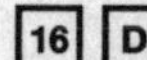

Luscious smoky richness, woodiness, softness and great balance. A lovely texture, aroma, solidity, finish and overall aplomb. Terrific value for money.

Chilean Sauvignon Blanc 1997 

Montes Alpha Chardonnay 1996 17.5 E

Chile's greatest burgundian smell and taste alike? As if! This is better than any Montrachet I've tasted for twenty years. Except, of course, the great names (Comte Lafon etc). So – do you spend nine quid on this or £40 on a Lafon? True, the wines are different in mood. The Chilean has more verve.

Santa Carolina Cabernet Sauvignon Rosé 1998 14 C

Has substance, texture, flavour and depth.

Stowells Chilean Sauvignon Blanc NV (3-litre box) 13 B

Almost good enough, but not quite. Price bracket is the 75cl equivalent.

Villa Montes Sauvignon Blanc 1997 14 C

Crisp concentrated fruit with a lovely mineral undertone.

ENGLISH WINE — WHITE

Three Choirs Estate Premium 1997 14 C

Possibly the most drinkable English wine.

FRENCH WINE — RED

Beaujolais NV 13 C

Beaujolais Villages 1998 10 C

Bouches du Rhone Merlot NV 15 B

Terrific bargain here. Great warmth of texture, savoury fruit and rich chewy tannins.

Chateau Cadillac Legourgues Bordeaux Superieur 1995 16.5 D

Superbly savoury tannins as ornate and complex as the gothic label. The fruit is tautologically blackcurranty and well spread and it packs a dry yet friendly fruity finish.

Chateau de Candale Haut Medoc 1996 15 E

Distinguished warmth. A most softly textured claret.

Chateau du Petit Thouars Touraine 1996 13.5 C

Touch sweet on the finish.

Chateau Jougrand St Chinian 1997 12 C

Odd aroma of ripe compost-fruited grapes.

Chateau Le Fage Bergerac 1996 14.5 C

Richness and dryness, scrubby fruit with good tannins.

Chateau Saint Galier Graves 1997 15.5 C

Perfectly rounded, savoury depth.

Chinon Domaine de Briancon 1997 16 C

What a bargain! Tobacco and wild raspberries with gorgeous

tannins, this is a classic Chinon of great wit and warmth, at a terrific price.

Claret, Morrisons 13 B

Coteaux du Languedoc NV 14.5 B

Lovely herby dryness and gentle, tannically coated richness. Great texture and savouriness.

Cotes de Luberon 1997 14 B

Cotes du Rhone NV 13 B

Cotes du Roussillon, Morrisons 15 B

Cotes du Ventoux La Pierre du Diable 1997 13 B

Falcon Ridge Cabernet Sauvignon, VdP d'Oc 1997 16.5 B

What staggeringly toothsome fruit here for the money. Quaffable yet complex, full yet dry, this combines cassis richness with marvellous tannins. A terrific cab.

Falcon Ridge Merlot 1998 16 B

Hint of ripe cherry and summer pudding but the tannins are so good and gorgeously rich the overall effect is of dry, serious, high class fruit. Huge charm.

Falcon Ridge Syrah 1998 16 B

Utterly resounding fruit – strawberries, raspberries and damsons – well baked and warm plus gentle meaty tannins. Overall, one of the most gluggable syrahs I've tasted yet it has the heft to handle robust food.

Fitou NV 13 C

Gigondas Chateau St Andre 1997 15 D

Big bonny bouncing fruit of lushly controlled meaty depth.

La Chasse du Pape Reserve Cotes du Rhone 1997 15.5 C

Amazing price for such classy texture and richly rounded, yet gently earthy, fruit. A lot of wine for not a lot of money.

La Passion VdP Vaucluse Red 1997 10 B

Le Pigeonnier Bergerac 1996 12 B

Minervois Cellier la Chouf NV 13 B

Rhone Valley Red 1998 14 B

Touch of bitter cherry to the sweet fruit. Hugely gluggable (and chillable).

Rhone Villages St Jean d'Ardieres 1996 14 C

Gently jammy, warmly textured, handsomely smoothly-shaved and fruity.

Sichel Medoc NV 13 D

St Emilion, Morrisons 13 C

Vacqueyras Domaine de Ameleraies 1998 14.5 D

Meaty and rich. Has some rippling tannins finely evolved.

Vin de Pays de l'Hauterive NV 12 B

Basic stuff and sweetish.

Winter Hill Red VdP de l'Aude 1997 15.5 B

FRENCH WINE WHITE

Bordeaux Blanc NV 14 B

Chablis La Lotte 1996 12 D

Chateau Le Fage Bergerac 1997 14 C

Dry and charmingly wry, underfruited perhaps, but with a fat, greasy mackerel from the grill – perfect.

Chateau Loupiac Gaudiet 1995 (50cl) 15.5 C

Superb toasty, sesame-seedy, honeyed sweetness. Great texture and ripeness and lovely complexity. A great wine for sweet pastries.

Domaine du Rey VdP Gascogne 1998 13 C

Escoudou VdP de l'Herault Blanc 1997 13.5 A

Falcon Ridge Chardonnay, VdP d'Oc 1998 15.5 B

Fantastic value: real smoky, buttery, melon soft ripeness of fruit, gentle acidity, and thus a strident, dry yet rich finish. Terrific.

Falcon Ridge Marsanne, VdP d'Oc 1997 14.5 B

The least convincing of the Falcon Ridge wines, made for Morrisons by Michael Goundrey (a benign Aussie), but still terrific value for such accommodating fruit. I suspect further vintages of this grape will improve hugely.

Falcon Ridge Rosé VdP d'Oc 1997 14 B

Delicious cherry-fruited rosé of dryness and style.

Falcon Ridge Sauvignon Blanc, VdP d'Oc 1997 15.5 B

Superb tenseness between fruit and acidity makes for an elegant sauvignon more satisfying at this money than many a Sancerre at twice the price.

Gewurztraminer Preiss-Zimmer 1998 14.5 D

Soft, gently spicy, restrained richness, and brilliant with Peking duck.

Ginestet Oaked Bordeaux 1997 14 C

Rather classy in a quiet way. Has touches of le vrai Bordeaux blanc: dry, gently pebbly and vegetal.

Haut Poitou Sauvignon Blanc NV 14 B

Interesting fish wine: nice fat grass-fed grapes, well chewed, make for a chewy, edgy wine.

James Herrick Chardonnay 1997 15 C

One of southern France's most accomplished, classically styled, bargain chardonnays.

La Passion VdP de Vaucluse 1997 14 B

Very floral and perky and full of fruit. Bargain tippling.

Le Pecher Viognier VdP Vaucluse 1998 14.5 C

Apricot fruited, good viognier always are, and perhaps it's a touch fat but it isn't blowsy and it would be great with Thai food.

'M' Muscadet Sevre et Maine 12 B

Macon Villages Teissedre 1998 13 C

Touch uncertain on the finish.

Pinot Blanc Preiss Zimmer 1998 15.5 C

Delicious ripe fruit, beautifully plump and rich.

Rhone Valley White 1998 14 B

Has some cheering fruit to it.

Rosé d'Anjou, Morrisons 14 B

Saint Veran Pierre Thomas 1997 14 D

Soft and stylish. A decent white burgundy at a decent price.

Sancerre la Renardiere 1998 15 E

One of the better Sancerres around. Drink it all by Christmas, though. That mineral tinge to the fruit won't last. The vintage, 1998, is exceptional.

Winter Hill White 1998 14 B

Some dry, lemony fruit in good form.

GERMAN WINE — WHITE

Bereich Bernkastel 1996 11 B

Devil's Rock Riesling Kabinett 1997 14 C

Good new vintage, maturing early. Crisp and clean.

Fire Mountain Riesling 1997 14 B

Brilliant price for such perky, crisp fruit.

Franz Reh Auslese 1997 14 C

Delicious honeyed aperitif – or try it as a spritzer ingredient.

Kendermanns Dry Riesling 1997 13 C

Klussterather St Michael Spatlese 1996 11.5 C

Kurt Darting Durkheimer Nonnengarten Weissburgunder Beerenauslese 1992 (half bottle) 16 C

Still young and will age for another dozen years. Lots of ripe acids here which subsume the honeyed sweetness, but with fresh fruits or fruit tarts this is a terrific partner.

'M' Mosel Light & Flinty 11 B

Wehlener Sonnenuhr Riesling Spatlese 1997 11 D

Very sweet and one-sided.

Zimmermann Bereich Bernkastel Rivaner 1997 10 B

Zimmermann Riesling NV 13 C

GREEK WINE RED

Boutari Xinomavro 1995 14 E

Mavrodaphne of Patras 14 C

HUNGARIAN WINE RED

Chapel Hill Pinot Noir 10 B

HUNGARIAN WINE WHITE

Chapel Hill Irsai Oliver 13.5 B

River Duna Chardonnay 1997 13 C

River Duna Gewurztraminer 1997 12 B

River Duna Pink Pinot Noir 1998  C

ITALIAN WINE — RED

Barbera Piemonte 1997 12 B

Casa di Monzi Merlot 1997 12 C

Chianti Colli Fiorentini Uggiano 1995 13.5 C

Dry and sweet.

Chianti Uggiano 1998 13 C

Bit austere.

Falconeri Cabernet Sauvignon di Toscana Uggiano 1995 13.5 F

A lovely tannic wine, touch of baked rich fruit, but thirteen quid takes a lot of thinking about. If the wine provided concomitant fruity complexity, in spite of its undoubted quality, I would rate it higher. But I can't.

La Casona Bardolina Classico 1996 14 C

Light cherry fruit with a hint of toffee.

La Quercie Montepulciano Uggiano 1996 14 C

Montepulciano d'Abruzzo 1997 15 B

Ritratti Merlot Trentino 1997 15 D

Lovely depth of tannins and richly textured fruit.

Segesta 1997 14 C

Light and very cheering. Has a dry edge.

Valpolicella NV 12 B

Vino Rosso di Puglia NV 10 B

Fruit juice.

ITALIAN WINE WHITE

Casa de Monzi Chardonnay 1997

Curiously dry and palate-stretching on the finish from an entrance which is bold and softly striking. Very convincing chardonnay.

Chardonnay di Puglia NV

Ponte Vecchio Oaked Soave 1997

Ritratti Pinot Grigio Trentino 1997

Delicious change from chardonnay. Here it isn't cheap but gamine and good-hearted, rich, deep and brilliant with food.

Segesta Italian White 1997

Elegant, rich, balanced, aromatic, brilliant value.

Soave NV

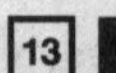

Verdicchio di Jesi Classico 1998 15 B

Great green label but nothing green about the ripe fruit. It plummets, it soars, it enriches the taste buds all the way to the rear of the throat.

MEXICAN WINE RED

L A Cetto Zinfandel 1997 13 C

Bit dry and dusty.

MOROCCAN WINE RED

Le Chameau Grenache Cinsault NV 11 B

Terribly terribly juicy.

NEW ZEALAND WINE WHITE

Canterbury House Chardonnay 1997 10 D

Dull.

Canterbury House Riesling 1997 11 D

Canterbury House Sauvignon Blanc 1997

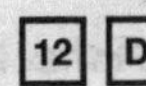

Grassy and ragged with it. No finely manicured lawn here.

Cooks Sauvignon Blanc, Marlborough 1998

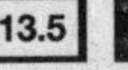

Always a bit too raw and grassy for me to rate it higher.

Montana Chardonnay, Marlborough 1998

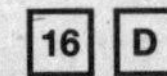

Utterly delicious. Superb fruit. Great balance. Commanding texture.

Montana Sauvignon Blanc 1998

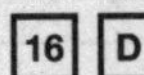

A rich vintage – fewer cold nights to build up acids – has resulted in Marlborough's sauvignons for '98 being fatter than normal, but there is good balancing acidity. A very elegant wine.

Whitecliff Sacred Hill Sauvignon Blanc 1997

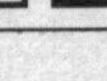

PORTUGUESE WINE — RED

Dao Meia Encosta 1996

PORTUGUESE WINE — WHITE

Sinfonia White Alentejo 1998

 C

Vinho Verde 10 B

ROMANIAN WINE RED

'M' Ideal with Friends Cabernet Sauvignon 1997 14 B

Nicely tannic and savoury. One's friends need to have dry palates and fruity dispositions.

Romanian Border Pinot Noir 1996 11 B

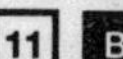

Odd – vanishes by the time it hits the throat.

Romanian Country Red 12 B

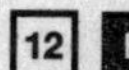
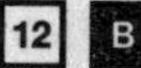

ROMANIAN WINE WHITE

Late Harvest Chardonnay 1987 (yes, 1987!) 13.5 C

Curious pastry-edged fruit-tart fruit. Will it accompany such a dessert? Hmm . . .

Romanian Classic Chardonnay 1997 12 B

Touch cabbagey.

Romanian Classic Pinot Gris 1998 13 B

Needs Thai spicy food.

SOUTH AFRICAN WINE RED

Backsberg Klein Babylonstoren 1996 13 E

A lot of money for such glum fruit.

Cathedral Cellars Merlot 1996 13 E

Bit juicy for eight quid.

Kleindal Pinotage 1997 15 C

Terrific value for meaty grills. The tannins are hair-raisingly rich and active.

Neil Joubert Cabernet Sauvignon 1997 13 C

Very soft and slippery – you only catch it if you concentrate hard.

South African Red NV 13 B

SOUTH AFRICAN WINE WHITE

Arniston Bay Chenin Chardonnay 1998 15.5 C

Extremely forward but not flashy. Has warmth and piles of soft fruit but manages to stay refreshing and engagingly plump without being obscenely Rubenesque.

Black Wood Chenin Blanc 1998 14.5 B

Great value fish wine. Dry and mineral-edged.

Dukesfield Chardonnay 1997 13.5 C

Fair Cape Chenin Blanc 1998 15.5 B

Superb individuality here: texture, richness, complexity and concentrated finish.

Fair Cape Sauvignon Blanc 1998 15 B

Excellent throughput of crisp fruit here.

Laborie Chardonnay 1997 15 C

Chewy food wine of nervosity yet rich intentions. Has touches of woody elegance even if the finish is a bit tremulous.

'M' South African White Crisp and Fruity 13.5 B

SPANISH WINE RED

Chateldon Cabernet Sauvignon Reserva 1994 15 C

Good Spanish Red 13.5 B

Remonte Crianza Cabernet Sauvignon, Navarra 1996 14.5 C

Juicy with hints of warm cheroot. Great glugging here.

Rio Rojo Tinto NV 14 B

A light and versatile red which can be drunk with casseroles or chilled to accommodate grilled fish.

Rioja NV, Morrisons 16 C

Great vanilla-edged ripeness and richness. Full, deep, balanced and deliciously fruity.

Stowells Tempranillo NV (3-litre box) 12.5 B

Price bracket has been adjusted to the 75cl equivalent.

Torres Sangre de Toro 1996 15.5 C

In great form, this old bull of a wine. Has firm tannins undercoating rich, gently jammy fruit. Hugely drinkable.

Vina Albali Gran Reserva 1991 16 D

Vanillary, spicy, nicely warmly textured and softly, savourily tannic. Has an almost yoghurt touch on the finish.

Vina Albali Tempranillo 1998 14.5 B

Lovely rounded plummy fruit.

SPANISH WINE WHITE

Torres Vina Sol 1998 13 C

Vina Albali Rosado 1998 12 B

Light as light can be.

USA WINE RED

Blossom Hill California Red NV 10 C

Extremely juicy and synthetic.

Californian Red NV 10 B

Very sticky and puerile.

Glen Ellen Proprietor's Reserve Zinfandel 1997 12 C

Slips down well, without leaving a huge impression.

Ironstone Shiraz 1996 13.5 D

Ironstone Vineyards Cabernet Franc 1996 15.5 D

Fleshy yet firm, controlled yet full of wise old franc fruit.

Murieta's Well, Livermore Valley 1995 14.5 F

Sutter Home Zinfandel 1996 13 C

Juicy.

Wente Reliz Creek Pinot Noir 1998 13.5 E

Very good up to the finish – it pales here.

USA WINE WHITE

Blossom Hill White Zinfandel Rosé 1997

Those who commit the heresy of making rosé from zinfandel grapes have only Hell to look forward to when hot irons will apply eternal torture.

Californian White NV

Gallo Turning Leaf Chardonnay 1997

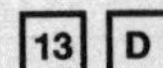

Bit blowsy on the finish.

Glen Ellen Chardonnay 1996

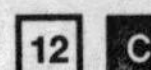

Very sticky and rich.

Ironstone Chardonnay 1997

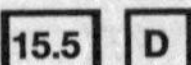

Lovely rich fruit, polished and buttery, and with great litheness. It's a muscular yet very spry wine of depth and decisiveness. Very good price.

Mission Hill Chardonnay Reserve 1996

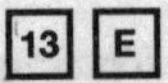

Drinkable and almost very fine. But lacks punch on the finish for a tenner and it isn't especially complex.

Sutter Home Chardonnay 1997

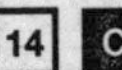

Under-a-fiver Cal chardonnay? When it's good, it's creamy and rich and great with food.

Talus Chardonnay 1995

Gorgeous rich, ripe fruit combining dry, sticky-toffee texture with huge dollops of melon and pear.

Wente Chenin Blanc, Le Blanc de Blanc 1997 15 C

Again, a Wente which is rich, almost sweetish, and not subtle but with Thai fish cakes, herby and heavy, I can't think of anything better for the money.

Wente Johannesburg Riesling 1996 16 C

Superb rich fruit here, absolutely full of itself, true, but has bounce, has creamy depth, is great for reviving quaffing and for oriental food.

FORTIFIED WINE

Rozes Special Reserve Port NV 14 D

SPARKLING WINE/CHAMPAGNE

Asti Spumante Gianni (Italian) 14 C

Barramundi Sparkling NV (Australia) 15 D

One of the crispest, most entertaining Aussie bubblies around.

Brut de Channay NV (France) 11 D

Boring.

Chapel Hill Chardonnay-Pinot Noir NV (Hungary) 12 C

Bit numb.

Chapel Hill Sparkling NV (Hungary) 11 C

Tedious.

Green Ridge Chardonnay Spring NV (England) (low alcohol 1.2% proof)) 0 A

Utterly absurd price for what soft drinks do better.

Green Ridge Sauvignon Spring NV (England) (low alcohol 1.2% proof) 0 A

Undrinkable, thin, jejune, spineless, vapid, unattractive, anorexic, utterly . . . Oh, words fail me.

Millennium Cava NV 14 E

Has some very dry elegance.

Mumm Cuvee Napa Brut (California) 16 E

So much more assertive, refined, tasty and sanely priced than its French cousin I'm surprised there aren't serious riots in Rheims.

Nicole d'Aurigny Brut Champagne 14 E

Paul Herard Champagne Brut NV 12 F

Paul Herard Demi Sec Champagne (half bottle) 13.5 D

Reminger Sparkling Brut NV (France) 10 C

Difficult to swallow.

Rondel Cava Rosé 14 D

Santa Carolina Chardonnay Brut 1996 (Chile) 14 D

A fruity bubbly which is not remotely champagne-like in its style.

Seaview Brut NV (Australia) 14 D

Lithe and light. Delicious simplicity.

Seaview Brut Rosé (Australia) 14 D

Delicate little rosé.

Sparkling Zero (alcohol free) 15 

SAFEWAY PLC

Not just fresh fish, but Mr Fish too.

One doesn't hear very often of people being nabbed by store detectives while trying to steal bottles of wine. This could be because winelifters are particularly skilled at their craft but could owe more to the fact that wine bottles are simply harder to steal – bulky items with the annoying tendency to clunk at the wrong times. (I am at this juncture reminded of the octogenarian shoplifting pensioner who died of hypothermia after having to conceal two frozen turkeys under her overcoat for too long. There is also Margaret Rutherford's vintage performance as an elderly kleptomaniac in the British comedy, *Trouble in Store*, in which Ms Rutherford steals a toy train being displayed in the toy department by simply putting her arm down onto the track and allowing the train to speed up her cavernous sleeve. A lesson that nothing is safe from the determined larcenist.)

But why this discourse on what retailers sometimes charmingly refer to as shrinkage? Because I understand that Safeway was one of the retailers experimenting with civil recovery from those found to be shoplifting. This means that those caught shoplifting are sued in the civil court for the cost of the goods as well as the cost of the arrest and prosecution. I learned from the *Grocer* magazine that Safeway was last year testing the efficacy of civil recovery at its stores in Wolverhampton, Dudley and Brierley Hill. Among the other retailers in the West Midlands involved in the project were Sainsbury's, Tesco and the Co-op.

Deterrent, we are generally told, is the most effective weapon against crime and what better deterrent can there be in a supermarket than the presence of plenty of staff on the shopfloor? Rather more importantly from the honest consumer's point of view it allows us to ask for help, though one will generally expect a more intelligible response to the question 'Where can I find the pickled gherkins?' than to 'What wine would you recommend with monkfish slices stuffed with pesto sauce and shredded kohlrabi?' Safeway is aiming to do something about this with changes it has made to its approach to wine merchandising. *Off Licence News* last year reported that Safeway had overhauled its wine merchandising system, pinning its hopes on full-time drinks aisle staff with a working knowledge of drinks products. The company, which abandoned its gold, silver and bronze grading system in 1997 (a move which when it was initiated I forecast would die a rapid and anonymous death), said that it found shoppers did not want to be bombarded with information. Ms Liz Robertson, the company's wine department controller, said consumers wanted fast advice and Safeway has appointed 186 wine advisors to provide it.

While on the subject of off-licence displays it was reported by *Supermarketing* magazine at about the same time that Safeway was re-vamping its beer units to make them more appealing to women. The aim is to boost sales of premium bottled beers by making the shelves as interesting as the wine and spirits shelves. The aim was also to use shelf-edge labelling to give more information about the beers.

Safeway has been making an effort to become better informed itself. Last year, it signed a £300,000 deal with the Met Office which will give the retailer in-depth weather forecasting to allow it to plan ordering of weather-dependent lines. Medium and short term graphical and textual forecasts are broken down by region and store clusters. Safeway hopes it will be able to better predict surges in demand for products such as ice cream and salads. According to *The Times*, Safeway believes the Met Office to be the world's leading authority on forecasting information, choosing to ignore its darkest hour in 1987 when a few hours before Britain's worst storm in living memory, Michael Fish told viewers 'Rest assured there isn't going to be a hurricane'. I'll never forget the 100-plus-year-old plane trees opposite my house being shaken like blades of grass a few hours after Mr Fish's assurance.

It was revealed in February this year that Safeway was funding research to find out which of the fruits and vegetables it sells are the richest in flavonols and therefore most healthy to eat. Studies have revealed that a flavonol-rich diet can reduce the chances of heart disease, stroke and cancer. This was also extended to the wine shelves when Glasgow university chemists revealed that Chilean red wines, cabernets and merlots, were amongst the highest in these flavonols and perhaps it was this which inspired Ms Robertson to precede the spring press tasting of her department's new wines with a seminar on wine and health at which this aspect of the subject was explored in depth.

Talking of in-depth exploration, just as we are getting used to the idea of shopping via the internet, Safeway tested a computerised ordering system which bypasses the net altogether. Early in 1999, the company began trials of a new electronic system called Easi-Order which involves giving consumers a special hand-held gadget. With this gizmo, which is about the same size as an electronic personal organiser, the shopper can compose a shopping-list, download it directly over the phone when it will be picked in the store and readied for collection. There were, according to *The Grocer* magazine in February, hundreds of Safeway consumers eager to get their hands on the gadget. However, just 200 consumers currently using the company's Collect & Go Home Shopping service were invited to participate in the trial at the company's Basingstoke store.

Clearly keen to promote the one-stop shop concept, Safeway announced last year that it was collaborating with Abbey National to create the UK's biggest in-store banking operation. After three pilots, branches will be rolled out in 25 stores over the next 12 months. The retailer has also been expanding its in-store creche facilities and opened its 100th creche at its Cromer store in February 1999.

Expect to see the Safeway fascia at more petrol stations in the future thanks to another collaboration. In July 1998, the retailer announced that it is teaming up with BP to roll out 100 forecourt stores over the next four years in a £100 million investment creating 2,000 jobs. Quite what their new petrol-selling partners would have made of the tests being made at Safeway's Welwyn distribution centre at about the same time I cannot say. Safeway was apparently trialling 10 trucks which can operate without ever visiting a petrol station, BP or anyone else's. They are gas-powered.

Less welcome news for the retailer came in December when it was reprimanded by the Advertising Standards Authority for a series of local press ads in which the retailer compared prices between Safeway and Tesco. The price comparison was said to have been misleading and unfairly denigratory.

Whether unfair advertising had anything to do with it or not, Christmas 1998 proved prosperous for Safeway. According to the *Guardian*, like-for-like sales rose by 3% in the 17 weeks to February 6th. The same report put Safeway's share of the £100 billion UK grocery market at about 8%. Although Safeway recorded a 5% drop in pre-tax profits to £57 million in the year to April 1999, like-for-like sales growth was 3.5%. Shares in the retailer surged after speculation that the US retailer Wal-Mart was preparing a £4 billion bid for the retailer which, as we all know by now, ended up knocking at Asda's door. A report the month before suggested that Safeway was being stalked by the Dutch group, Ahold. Safeway announced in May that it was planning to re-merchandise two of its superstores every week in the coming months as part of the final phase of its 'category management programme' begun as far back as the beginning of 1998.

How well did the wine department perform? Well, from my point of view very well. It is true the supermarket does not have an abundance of own-label ranges and it is often outmanoeuvred on dirt-cheap bargain wines by the severe competition from other retailers, but there is a huge amount of enthusiasm within the department to get interesting wines on to the shelves and to communicate their virtues. The strong ranges are south and north America, South Africa (including a terrific 3-litre wine box Quagga Cape Red), and Australia.

But under the surface there is a bubble waiting to burst at this retailer. This is total speculation on my part but I feel something drastic will occur in Safeway's wine buying ambitions over the year 2000 but exactly when or what I have no idea.

Safeway plc
Safeway House
6 Millington Road
Hayes
Middlesex UB3 4AY
Tel: 0181 848 8744
Fax: 0181 573 1865

SEE STOP PRESS SECTION AT END OF BOOK FOR LAST-MINUTE ADDITIONS OR UPDATES TO THIS RETAILER'S RANGE.

ARGENTINIAN WINE RED

Balbi Malbec 1998 13 C

Juicy.

Caballo de Plata Bonarda-Barbera 1998 13 B

Intensely soft and juicy. Might do a brinjal and curried rice proud.

Diego Murillo Malbec, Patagonia 1997 17 D

Fabulous roast fowl wine. Combines rich baked spicy fruit and evolved tannins. Incredible richness.

Fantelli Barbera/Cabernet, Mendoza 1998 14.5 C

Bitter cherry and fruit, plummy yet dry, rather soft yet has some underlying character and very warm and cosy on the finish. Excellent quaffing here.

Mendoza Merlot 1997, Safeway 13.5 C

Rafael Estate Malbec, Mendoza 1997 16 D

Good heavens what nerve! It's the cheekiest amalgam of fruit and tannin I've tasted for years.

Santa Ana Cabernet/Malbec, Mendoza 1997 14.5 C

Simonassi Lyon Barbera 1998 14 D

Dry, dark, savoury jam.

ARGENTINIAN WINE WHITE

Alamos Ridge Chardonnay, Mendoza 1996 15.5 D

Caballo de Plata Torrontes 1998 12 B

Rafael Estate Chardonnay/Chenin, Mendoza 1997 14.5 C

Santa Ana Chardonnay/Semillon, Mendoza 1997 15.5 C

Santa Ana Malbec Rose 1998 14 C

A very rich dry rose of some weight and serious food compatibility.

AUSTRALIAN WINE RED

Australian Cabernet/Shiraz 1998, Safeway 15.5 C

Contains hints of cabernet's peppery vegetality but this is subsumed under the lush shiraz fruit.

Australian Oaked Cabernet Sauvignon 1998, Safeway 16 C

Seems to hint at ripeness and juiciness but the lovely soft tannins cruise in and take command.

Australian Oaked Shiraz 1998, Safeway 14 C

Smoky rubbery fruit, hint of vegetality, good tannins, rich polish.

Australian Shiraz 1998, Safeway 15 C

Juicy yet attitudinal and fully charged. Terrific quaffing.

Australian Shiraz/Ruby Cabernet 1998, Safeway 13.5 C

Highly cooked and rich. Like a gravy for roast grouse.

Banrock Station Mataro/Grenache/Shiraz 1998 13 C

From the very overripe sticky Banrock '98 stable.

Capel Vale Shiraz 1997 13.5 E

Top 130 stores.

Chateau Reynella Basket-Pressed Shiraz 1995 17 F

Wonderfully rich beast of race-horse lithness with cart-horse endurance and muscle. It is highly aromatic, maturely fruity, deeply complex as it crushes all resistance from the taste buds, and the finish makes a much vaunted northern Rhone syrah seem positively peaky.

Conundrum Vineyards Shiraz/Malbec 1997 12 D

Like fruit juice – without attitude.

Dawn Ridge Australian Red (3-litre box) 15 B

Hardys Coonawarra Cabernet Sauvignon 1995 15 E

Impressive caressing fruit which has lovely tannic bite on the finish. Meaty and mouthwatering.

Jacob's Creek Grenache Shiraz 1998 14 C

Raunchy, restless and deeply engaging.

Knappstein Cabernet Franc 1996 16.5 E

Wonderful concentration and richness here. Quite marvellous layered fruit – utterly superb and magically drinkable. Top 130 stores.

Knappstein Cabernet/Merlot 1996 13.5 E

Too juicy for eight quid. Top 130 stores.

Mamre Brook Cabernet Sauvignon 1996 16 E

Now here the juice of the blackcurrants is firmly textured by great tannins. Top thirty-six stores.

McPherson Croftwood Vineyard Shiraz, SE Australia 1998 15 C

Metala Shiraz/Cabernet Sauvignon 1997 11 D

Top 130 stores.

Normans Old Vine Shiraz 1997 14.5 E

Spice and meatiness, deftly conceived, and soupy. Not at all stores.

Oxford Landing Cabernet/Shiraz 1998 15 D

Juicy and rich, wery wery (sic!) soft and sibilant tannins and altogether once in a glass the glass is drained. And you feel the opposite.

Penfolds Bin 389 Cabernet Shiraz 1996 17 F

Sufficient unto itself. Settle down with a rich, tannic author and relish the intricate plot of this stunning wine. Top thirty-six stores.

Peter Lehmann The Barossa Cabernet Sauvignon 1996 16.5 E

Fabulously good value for an Aussie nowadays: dry, balanced, witty, rich, lengthy, deep and fully dimensional. Great stuff.

Peter Lehmann Vine Vale Grenache 1998 15.5 

Hint of leather, spice and rich, very rich, damson fruit. Jam of a highly sophisticated kind.

Rosemount Estate Grenache Shiraz 1998 15 D

Yes, it's immensely juicy but fine tannins interrupt the flood – well in time.

Rosemount Estate Shiraz 1998 14.5 E

In the Rosemount tradition of juice with an adult attitude. Totally quaffable.

Rosemount Estate Shiraz/Cabernet Sauvignon 1998 15.5 D

The jamminess is extraordinarily toothsome and charming.

Rosemount Estate Show Reserve Cabernet Sauvignon 1996 13 G

Too juicy and characterless for fifteen quid. Top thirty-six stores.

Taltarni Merlot/Cabernet Sauvignon 1997 16 D

Curiously dry for an Aussie red. Classic touches of Bordeaux! Top 130 stores.

Woolshed Cabernet/Shiraz/Merlot, Coonawarra 1996 15.5 D

Delicious, quite delicious. Nothing quite, however, or quiet about the fruit which is rich, ripe and full. Top 220 stores.

AUSTRALIAN WINE WHITE

Annie's Lane Semillon, Clare Valley 1996 17 D

Absolutely hums with multi-layered flavours (peaches, plums, hint of strawberry).

Australian Chardonnay 1998, Safeway 16 C

Lovely ripe, soft fruit with a nutty edge and attendant acidity of delicacy yet bite. Brilliant value.

Australian Dry White 1998, Safeway 14.5 B

Australian Marsanne 1997, Safeway 13.5 D

Australian Oaked Chardonnay 1998, Safeway 16 C

Wonderful plumpness and textured freshness. Superb chardonnay for under a fiver.

Australian Oaked Colombard 1998, Safeway 14 B

Basedow Semillon, Barossa Valley 1997 15 D

Wonderful fish supper treat, this wine. It manages to offer health and wealth, freshness and fruit, fullness and delicacy. Top 120 stores.

Breakaway Chenin/Sauvignon 1998 11 C

Top 280 stores.

Capel Vale Unwooded Chardonnay 1998 16 E

Better, in its steely yet rich fruit, than so many vaunted Chablis. Top 120 stores.

Capel Vale Verdelho 1998 16 E

This is a lovely, softly textured, gently spicy artefact of immense charm. Top twenty-three stores.

Chardonnay/Colombard 1998, Safeway 15 C

Geoff Merrill Reserve Chardonnay 1996 16 E

Real treat. Mature, vegetal, Meursault-like acidity with a coating of Aussie warmth. Top 120 stores from June.

Hardys Nottage Hill Chardonnay 1997 16.5 C

Fantastic oily/buttery texture, ripe fruit, just terrific.

Lindemans Bin 65 Chardonnay 1998 16 C

One of the chicest, most expressive chardonnays under a fiver out of Australia.

Lindemans Winemaker's Reserve Padthaway 1995 13 G

Loxton Low Alcohol Chardonnay (1.2% vol) 11 B

Makes a brave stab at tasting like wine but do chardonnay grapes need to go through this?

Loxton Lunchtime Light Chardonnay (4% vol) 12 B

Very light for a miserable lunchtime.

Mount Hurtle Chardonnay 1996 15 D

Ninth Island Sauvignon Blanc, Tasmania 1998 13.5 E

Four quid wine. Top fifty-three stores.

Oxford Landing Chardonnay 1998 15.5 C

Delicate balancing act, successfully achieved, of some ripe fruit and some herby acidity. The result is excellent, warm, winning and stylish.

Oxford Landing Estate Viognier 1998 15 D

Develops, from a demure start, into a lovely calm apricot-tinged, dry wine of some class. Will cellar well for three or four years. Top fifty-three stores.

Oxford Landing Sauvignon Blanc 1998 14 C

Amazingly fresh and cheeky for a warm climate sauvignon.

Penfolds The Valleys Chardonnay 1997 14.5 D

Polish Hill River Vineyard Riesling, Clare Valley 1998 15 E

Quirky, mineral fruit of style. Not at all stores.

Rawsons Retreat Bin 202 Dry Riesling 1998 

Has the capacity to age gracefully, refresh fully, to partner complex fish dishes with vigour and, lastly, not to discomfort the pocket. A great bargain.

Rawsons Retreat Bin 21 Semillon/ Chardonnay/Colombard 1998 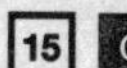

Fat and full of fun. Great striding style of behaviour over the taste buds.

Riddoch Chardonnay, Coonawarra 1996 16 D

Super mouth-filling plumpness of ripe fruit here, hint of caramel cream even, but the acidity surges alongside in support and the finish is regal. Very classy wine.

Rosemount Estate Chardonnay 1997 (1.5L) 16 D

A classy beast of true pedigree feel from start to finish. Superbly chic and classy. Price bracket has been adjusted to show bottle equivalent.

Rosemount Show Reserve Chardonnay 1997 16 E

Such style and wit here. And it'll age for two or three years and grow more pointed. At most stores.

Rothbury Estate Hunter Valley Verdelho 1998 15.5 D

Something different, spicy and plump and food friendly, to purge the blues at the end of the day. A florid wine, fit for choosy throats.

Taltarni Sauvignon Blanc, Victoria 1998 14 D

Dry, restrained richness, a hint of under-ripe melon. Has class. Will cellar well for two or three years. Top 110 stores.

AUSTRIAN WINE WHITE

Cat's Leap Gruner Veltliner 1997 12.5 C

At most stores.

BULGARIAN WINE RED

Azbuka Merlot 1996 16 D

Highly perfumed and individual, this luscious merlot offers

blackcurrants and spicy plums and soft leather. Improving enormously in bottle. Top 121 stores.

Bulgarian Country Wine, Merlot/Pinot Noir 1997, Safeway 15.5 B

Huntman's Red, Cabernet/Merlot 1997 15.5 B

Musika Merlot 1995 16 C

Brilliant dry fruit of great depth and charm. Has oodles of flavour and layers of warmly textured richness.

Oaked Merlot, Rousse 1997, Safeway 13.5 C

Silistra Cabernet Sauvignon 1997 13.5 B

Very juicy and ripe.

Vinenka Merlot/Gamza Reserve, Suhindol 1993 14 B

BULGARIAN WINE WHITE

Bulgarian Chardonnay, Rousse 1998, Safeway 16 B

Deliciously proper and posh. Better than many a white burgundy.

Bulgarian Oaked Chardonnay 1997, Safeway 15.5 C

Delightful amalgam of gentle wood and firm fruit.

CHILEAN WINE RED

35 Sur Cabernet Sauvignon 1998

16.5 C

Superb cabernet of wit, warmth, character, concentration, softness yet dryness, approachability yet seriousness and a great potency of flavour on the finish. A vivacious cabernet of punch and pertinacity.

Caballo Loco No 2, Valdivieso NV

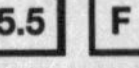

15.5 F

Carta Vieja Merlot 1998

16 C

Superb turn of speed as the fruit surges across the taste buds in Protean layers of richness. Most stores.

Casa Lapostolle Cuvee Alexandre Merlot, Rapel 1997

18 F

Who gives a toss for £100 Petrus when there is this rich, hugely complex beauty on sale for eleven pounds? Top 119 stores.

Castillo de Molina Cabernet Sauvignon Reserva, Lontue 1996

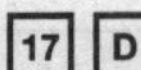

17 D

A stunning cabernet with piles of rich tannic fruit and cassis/chocolate undertones. A marvellously fluent yet dry wine of massive charm, depth, complexity and lingering fruit. Selected stores.

Chilean Cabernet Sauvignon 1998, Safeway

16 C

It's not classic and peppery but it is cabernet. But cabernet as soft, rich, deep and utterly quaffably delish.

Chilean Red 1998, Safeway 15 C

Terrific buzz about this wine: fruity and full. Great frolicsome fun.

Concha y Toro Casillero del Diablo Cabernet Sauvignon, Maipo 1998 16.5 C

Superbly classy tannins allied to ruffled corduroy textured and lovely chocolate, cassis and tobacco flavours.

Errazuriz Syrah Reserve, Aconcagua 1997 17.5 E

Big, berried fruit, rugged yet immensely soft, huge depth, flavour and commanding richness. This is even better than it was in the summer of '98 when I first tasted it.

Genesis Vineyards, Palmeras Estate Oak Aged Cabernet Sauvignon, Nancagua 1996, Safeway 16 C

Brilliance and bite here from the vigour of the fruit, dry and lingering, to the cigar-box finish. Very classy stuff. Astonishingly good value.

Isla Negra Merlot 1998 16.5 D

What superb dryness yet riveting rich leathery fruit! It's marvellous drinking. Top 219 stores.

Soleca Cabernet/Merlot, Colchagua 1997 15 C

TerraMater Merlot 1998 13 C

Bit juicy – tannins all in very late. Most stores from June.

TerraMater Zinfandel/Syrah, Maipo 1998 

Superb clashing of spice and bright hedgerow fruitiness. Wonderful deep texture and tension here. Scrumptious. Top 117 stores.

Valdivieso Cabernet Franc Reserve, Lontue 1997 

Touch sedate for a Chilean cab franc but truly wonderful tannin control and soft layers of fruit.

Valdivieso Malbec Reserve, Lontue 1996 

A soft, caressing malbec of lushness yet never soppiness. Delicious quaffing. Top 119 stores.

Valdivieso Merlot Reserve, Lontue 1997 

Utterly gorgeous: cassis and toffee, brilliant earthy tannins, old leather and lush plums. Superb world class recipe.

Villard Vineyards Cabernet Sauvignon, Maipo 1997 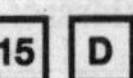

Vegetality flooded with ripe fruit. Yet it has a kind of great maturity and richness.

Vina Morande Merlot 1998 

This has fruit so textured and rich it surprised like fluid grease. Incredible leathery lushness here.

CHILEAN WINE WHITE

35 Sur Sauvignon Blanc 1998

C

Superb! The grassiness of the acidity and the richness of fruit, still classic dry sauvignon, make for a wonderful crisp mouthful. Selected stores.

Casa Lapostolle Cuvee Alexandre Chardonnay, Casablanca 1996

One of the best chardonnays in the world. Simply gorgeous texture, complex fruit and sheer charm. Top twenty-nine stores only.

Castillo de Molina Reserva Semillon, Lontue 1997

Chilean Sauvignon Blanc Lontue 1998, Safeway

Delicious under-ripe greengage and gooseberry fruit, hint of pineapple, and the acids are firm and mineralised. Delicious, classic, classy, cheap!

Chilean Semillon/Chardonnay 1998, Safeway

Baked fruit mixed with fresh. Wonderful stuff!

Chilean White, Lontue 1998, Safeway

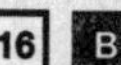

What a price for such depth, elegance, freshness and flavour.

Cordillera Estate Oak Aged Chardonnay Reserva 1997, Safeway

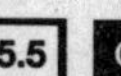

Soleca Semillon/Chardonnay, Colchagua 1997 16 C

Clever winemaking here. Modern wizardry creating class, richness and style.

TerraMater Chardonnay, Maipo 1997 16 C

Astonishing richness yet charm (of relaxed manners) here. Selected stores.

Vina Gracia Chardonnay 'Reposado', Cachapoal 1997 14 C

ENGLISH WINE — WHITE

Stanlake, Thames Valley Vineyards 1996, Safeway 13.5 C

FRENCH WINE — RED

Beaujolais 1998, Safeway 12 C

Rather dull.

Beaune 1996, Safeway 10 E

Bergerie de l'Arbous Coteaux du Languedoc 1996 14 D

Tobacco-scented, herby, very dry and great with casseroles and cheeses. Top 220 stores.

Bordeaux Merlot 1998 13 C

Bit austere. At most stores.

Cadet Claret, Bordeaux 1998 13 C

Not bad. Has pleasant tannins and some assertive qualities.

Calvet Reserve, Bordeaux 1996 12 D

Always such dullness here. Like chewing a monk's habit.

Calvet St Emilion 1997 13 D

Oddly untypical, stickily rich, and is far too pricey.

Chateau Barde-Haut, St Emilion Grand Cru 1995 13 F

Yes, it's an odd vintage and it shows how ill-knitted together it is in spite of some fine rich-edged tannicity. But the price . . .

Chateau des Cordes, Minervois 1997 16 C

Superb rich fruit, tobacco-edged and subtly spicy, with herbs and hedgerows and loads of character.

Chateau du Grison, Bordeaux 1995 12.5 D

Chateau du Piras, Premieres Cotes de Bordeaux 1994 14 D

Chateau Maison Neuve Montagne St Emilion 1996 15 E

Gets a bit rugged and crotchety on the finish but the tannins and leathery fruit are in rip-roaring form. Very, very classy, dry and rich and firmly concentrated. Very clarety.

Chateau Soudars, Cru Bourgeois 1994 

Corbieres 1998, Safeway 

What a fleshily fruity, very civilised bargain. Herbs, sun, gentle tannins and real style.

Cotes du Rhone Oak Aged 1997, Safeway 

Crozes-Hermitage, Domaine Barret 1997 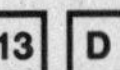

Close to being rather good, but the price demands we must take it seriously. The fruit is soft and plump, with some earthy character, but it seems to be perfunctory on the finish.

Domaine Chris Limouzi, Eleve en Futs de Chene Corbieres 1997 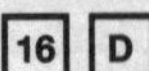

Ripe yet dry, cosy yet argumentative, this is a hugely approachable wine of great class. Top 220 stores.

Domaine de Boriettes Syrah, VdP d'Oc 1998 

Very fresh and dry on the finish but the tannins are active and flowing.

Domaine de Condamine, Fitou 1997 

Gruff yet sweet tempered.

Domaine de Tudery Saint Chinian 1997 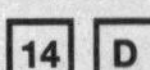

Finishes strongly, from a juicy start. Top 219 stores.

Domaine des Bruyeres, Cotes de Malepere 1998 

What effrontery to be so rich and complex, dry and decisive, for such a small sum of money. It's a lovely wine.

Domaine des Lauriers, Faugeres 1996 16.5 D

Superb texture here. It resounds with aromatic and fruity hints of the Midi scrub and hedgerows, orchards and earth. Wonderful tannins. Top 220 stores.

Domaine Vieux Manoir de Maransan Cuvee Speciale 1998, Safeway 15.5 C

Delicious. Not a hint of earth, only lush fruit Mingling amicably with dry tannins.

Fleurie Domaine des Raclets 1998 13 E

Very drinkable, but pricey.

Gevrey Chambertin Domaine Rossignol-Trapet 1996 10 G

Intensely dull for the money. Well, it would be dull at £2.99. Does it try? A bit. But its outlandish price makes enthusiasm impossible.

Graves Cuvee Prestige 1994 13 D

Hautes Cotes de Nuits Cuvee Speciale 1996 10 E

Very raw and juicy.

L'If Merlot/Carignan, VdP du Torgan 1998 14 C

Intensely dry and firmly tannic. Will soften beautifully over the year.

'La Source de Mirail' Grenache/Syrah, VdP de Vaucluse 1997 15 B

La Source Merlot/Syrah VdP d'Oc 1998 

Herbs and rocks, hillside scrub and well cooked fruit. Finishes dry yet very satisfyingly.

Le Haut-Medoc de Giscours 1995 

Les Hauts de Montauriol, Cotes du Frontonnais 1996 

March Hare VdP d'Oc 1998 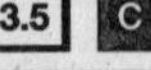

Mercurey Raoul Clerget 1996 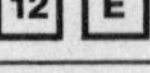

Merlot 24 Selection Frederic VdP d'Oc 1998 

Very dry yet also curiously rounded and ripe. Beautifully textured and plump with a raisiny finish.

Minervois 1998, Safeway 

Terrific herby, dry yet textured richness.

Oak-aged Medoc 1996, Safeway 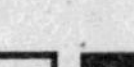

Organic French Red VdP du Gard NV, Safeway 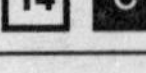

Pommard 1er Cru 'Les Clos des Boucherottes' 1996 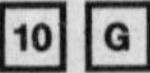

Red Burgundy 'Les Vignes de la Croix' 1997 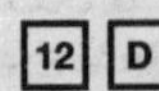

Richemont Montbrun Old Vine Carignan VdP de l'Aude 1995 14 D

Richemont Reserve Merlot, VdP d'Oc 1996 14 C

Saint-Emilion 1997 12 D

Saint-Joseph 'Cuvee Cote-Diane' 1995 14 E

Savigny du Domaine du Chateau de Meursault 1996 11 E

Syrah VdP d'Oc 1998, Safeway 14.5 B

Juicy fruits yet wry and dry on the finish.

Winter Hill Merlot/Grenache, VdP d'Oc 1998 15 B

Very dry and richly characterful. Not a pussycat at all. But it still purrs. At most stores.

Young Vatted Syrah VdP de Vaucluse 1998, Safeway 14.5 C

Very dry and tongue-puckering, but great chilled with fish.

FRENCH WINE WHITE

Bordeaux Blanc Sec Aged in Oak 1997, Safeway 13 C

Bordeaux Sauvignon, Calvet 1998 13 C

Bit austere on the finish.

Chablis Premier Cru Mont de Milieu 1997 12.5 F

Too expensive.

Chardonnay VdP de l'Herault 1998, Safeway 15 C

Delicious layered wine, lemony and ripely edged, with a dimension of real refreshing fruitiness.

Chardonnay VdP du Jardin de la France 1998, Safeway 12.5 C

A shadow of a chardonnay.

Chateau du Plantier Entre Deux Mers 1997 13 C

Chateau du Roc Bordeaux Sauvignon 1998 10 C

The specimen I tried tasted 'of old peapods' according to one Safeway wine buyer.

Chateau Magneau, Graves 1997 14 D

Chenin VdP du Jardin de la France 1998, Safeway 13 B

Touch juicy and raw on the finish.

Cotes du Luberon Rosé 1998, Safeway 14 C

Brilliant texture and ripe, rich fruit. Great with food.

Domaine du Rey, VdP des Cotes de Gascogne 1997 (vegetarian) 13.5 C

En Sol Kimmeridgien, Bourgogne Blanc 1997 11 D

Pretty dull for seven quid. Top 280 stores.

Gewurztraminer d'Alsace 1997, Safeway 16.5 D

Stunning smoky fruit redolent of gently spicy crushed rose petals. Captivatingly fruity.

James Herrick Chardonnay 1998 16.5 C

Cracking performer: elegant toasty fruit, firm balance of fresh acid (lemon-edged) and an overall politeness of manner and form. Has well-established credentials which the '98 vintage only amplifies.

Kimmeridgien Chardonnay, Bourgogne 1998 13 D

A pretentious try at claiming a unique provenance. Overpriced, unexciting.

L'If Grenache Blanc, VdP du Torgan 1998 16.5 C

What a wonderfully rich and refreshing change from chardonnay! It's a triumph of layered complexity.

La Baume Sauvignon Blanc, VdP d'Oc 1997 14 C

La Loustere VdP du Gers 1998 14.5 B

Lovely gentle, exotic undertone. At most stores.

La Source Chardonnay/Roussanne VdP d'Oc 1998 14 C

Soft and hinting at nuttiness.

Les Caudanettes Anjou Blanc 1998 13.5 B

A dry echo of a sweet wine it's trying to be.

Macon Villages 1998, Safeway 15 C

A bargain minor white burgundy of genuine vegetal charm and soft/crisp fruit. Such a paradox is Macon's trademark.

Montagny Premier Cru 1998, Safeway 14 E

Big woody fruit of some stealth and richness. Drink it young, before Christmas 1999.

Muscadet 1998, Safeway 11 B

Very raw and skinny. Needs to meet a rich Chilean and produce offspring.

Pinot Blanc Alsace 1998, Safeway 13.5 C

Needs a six month lie-down to knit its ragged edges together. Will be fine for Christmas smoked salmon.

Puligny Montrachet 'Les Charmes' 1996 13 G

Has some charm, but not seventeen quids' worth.

Rochemartain Sauvignon Touraine 1997 14 C

Sancerre 1998, Safeway 12.5 E

Touch dull for £7.50. More than a touch, in fact.

Sancerre 'Les Bonnes Bouches' Domaine Henri Bourgeois 1997 12.5 E

Sauvignon Blanc Cuvee Reserve VdP d'Oc 1998 16 C

Lovely dry nuttiness and a crisp, decisive edge. Sullen richness here, good in a sauvignon, makes it a classic. Top 280 stores.

Vin Blanc VdP de l'Herault 1998, Safeway 13 C

Bit cheesy on the finish.

Vin de Pays de Vaucluse 1998, Safeway 14.5 B

Real bite and freshness here. Gentle fruit with a nutty tang. Has character to it.

Viognier Cuvee Reserve, VdP d'Oc 1998 15.5 C

Delicious apricot and peardrop-tinged fruit. Young, rich and energetic, this is an immensely quaffable wine.

Wild Trout VdP d'Oc 1998 15.5 C

Dignified and dainty, rich yet controlled. Outstanding blend of tasty grapes.

GERMAN WINE — WHITE

Fire Mountain Riesling, Pfalz 1996 13.5 C

Hattenheimer Heiligenberg Riesling Kabinett, Rheingau 1996 13 D

Heinz Frank Auslese, Pfalz 1996 15 C

A brilliant aperitif with its richness yet lightness. Not a great finish, but attractive.

Kenderman Dry Riesling, Pfalz 1997 13 C

Oppenheimer Sacktrager Riesling Kabinett, Rheinhessen 1996 12 D

Pudding Wine, Pfalz Auslese NV (half bottle) 15 C

Riesling Classic, Pfalz 1996 15 B

Rupertsberger Nussbein Riesling Kabinett 1995 14 C

Still young and searching for its soul (mineralised acidity like licking a slate tile). But it's still got some crisp class to it – but wait five or six years . . .

Weinheimer Sybillenstein Beerenauslese, Rheinhessen 1993 (half bottle) 16 D

Superb, honeyed, nutty, sweet wine with rampant fruitiness and compatibility with fresh fruit and desserts. Selected stores.

GREEK WINE RED

Mavrodaphne of Patras NV 14.5 C

HUNGARIAN WINE RED

Bull's Blood 1997 13 B

Hungarian Cabernet Sauvignon, Villany 1996 15.5 C

River Duna Kekfrancos, Szekszard 1997 14.5 B

HUNGARIAN WINE WHITE

Chapel Hill Barrique-fermented Chardonnay 1996, Safeway 15 C

Hilltop Bianca 1998 (organic) 15.5 B

Superbly textured and richly polished organic wine of great integral freshness yet fruitiness. At most stores from mid-July.

Hungarian Chardonnay, Buda 1997, Safeway 13.5 B

Hungarian Dry Muscat Nagyrede 1997, Safeway 14 B

Hungarian Irsai Oliver, Neszmely 1998, Safeway 15 B

Compelling aperitif. Daintily floral fruit. Terrific picnic wine.

Matra Mountain Oaked Chardonnay, Nagyrede 1998, Safeway 13 C

Matra Mountain Sauvignon Blanc 1998, Safeway 13.5 C

At most stores.

Matra Mountain Unoaked Pinot Grigio 1998, Safeway 14 C

A good shellfish partner. Very knife-edged and fresh.

Nagyrede Oaked Zenit 1998 12 B

Riverview Chardonnay 1998 14.5 C

Bruised and rich, the fruit to make this gallant wine was obviously at the peak of pickability.

Riverview Gewurztraminer 1997 12.5 C

In the top fifty-five stores from mid-July.

Woodcutter's White, Neszmely 1998 15 B

Doesn't develop a gripping finish but it gets there deliciously fruitily and charmingly.

ISRAELI WINE RED

King David Sacramental Medium Sweet Red NV (kosher) 15 C

Screwcapped and very sweet and pruney. Great, ironically, with a slice of Christmas cake.

ITALIAN WINE RED

Alto Varo Rosso di Puglia 1997 13 C

Sweet and dry contrast – ends dryly. Needs pasta (with bacon bits).

Amarone delle Valpolicella Classico, Tedeschi 1995 16.5 F

Expensive treat: prunes, liquorice, almonds, spicy cherries, and consummate smoothness yet alert tannins make for a lovely Christmas lunch wine of utter downability and food matchability.

Cecchi Barrique Aged Cabernet Sauvignon, Toscana 1996 14 E

In spite of the very fancy French grape, it still comes out with terracotta warmth and dry richness.

Chianti Classico 1997, Safeway 15 D

Lovely ripeness and terracotta-rich tannins.

Di Giorno Merlot/Corvina, Veneto 1997 13.5 B

Mimosa Maremma Sangiovese 1997 15.5 C

Juicy undertone controlled by good assertive tannins. Modern yet traditional. Lovely stuff. Top 289 stores.

Salice Salento Riserva 1994 14 D

Serina Primitivo, Tarantino, Puglia 1996 

A gutsy red with weight and wit – odd dry plum finish – a hint if not an echo of slice – but a welcoming brew of a bottle on a cool evening.

Sicilian Red 1998, Safeway (1.5 litre) 

Brilliant value for money: dry, stalky, rich to finish, earthy and very very food friendly. Great stuff for big pasta partners. Price band is for the 75cl equivalent.

Valpolicella Valpatena 'Corte Alta' 1997 

ITALIAN WINE WHITE

Casa di Giovanni Grillo 1997, Safeway (Sicily) 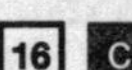

Utterly gorgeous fruit! Terrific opulence and gently toasty lemon.

Chardonnay del Salento Barrique-aged, Caramia 1996 15 D

Marc Zero Chardonnay Salento 1997 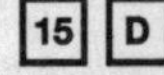

Like the screwcap. The fruit's like linctus-thick puree.

Orvieto Classico Secco 1998, Safeway 

Quintessential Italianate in its dryness yet richness, nutty quaffability and terrific food friendliness.

Serina Chardonnay, Puglia 1998 13.5 C

Very thick and unsubtle.

Sicilian Dry White 1998, Safeway (1.5 litre) 13.5 B

Bit weak on the finish, making it tough to pair with food, but as a party glugging wine it has some virtues. Price band is for the 75cl equivalent.

Tenuta 'Pietra Porzia' Frascati Superiore 1998 14.5 C

As good a Frascati as you can get under a fiver. Has gentility, charm and dainty fruit.

Verdicchio dei Castelli di Jesi Classico, Terre Cortesi 1998 15.5 C

An exceptionally fruity, richly textured and fully committed Verdicchio. Lovely balance and purpose.

MEXICAN WINE RED

L A Cetto Malbec 1997 15.5 C

MONTENEGRAN WINE RED

Monte Cheval Vranac 1993 13.5 C

NEW ZEALAND WINE RED

Church Road Cabernet Sauvignon/Merlot 1996

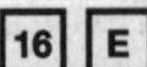

Still green and austere by the standards of New World orchards, this has some peppery class to make up for the vegetality.

Delegat's Reserve Cabernet Sauvignon Barrique Matured 1997

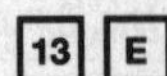

Vegetally elegant, savoury, polished and a touch feral. An individual cabernet of some style.

Ninth Island Pinot Noir, Tasmania 1998

13 E

Top forty stores.

NEW ZEALAND WINE WHITE

Delegat's Reserve Chardonnay, Barrel Fermented 1997

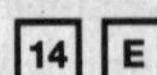

Rich, fat, plutocratically textured, luxuriously perfumed, and altogether too rich for the likes of a plonker like me. Not at all stores.

Goldwater 'Dog Point' Sauvignon Blanc 1998

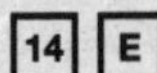

Dainty, possessing poise and finesse, expensive, dry. Top fifty-three stores.

Montana Chardonnay, Marlborough 1998 16 D

Utterly delicious. Superb fruit. Great balance. Commanding texture.

Montana Sauvignon Blanc 1998 16 D

Not remotely like the old style Kiwi grassy sauvignons, this specimen is warm and fruity with a striking finish.

Oyster Bay Chardonnay, Marlborough 1998 16 D

Delicate, decisive, delicious, utterly quaffable – has finesse, flavour and is not remotely flash. Top 120 stores.

Villa Maria Private Bin Chardonnay 1998 14 D

Needs a year to deliver its closed complexity. Top 235 stores.

Villa Maria Private Bin Sauvignon Blanc, Marlborough 1998 14.5 D

Quiet, reserved and very dainty. A thought provocative wine which needs no food.

Villa Maria Reserve Wairau Valley Sauvignon 1998 15.5 E

Keep it for eighteen months. Sure, it's lovely and elegant now but it will richly develop in bottle and possibly rate 17/18 points in a couple of years. Top fifty-three stores.

PORTUGUESE WINE RED

Bela Fonte Baga 1998 16 C

From the great '98 vintage; drink it before spring 2000. The wine has lovely immediacy and rapid, fine tannins. It's immensely food friendly.

Falua, Ribetajo 1998, Safeway 14 B

Dry, hint of earth, cherries well baked. Most stores.

Miradouro Portuguese Red, Terras do Sado 1996 13 B

Sinfonia, Alentejo 1997 16.5 C

The sheer polish of this wine as taste-bud-tinglingly rich and well textured. Superb fruit of great class for the money.

Vila Regia Douro 1995 14 C

PORTUGUESE WINE WHITE

Fiuza Sauvignon Blanc, Ribatejo 1998 14 C

Has some interesting edges. Good with food.

ROMANIAN WINE RED

Pinot Noir Special Reserve 1995, Safeway 14.5 C

SOUTH AFRICAN WINE RED

Bouwland Cabernet Sauvignon/Merlot, Stellenbosch 1997 14 D

Gobbets of rich earth and ripe fruit. Top 210 stores.

Delaire Cabernet Sauvignon Merlot 1997 15 E

Expensive treat. Has edges of tobacco and cassis, rather ripely in cahoots, and a finish of soft leather and baked plums. Not a classicist's cabernet but superbly gluggable. Top fourteen stores.

Fairview Pinotage 1998 16.5 D

Utterly compulsive glugging here: rich, smoky, beautifully intertwined spicy fruit and tannins. Wonderful! Top 292 stores.

Kanonkop Cabernet Sauvignon, Stellenbosch 1994 13.5 F

Kanonkop 'Kadette' Estate Wine, Stellenbosch 1996 14 D

Kleinbosch Young Vatted Pinotage, Paarl 1998 16 C

So vibrant and perky it shakes one's teeth to their roots! Lovely ripe fruit here.

Kleindal Pinotage 1997, Safeway 15 C

Kumula Cinsault/Pinotage 1998 15 C

Lovely softie – ripe, ready, rampant and rolling.

Landsdowne Cinsaut/Pinotage 1998 15 C

Landskroon Cinsaut/Shiraz, Paarl 1998 16 C

What an improvement on the '97! This is jammy, spicy and soft (yet fresh) but with good tannins. A masterly food wine.

Long Mountain Cabernet Sauvignon 1998 13.5 C

Very juicy and dry to finish.

Plaisir de Merle Cabernet Sauvignon, Paarl 1995 15 F

Plantation Ruby Cabernet, Stellenbosch 1998 15.5 C

Simonsvlei Shiraz Reserve 1998 15 C

Savoury and deep, dry to finish. A terrific energy here, faintly cigar-edged.

South African Cape Red 1998, Safeway 13 B

Sweet and juicy.

South African Cinsault 1998, Safeway 16 C

A wonderful wine which remind this drinker of great Beaujolais and stunning Cotes du Rhone. Brilliant softness and richness.

South African Oak Aged Pinotage 1997, Safeway 15 C

Tastes just like a fine Cotes de Brouilly thirty years ago, plus excitement.

Stellenbosch Cabernet Sauvignon 1998 16.5 C

Superb colour and concomitant depth of rich fruit. A wonderfully textured, warm yet gentle wine of utter sippability.

Stellenbosch Merlot 1998 13.5 C

Soft and supple.

The Pinotage Company Selected Bush Vine Pinotage 1998 16 D

Tasted the morning after Bill Clinton's televised squirmings, I found this wine fruitier by far.

SOUTH AFRICAN WINE WHITE

Arniston Bay Chenin Chardonnay 1998 15.5 C

Extremely forward but not flashy. Has warmth and piles of soft fruit but manages to stay refreshing and engagingly plump without being obscenely Rubenesque.

Bouchard Finlayson Oak Valley Chardonnay, 1996 10 E

Handsome polished floorboard aroma, strictly for the classically nasal, and the fruit is confected and stuck up, pretentious and over-engineered; it's refined yuk.

Brampton Sauvignon Blanc 1997 14 D

Wonderful fresh cut cricket pitch aroma. Is South Africa good at this sport? Must be, if this wine is any indication. Finishes flatly, though, and doesn't avoid the follow on.

Chenin Blanc Stellenbosch, Safeway 1998 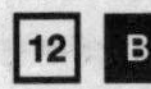

Delaire Chardonnay, Stellenbosch 1997 

Toasted nuts, hint of gunsmoke, tight gooseberry and melon fruit, gently viscous texture, terrific finish. A very convincing wine.

Early Release Chenin Blanc 1999 

Fresh and charmingly gauche.

Fairview Estate Semillon, Paarl 1997 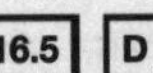

Wonderfully concentrated and freshly turned out. Has great lingering dry peach, vanillary and icy mineral undertones all packed together stylishly and sagely. Utterly delicious wine of class and composure.

Fairview Estate Semillon/Sauvignon Blanc, Paarl 1998 

Smells like an alluring old white burgundy but the fruit is plump and richer than o.w.b. and strikes the palate wonderfully.

Kleinbosch Bush Vine Dry Muscat 1998 

Gorgeous aperitif of floridity yet dryness and wryness. Great way to begin a meal. It says Grace for you.

Kleinbosch Chenin Blanc/Sauvignon Blanc 1998 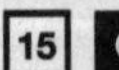

Stickily rich yet not OTT because of the pert pineapple acidity. It motors smoothly and charmingly.

Kleinezalze Sauvignon Blanc 1997 

Namaqua Colombard, Olifantsrivier 1998 

Plantation Semillon 1998 

Gorgeous concentrated gooseberry juiced wine with a further fruity layer, subtle, of lime. Utterly delicious – quenching and thought provocative.

Robertson Barrel Fermented Chardonnay 1997 

Chardonnay in the new-world, sub-citrus, gently woody style where the fruit is freshly picked, never cloying or taut, but just giving, clean and delicious.

Robertson Barrel Fermented Colombard 1998 

Good polish and ripeness, woody edge, fine texture and a classy finish. Very good value for soothing quaffing. Most stores.

South African Cape White 1998, Safeway 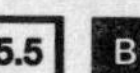

Superbly rich, energetic fruit – creamy, nutty, ripe yet dry, plus a wondrous texture. Individual and invasive.

South African Chardonnay 1998, Safeway 

Swartland Reserve Bush Vine Chenin Blanc 1998 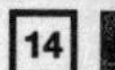

Dry yet full of compressed fruit – almost dares to be elegant.

Vergelegen Chardonnay, Stellenbosch 1997 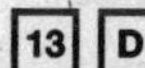

Very lemonic and fresh. Not complex. Top fifty-one stores.

SPANISH WINE RED

Agramont Tempranillo/Cabernet Sauvignon Crianza 1995 15 C

Very juicy for Agramont but still adult and audaciously fruity. Great slurping here.

Bach Merlot, Penedes 1996 16.5 D

Beware! Tannin attack! Oh what heaven! The squeamish are warned! Selected stores.

Berberana Tempranillo Rioja, 1996 14 C

Cosme Palacio y Hermanos Rioja 1996 13.5 D

Drying out a touch and getting a little grouchy.

El Leon, Bierzo 1998 15 C

Made from the local mencia grape, this is an interesting wine. It has bite and freshness and a cherry/plum dryness. Most attractive.

El Leon Mencia, Bierzo 1997 14 C

El Velero Monastrell, Murcia 1997 12 B

Marques de Murrieta, Rioja Reserva 1993 13.5 E

Marques de Riscal Rioja Gran Reserva 1989 16 G

A pound for every penny it costs. The acme of old style, vanilla rich, tannic Rioja. Fabulous stuff. Top thirty-three stores.

Muruve Toro 1997 15.5 C

Santara Cabernet/Merlot, Conca de Barbera 1996 16.5 C

One of the great under-a-fiver reds of supermarketing and Spain. Rich, mature, Claret-like aroma, big, dry, cassis-edged fruit with a hint of chocolate and tobacco and a roaring, handsomely dishevelled finish. A smooth rough diamond of deliciousness. Only a few bottles left – if any.

Torres Coronas Tempranillo, Penedes 1996 16.5 D

Wonderful vintage for this wine, full of rich, subtle complexity and classy layers of fruit. Very beautifully textured and stylish.

Young Vatted Tempranillo, La Mancha 1998, Safeway 15 B

Big and rubbery, loads of supple rich fruit undercut by smoke and acids. Grand glugging here.

SPANISH WINE WHITE

CVNE Monopole Barrel-fermented Rioja 1995 12 D

El Velero Dry White, Valdepenas 1998 13.5 B

Cheap and almost cheerful.

El Velero Rosé, Valdepenas 1998 15 B

Superb rosé: rich, plump and dry fruit. Great with all sorts of food. At most stores.

Moscatel de Valencia 1998, Safeway 

Screwcapped perfection! Wonderful marmalade freshness with a hint of spicy pineapple as it finishes.

USA WINE RED

Dunnewood Zinfandel, Barrel Select 1994 

Fetzer Barrel Select Cabernet Sauvignon 1994 

Great opulence and richness here. Coats the teeth like emulsion. Has bite and backbone.

Kenwood Lodi Old Vine Zinfandel 1996 

Touch overbaked and soupy. Top forty stores.

USA WINE WHITE

Californian Oak-aged Chardonnay 1997, Safeway 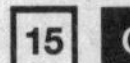

Dunnewood California Chardonnay 1996 

Gorgeous texture and great litheness with the balance of wood and fruit in perfect harmony. A hugely impressive Californian chardonnay without being attached to an obscene price tag.

Fetzer Chardonnay Reserve 1995 16 F

Did white burgundy, Montrachet say, ever taste this good in the good old days? Nope, never. This is a white wine of great class, richness, balance, and sheer world-class finish. Surely, little left on shelf now.

Fetzer Echo Ridge Sauvignon Blanc 1997 15.5 C

If Pouilly Fume tasted like this, it'd cost twenty quid a bottle.

Fetzer Viognier 1997 16 E

Exuberant, spicy, richly elegant yet expressive of fun and roses, with gooseberries and apricots, this is a deliciously swirling, all-dancing viognier of great charm.

Fetzer Viognier 1998 16.5 E

Lovely limpid, lush, lively – a wine of ineffable finesse yet apricot-scented and fruited richness. A rare treat. Fruit to read by, think by, listen by.

Ironstone Chardonnay 1997 15.5 D

Lovely rich fruit, polished and buttery, and with great litheness. It's a muscular yet very spry wine of depth and decisiveness. Very good price.

FORTIFIED WINE

10 Year Old Tawny Port, Safeway 14.5 F

Amontillado, Safeway 13 C

Barbadillo Solear Manzanilla 14 D

Dow's 20-year old Tawny 16 H

What a price! What a wine! To be drunk the night before the morning you get taken out and shot.

Fino, Safeway 14 C

Fonseca Guimaraens 1982 13 G

Marsala Superiore, Garibalde Dolce NV (18% vol) 16 D

Staggeringly rich and figgy. Wonderful for desserts of all descriptions (even if they all come served at once on the same grand plate). Or pour it over ice cream.

Penfolds Magill Tawny (half bottle) 14 D

Warre's Traditional LBV 1984 14.5 G

Warre's Vintage Port, Quinta da Cavadinha 1997 16 H

Superb for such youth. Lovely bucketload of crushed fruit, textured, sweet (but never cloying) and immensely polished and warm. A fabulous treat for ripe cheeses.

Warre's Warrior Finest Reserva 14 E

SPARKLING WINE/CHAMPAGNE

Albert Etienne Champagne Vintage 1993, Safeway

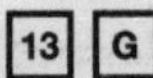

Canard Duchene Champagne Brut NV 14 G

Dry and classically styled.

Charles Heidsieck 'Mis en Cave 1994' Champagne Brut Reserve 16.5 H

A marvellous toasty and hugely biscuity Champagne which manages to end up dry and delicious – and demanding you try another glass. An expensive treat.

Chenin Brut, Vin Mousseux de Qualite (France) 14 C

Conde de Caralt Cava Brut NV 16.5 D

As elegant a cava as they come. Knocks a thousand Champagnes into oblivion. Top 280 stores from mid-June.

Cuvee Signe Champagne, Nicholas Feuillate NV 14.5 G

Undeniably possessed of great haughty finesse and class. Top 235 stores.

Freixenet Cava Rosada Brut NV 13.5 D

Very dry. Doesn't seem to this palate to justify the rosé tag (or price).

Graham Beck Brut NV (South Africa) 14 D

Crisp and gently fruity.

Lambrusco Rosé Light, Safeway (4%vol) 13.5 A

Lightly sparkling wine for old dears and young pretenders.

Lanson Champagne Demi-Sec Ivory Label NV 12 G

Bit too brutal for the classicist and the price sucks.

Lindauer Brut NV (New Zealand) 14.5 E

Expressive of nothing but great value for money and utterly charming sipping.

Louis Roederer Champagne Brut Premier NV 13 H

Top fifty-three stores.

Merlot/Gamay Brut NV (France) 14 C

Different, daring, not subtle – it's great with grilled meats and curries. At most stores.

Nicholas Feuillate Champagne Blanc de Blancs NV 14 G

Piper-Heidsieck Champagne Vintage 1990 13 H

Yes, it has charm. But twenty-three quid's worth? Nope. Top 235 stores.

Pol Acker Chardonnay Brut (France) 14 C

Pommery Brut Royal Champagne NV 12 H

Too expensive for the money. Twenty-one quid!!!! Cava rather. Top fifty-three stores from mid-June.

Seaview Pinot Noir/Chardonnay 1995 (Australia) 15 E

Expands in the mouth on the finish with sesame seeds and some uncategorised fruit. It is dry, very classy and works well from nose to throat.

Segura Viudas Cava Brut 1994 13 E

Selection XXI, Champagne, Nicholas Feuillate NV 13 G

At most stores.

Veuve Clicquot Champagne Vintage Reserve 1991 14 H

A rare treat. A fabulously priced Champagne which shows its class. Top fifty-three stores.

Veuve Clicquot Champagne Yellow Label Brut NV 11 H

Vintage Cava Brut Rosé 1997, Safeway 15 D

Very dry with a delightful, subtle fruity edge.

SAINSBURY'S

End of an era? Or the beginning of a new one?

Manchester United without Matt Busby. It took some getting used to. However, Sir Alex Ferguson has partially overcome the memory of Sir Matt's greatness by creating an even more glittering football team. What has this to do with Sainsbury's? Everything. After twenty-eight years at the retailer, Mr Allan Cheesman had left its wine department (where he spent all of twenty-six of those years). Will the department be rattled? Or will a new director take it on to greater glories? We shall see.

The news that Sainsbury's commercial director for beverages and ambient foods (no, I didn't make it up, that was Allan's real title), was leaving the company in June to join the Australian wine group, BRL Hardy, came as quite a shock. Allan was not just JS's wine guru, he was the inspiration behind many other supermarkets' approach to wine buying and selling. He was a Sainsbury's man through and through, having been with the company for so long. More importantly, he was doing rather well and patently loved wine from the tip of his neatly knotted tie to the toe of his grey cotton socks. His early successes heading up the wine department were arguably what kick-started his Sainsbury's career and while he had left the off-licence arena to run fruit & veg for a few years – in order to accommodate, I suspect, the Sainsbury's ethos that a man clearly intended for the top board could not get there having managed only one department – his most recent role at the company once again saw him in overall charge of wine. But this was obviously insufficient to meet Allan's deepest ambitions (I know him well enough to use his first name but not deeply enough to have insight into his thoughts).

Former retail wine buyers are much sought after by wine companies keen to recruit people who know how their most important customers tick – the cliché about poachers and gamekeepers irresistibly comes to mind and I shall not resist. BRL Hardy doubtless made him an offer he couldn't refuse. His solid French is certainly good enough to get him by in Adelaide and he sports a sort of Aussie no-nonsense thrust to his lower jaw.

Allan was, when asked, looking forward with what I can only describe as boyish enthusiasm to the exotic challenges he would now be facing as a director of a leading Aussie wine producer. 'The past three decades at Sainsbury's have been hugely rewarding', he said. 'I have thoroughly enjoyed working with the ever-dynamic wine and spirits buying team and I will miss them immensely.' He added: 'I am looking forward to working with them in my new capacity as Marketing Director at BRL Hardy Europe.' (It's not Sainsbury's wine department's only loss. The manager of the department under Allan, Mr Robin Tapper – a most charming and competent individual – has also gone, to become a senior manager of Sainsbury's fish and poultry department. Stepping into the breach caused by this departing double act is the very experienced Mr Allan Webb who has come over from directing at Savacentre.)

Allan will immediately notice the stark difference between the buyer and the seller – a power-struggle relationship if ever there was one. With huge volume contracts to offer, the supermarket wine buyer enjoys an enviable position in the wine industry hierarchy. Interestingly enough, Allan had been behind a new initiative at Sainsbury's which had seen the retailer try to build a more constructive and co-operative relationship with its suppliers in all areas.

A report appeared in *The Grocer* magazine in May about the Sainsbury's suppliers conference in Twickenham. Suppliers were left gobsmacked by the change in attitude at J. Sainsbury. Allan

Cheesman was said to be living up to the multiples' promise to work more closely with suppliers. 'We used to be arrogant. But now we want to know what you think we can do better,' he was reported as telling the conference. Allan has now taken the idea of working closely with suppliers as close as it is possible to take it, but the fact that he was linked with this initiative can hardly have counted in his disfavour with his then future employers.

Allan is not the only former head of off-licence buying to have departed Sainsbury's during the last year. It was announced in *Marketing* magazine in April that Mr Mike Connolly, whose latest job had been head of customer relations, had been made redundant as part of a 10% cutback in the Sainsbury's 230-strong head office marketing team. Another casualty was Mr David McNair, brand marketing director. His role was taken over by Sainsbury's head marketer, Mr Kevin McCarten, who became marketing and brand development director. Mr McCarten's own position was thought to be somewhat parlous after the less-than-howling success of the retailer's Value to Shout About ad campaign fronted by John Cleese in horrifically unfunny form. In March, *Retail Week* magazine reported that Sainsbury's moved to defend Mr McCarten after City speculation that a headhunter had been appointed to find a replacement.

Sainsbury's admitted in February that the Value to Shout About campaign had failed to meet its targets. The *Evening Standard*, a local London newspaper, on 5th February quoted Sainsbury's chief executive, Mr Dino Adriano: 'Our Value to Shout About campaign achieved its objective of improving customers' perceptions of value but did not meet its sales target.' But the group said it had no plans to curtail the campaign. Sainsbury's reported like-for-like growth in the 19 weeks to 30th January of 1.2%, against a figure of 3.1% reported by Tesco. Stripping out 1.5% inflation, this meant that Sainsbury's sales actually went down in comparison with the previous Christmas. Mr Cleese and his disagreeable commercials eventually got the chop. Personally, I felt it was the best thing Sainsbury's shelved all year (including putting on the ones marked Bordeaux the remarkable Clos Rene Pomerol 1994 – twenty-five quid at 18 branches but a stunningly concentrated 16.5 point red of such sublime tannicity I would have cheerfully shared a bottle with Mr Cleese if he had promised to shut up and sip quietly).

Things have never been the same for Sainsbury's since it lost its position as the UK's top retailer to Tesco four years ago and the retailer's management teams have been under pressure since then. To return to a football analogy, it was rather like M. United overtaking Liverpool as the dominant team in both England and Europe. In July 1998, Lord Sainsbury bowed out as chairman at the Annual GM, with Mr George Bull taking over as chairman from September. Lord Sainsbury left to take up a government position as a working peer (a concept which is not only homophonically incapable of being explained to a foreigner but is also defiant of elucidation to an intelligent child). His Lordship's appointment as Science Minister was in fact to lead him straightaway into controversy over the government's stance on GM food. Lord Sainsbury's great grandfather was the company's founder and this is the first time in the retailer's 129-year history that a family member has not been at the helm. When writing about Lord Sainsbury's decision to quit, the *FT* featured a photograph – taken back in the 1970s judging by the design of the tills – of seven pin-striped Sainsburys, most either knighted or ennobled, all seated in a line at the checkouts in a Sainsbury's store. It made an amusing picture but the idea of all the senior members of the Sainsbury family working for the Sainsbury's of today would appear to be an even more whimsical and anachronistic notion.

The tough times at Sainsbury's have diluted the personal wealth of Lord Sainsbury. According to *The Sunday Times* Rich List, published in April, he has seen some £200 million wiped off his personal fortune. He is now down to his last £3.1 billion. He is still Britain's second wealthiest person according to the list. The effects on some of Sainsbury's management staff have been rather more drastic. In April, Sainsbury's announced that it was closing the Wokingham head office of its Savacentre operation. Some 85 staff were to be relocated to Sainsbury HQ, but 230 faced redundancy. A month later it was revealed that the retailer planned to spend £150 million refurbishing its London head office. The appointment of Arsenal supporter Mr Dino Adriano as Chief Executive was another significant move. Mr Adriano is an unstuffy and committed individual – pity he doesn't support north London's greatest football team but let that pass – and he knows he has a job on his hands. However, as the son of an Italian accordionist he presumably loves food and music and I strongly suspect a new harmony and greater (and more intelligently directed) daring will begin to manifest themselves at Sainsbury's once everyone is singing from the same song sheet. Mr Adriano said in a *Guardian* interview that he is 'in a position to make the changes. I understand what really lies behind the success of the brand.'

Around this time, late spring '99, it was reported that Sainsbury's share of the UK grocery market had slid to its lowest point since the 1980s. Having lost leadership to Tesco three years ago, Sainsbury saw its share slip a whole percentage point to 19% in the first three months of 1999. *The Times* suggested it was further evidence of the failure of the company's Value to Shout About ad campaign. A few days later, Sainsbury's denied that 300 store managers could lose their jobs as part of a new strategy.

But the following week in *Marketing* magazine, it was reported that Sainsbury's was planning a radical new advertising approach focused on representing its ordinary customers with the strapline Making Life Taste Better. Four new TV commercials had been made and the new marketing strategy was to be unveiled as Sainsbury's announced its results. *Marketing* described the last Sainsbury's campaign, the notorious Value to Shout About commercials, as disastrous.

When not discussing the relative merits of its advertising campaign, the press found Sainsbury's a bountiful source of material over the past year or so. One particular innovation which attracted much media attention was the retailer's decision to sell its own brand merchandise to local village stores. It was not only that the retailer was undertaking this unprecedented course of action that made it such a good story but that it claimed to be doing so for quasi-charitable reasons. The *FT* reported the launch of the SAVE (Sainsburys Assisting Village Enterprises) initiative in August 1998. The trial scheme allows independent shopkeepers to use their local Sainsbury's as a wholesaler. They pay supermarket prices on most goods but earn loyalty points and receive bulk purchase offers. Shopkeepers are allowed to set their own prices. Sainsbury's said the intention of the scheme, run in association with the charity Village Retail Services Association, was to meet a demand for local convenience shopping. One shopkeeper, Brenda Erscott of Halstock in Dorset, said she was confident that she could make profits on the scheme. In many cases, she said, supermarkets' retail prices were cheaper than wholesalers.

But wholesalers such as NISA-Todays, as reported in CTN in August, were not surprisingly highly sceptical of the programme, advising retailers to leave well alone. *Nisa*'s managing director Mr Dudley Ramsden said Sainsbury's had quite a cheek to make such a patronising offer because many independents had already been driven out of the market by supermarket domination.

An *FT* comment also recognised the irony of the situation: 'Having contributed handsomely to the destruction of village stores, J. Sainsbury is now holding out a helping hand'. It added that the move had little downside for the retailer: 'it fosters incremental sales with few additional costs and the local retailers could become proxy home delivery centres in rural areas.'

According to *The Grocer* magazine, five more village stores had signed up to the scheme by September, while research published in *Supermarketing* last autumn suggested that more than a quarter of independent retailers would stock Sainsbury's own label products in their stores if the scheme were extended nationally. It was therefore no surprise to read in *The Times* in May 1999 that following the successful trial, Sainsbury's was planning to expand the scheme nationwide. The company said it expected to have Sainsbury's own label merchandise on sale in more than 200 rural stores by the end of 2001. *Supermarketing* magazine reported in the same month that through a link-up with Post Office Counters, the SAVE scheme was being extended to more than 200 village post offices and rural shops.

While keen to sell its merchandise through small independent shops, Sainsbury's has also been opening some new smaller shops of its own. As with loyalty cards, it has seen the success enjoyed by its arch-rival Tesco, with sub-brands as they are so cutely termed in marketing jargon, and decided to follow suit with the introduction of Sainsbury's Local and Sainsbury's Central. The first Local store opened in Fulham in July 1998. The concept carries only 2,000 lines out of the Sainsbury's 23,000-product range. Locals were later chosen as pilot stores to test Christmas Day opening. In January, Sainsbury's said Christmas Day trading had proved a great success. The Sainsbury's Local stores in Hammersmith in West London and Headcorn in Kent both opened from 10am to 6pm on Christmas Day attracting some 2,000 customers. However, Sainsbury's announced in February that it was cutting back on its wider 24-hour opening programme because of a lack of demand.

This year, the retailer has followed up the development of Sainsbury's Local with the Sainsbury's Central city centre concept. The first Sainsbury's Central store opened in Glasgow in March 1999 to be followed, according to *The Grocer*, by 30 others in prime city centre locations including Tottenham Court Road, Holborn and Edinburgh. In April, the retailer announced that it was planning to open a Sainsbury's Central opposite The Ritz in Mayfair early next year.

But probably the highest profile new store in the Sainsbury's portfolio will be its new supermarket at the Millennium dome site. The company beat off competition from Morrisons, Asda and Tesco to win the prestigious contract for the site. The 55,000 sq ft outlet will be an ultra-green store, requiring 50% of the usual energy requirements and will create 500 new jobs.

Last year, Sainsbury's said it wanted to increase its emphasis on staff training with the introduction of a new appraisal system for staff on the shop floor. Specifically mentioned in the report in *The Grocer* was the fact that 450 of its store staff had been trained to Wine & Spirit Educational Trust certificate level.

A few months later, it was reported in *Supermarketing* that Sainsbury's was aiming to give its wine fixture a more upmarket look. In larger outlets the fine wine selection was to be separately branded as Special Selection. Around 90 stores stock a range of 25 fine wines, with 20 larger outlets carrying 40 fine wine lines. The retailer said it planned to sell ultra-fine wines at its Savacentre store in Calcot, Reading and the Sainsbury's store in Swiss Cottage. The company described this as an experiment. Some of these wines will sell for £100-plus but the first one I persuaded the store to open for me to taste, a red burgundy, was corked (that is to say the fruit had been marred by a cork poisoned by cork taint) and had I been a paying customer presumably a refund would have been instantly available.

Quite what a supermarket is doing selling wines for £100 a time is something of a mystery – but only if you look at the larger picture. By the use of this book you can, I hope, find some superb Sainsbury's wines for a fraction of £100 but what of the well-heeled individual who regards his individual Sainsbury's store as his local wine shop? In the case of certain poshly sited Sainsbury's, like the one it was rumoured the late Princess of Wales had been spotted at in west London's Cromwell Road, the store is seen in this way and, especially at certain times of the year, highly expensive wines will move smartly off the shelves. Sainsbury's obviously feels that there are shoppers in its stores who can be seduced into such extravagance and I do not think they are mistaken. Identifying such arguably maladjusted individuals is what retailers call customer profiling and Sainsbury's believes it has reached new heights of excellence in this area. Aforementioned marketing supremo, Mr Kevin McCarten, last year came up with a new way of dividing up the Sainsbury's clientele, separating them into seven segments. Apparently, this approach involves segmenting consumers in terms of their needs though I must say I find it difficult to believe no-one has been struck by this insight before (it's surely been used in other businesses, like the American entertainment industry, for some years). Mr McCarten sees Customer Needs Segmentation (CNS) as a major analytical breakthrough which will deliver significant competitive advantages. He said in *The Grocer*: 'This allows us to dissect how customers behave, what motivates them and enables us to cluster this information back in a way that lets us act in a very focused way.' I must confess to feeling that CNS sounds like that classic preserve of the marketing researcher, which is to state the blindingly obvious in a linguistic manner which suggests that TOE* has finally been cracked. I am probably doing Mr McCarten and his researchers a grave injustice but Customer Needs Segmentation doesn't sound so different from what Sainsbury's and its rivals have been doing for years. (I cannot say for sure because the precise details of Mr McCarten's seven segments are being kept a closely guarded secret.) Most intriguingly, Sainsbury's was taking the precaution of not sharing the details with its employees. According to the article in *The Grocer*, only seven people in the Sainsbury's organisation were privy to the workings of the new system. 'One of the issues we've got is how far within our business we should deploy the level of understanding of the strategic elements of this model,' said Mr McCarten. 'It's quite complicated and we don't want to inspire the wrong action.'

Not everything Sainsbury's does is so coded, secret, or sounds remotely so eccentric. In fact, the retailer has brought in a number of sensible innovations during the past year or so. Coffee bars in its stores was a good move, though coffee shops have been a feature of many larger branches for some time. In July 1998, Sainsbury's launched trials for two branded in-store coffee bars at two stores. The introduction of the Costa and Perfection coffee bars put a question mark over the roll-out of the company's own J-Expresso concept. The Sainsbury's Bank appears to be going from strength to strength and is a positive development. At the end of last year, *The Sunday Times* reported that Sainsbury's Bank was about to sign up its one millionth customer and would have £2 billion on deposit to mark its second year of trading. At the same time, the retailer announced that it was extending its loyalty card scheme allowing consumers to spend their reward points at several high street retailers such as Dorothy Perkins, Burton, Top Shop as well as Burger King, British Gas and Blockbuster.

However, home shopping does not appear to be a high priority development for the retailer. While some retailers have been going gangbusters with the expansion of home shopping initiatives, it was reported in *The Grocer* in May 1999 that Sainsbury's was scaling down its Orderline home shopping service saying that customers did not want it. The retailer cut the number of stores offering the service to nine – all inside the M25 – and abandoned plans to expand the service further, though it said that home shopping was an area it would continue to investigate in spite of an apparent lack of demand.

The retailer was also highly commended in *Marketing* for the introduction of a new type of trolley. In January, a feature in this magazine praised the new Sainsbury's people-carrier trolley which allows a shopper with three children to transport them all in one trolley – two forward-facing seats for toddlers/small children and a rear-facing baby seat. Sainsbury's is testing the new style of trolley and said it was considering adding features such as play steering wheels and books or even designing the trolleys in the shape of popular children's characters. Also with the younger members of the population in mind – but their parents firmly in its sights – Sainsbury's announced in December that it was to give away more than a million books to babies over the next two years as part of a £6 million sponsorship of Bookstart.

On Green matters, the retailer has also made encouraging progress. In *Retail Week* in April 1999, it was reported that Sainsbury's was striving to catch up Tesco in the organic department by introducing a core range of 50 organic lines in all its stores. The full organic line-up was increased from 400 to 450 lines in May. The previous August, Sainsbury's had offered free car exhaust emission tests at 17 stores for a month as part of the government's Greener Vehicles Campaign. However, the retailer did incur the wrath of Green lobbyists over its approach to selling kangaroo meat. In 1998, *Supermarketing* reported that the vegetarian charity, Viva, was holding demonstrations at 110 Sainsbury's stores to protest against the company selling the meat of Australia's jumping beast. The charity said that the meat trade was wiping out kangaroo populations in Australia, but Sainsbury's said it sourced kangaroo meat, which was then selling in 200 stores, from legitimate culls.

The legitimacy of Sainsbury's supply sources was also brought into question in a quite different area of its operation. Like most supermarkets, the retailer has been selling branded merchandise at discount prices much to the chagrin of the brand owners. In 1998, Nike was threatening to take legal action against Sainsbury's to prevent the retailer from selling what it said were counterfeit Nike polo shirts. Sainsbury's said it was confident that the items were genuine and had no intention of removing them from its shelves. The move came at a time when Tommy Hilfiger was suing Tesco over similar claims. In this case, though, Sainsbury's quickly recanted. The day after the first report appeared in the *FT*, Sainsbury's bowed to pressure and withdrew the polo shirts from its shelves. It admitted that evidence produced by Nike had raised questions about their authenticity.

Sainsbury's reported that it had made progress in EPOS (electronic point of sale) during the last year. In September 1998, there were several reports about Sainsbury's holding trials of an electronic shelf-edge labelling system – allowing the retailer to vary prices at different stores with utmost ease – at one of its supermarkets in Berkshire. One can only hope that this system does not run into the same difficulties encountered by a Sainsbury's outlet in Fulham late last year, as reported in the *Daily Telegraph*. The newspaper wrote that a power cut had meant that checkout operators had to estimate all prices on customers' goods, rounding down to the nearest pound or 50p. Fulham residents are nothing if not opportunists (after all, they persuaded a store owner who shall remain nameless to buy the local football club). The report went on to say that some customers were sensibly milking the situation, leaving the checkout queue to fill up another trolley. Commenting on the resultant necessary mental arithmetic, an employee on the checkout was reported as saying 'I haven't had to do this since my training 15 years ago,' while the reporter remarked that he had 'not seen prices like this for about 15 years either.'

Another technical innovation which appears to have run into trouble is the so-called video wall which the retailer introduced with much hype at its store in Clapham. The £1 million display had been, quite literally, less than a glowing success. The idea was that rather than facing plate glass, people walking by the store would be treated to a massive high-tech video display along the entire face of the wall. It ran into problems, however, almost immediately – not least because the wall was very hard to see in daylight hours. It failed to attract the expected sponsorship and the retailer, according to *Supermarketing*, subcontracted the management of the wall to an independent production company in January.

Whether these things are successes or failures, what they do show is that Sainsbury is being innovative again. And this can only be good for the wine department which has, over the past year, been solid in its presentation of interesting own-label ranges. These are a departure from the Sainsbury norm and to explain why, I need to disinter a little piece of marketing history.

Let us, briefly, go back to the early eighties; to the chilling moment when the makers of the nation's most famous brand of frozen food realised that customers were more likely to buy the supermarket own-label product. The implications of this only began to sink in during the decade when the Big Brands discovered that shoppers actually trusted supermarkets more than manufacturers. Supermarkets were thrilled and began plastering their names over everything – including wine. What Tesco was the first to begin with its own-label sherry back in 1969 had by the twilight years of the Thatcher epoch become a flood when supermarkets' names appeared on all manner of bottles. Sainsbury's went the furthest. By 1989 Sainsbury's had some 300 wines in its range of which 169 all proclaimed themselves to be its own.

The degree to which this sort of branding was acceptable to drinkers reached its apogee during the recession of the 80s/90s. Conspicuous consumption was anathema. It was even seen as mildly fashionable to have supermarket own-label bottles at dinner parties; it demonstrated that though the hosts were tightening their belts they were still able to dish out decent wine.

Today, this is all wildly unhip. We have retained our recessionary attitudes when buying wine, and bargains are widely hunted out, but we don't wish to be patronised by supermarkets to the extent of seeing their names on every bottle. Sainsbury's Cotes-du-Rhone for midweek bangers and mash is okay but for the weekend, with more time to prepare food and experiment, or for entertaining, we want bottles which don't patronise us even with such mild possessiveness as the long gone Sainsbury's Chateau de Gourgazaud 1986 (£5.75 the magnum).

What has belatedly sunk in is that supermarket wine departments must be less overt in their branding. Hence, over the past year, a proliferation of wine ranges at supermarkets which though created specifically for the supermarket do not have the Name significantly emblazoned. Sainsbury now has the excellent Bankside range of southern French reds, the Spice Route range (though not all the wines in the range are exclusive to Sainsbury), Alteza from Spain, Stonybrook from California, and I expect to see many more over the next few years as wine buyers spread their wings and develop this concept. Many of these wines make for excellent drinking and, for those who care about appearances, there is often no evidence from a cursory glance at the front label that Sainsbury is behind it.

Many such wines I have been happy to drink to accompany the words I was forced to eat in 1999. I had written Sainsbury off as a supplier of £2.99 and under wines – wines of quality and pace – because I saw clearly that prices were not sustainable at this point for very much longer (except for price-reductions and special offers). From the wine department's point of view much more exciting ranges are possible to develop at £3.99 and £4.99. But Sainsbury's came up with a terrific pair of Vin de Pays de l'Audes, a red and a white, at £2.99 (still on sale) and never were my words so deliciously enhanced as they descended my gullet helped by these wines' well-formed 15-point fruit. I look forward to downing more examples of similarly priced wines at Sainsbury in future, though not, it is surely safe to speculate, from BRL Hardy – though with Mr Allan Cheesman now running the marketing here this may be a rash statement. Do I need to prepare myself for another plate of my own words, Allan?

* TOE sucking is the fashionable pursuit of theoretical physicists unravelling the ingrowing layers which it is believed conceal the Theory Of Everything from human grasp. TOE, naked, will show us how all the forces, all matter in the universe, is of a piece and so the minuscule components of quantum mechanics will merge smoothly with the massive concepts of cosmology – time, space, etc. It is also believed TOE will eventually yield the reason why certain persons spend £50 on a bottle of champagne rather than £5 on a cava when it is impossible for such individuals to tell them apart in the glass.

Sainsbury's Supermarkets Limited
Stamford House
Stamford Street
London SE1 9LL
Tel: 0171 921 6000
Fax: 0171 921 7925
Customer Care Line: 0800 636262
website www.sainsbury.co.uk.

SEE STOP PRESS SECTION AT END OF BOOK FOR LAST-MINUTE ADDITIONS OR UPDATES TO THIS RETAILER'S RANGE.

ARGENTINIAN WINE RED

Alamos Ridge Cabernet Sauvignon 1996 16.5 D

Gorgeous, meaty and rich. A most wonderfully textured and well polished wine. 170 stores.

Mendoza Cabernet Sauvignon/Malbec NV, Sainsbury's 15.5 C

Textured, tauntingly rich and ripe, dry and deep. Great food wine.

Mendoza Country Red NV, Sainsbury's 15 B

Superb value for money: a sticky rich yet accomplished and well-balanced fruity specimen of great charm.

Norton Malbec, Mendoza 1995 16 D

Juicy yet classy and full of busy tannins. These latter are subdued under the onrush of fruit – which is high quality. Selected stores.

Trapiche Oak Cask Reserve Cabernet Sauvignon 1995 17 D

Superb class here: richness, savouriness, thickness and utterly brilliant fruit. It is utterly lovely. 175 stores.

ARGENTINIAN WINE WHITE

Alamos Ridge Chardonnay 1997 16.5 D

Elegant, confident, subtly rich and very very good value. It has such calmness, such unhurried, restrained fruit. Not at all stores.

Mendoza Country White NV, Sainsbury's 14.5 B

Fantastic value: real rich, balanced, clean fruit.

Tupungato Chardonnay NV, Sainsbury's 13 C

Selected stores.

AUSTRALIAN WINE RED

Australian Cabernet Sauvignon, Sainsbury's 16 C

Superb fruit here. Has dash, dynamic fruit, lovely tannins and beautifully crunchy texture.

Australian Red Wine NV, Sainsbury's (3-litre box) 15 B

Price bracket has been adjusted to the 75cl equivalent.

Australian Shiraz 1997, Sainsbury's 14 C

Soft and squashy and very slurpable.

Banrock Station Mataro/Grenache/Shiraz 1998 13 C

From the very over-ripe sticky Banrock '98 stable.

Brown Brothers Tarrango 1998 13 D

They should put it on a lolly stick. Selected stores.

Cawarra Shiraz/Merlot/Ruby Cabernet 1998 13.5 C

Very ripe and jammy.

Clancy's Barossa Valley Red 1997 14.5 E

Cough linctus thick and rich. It needs spicy food to bring it in line. At most stores.

Eileen Hardy Shiraz 1995 13.5 H

Don't like the over-ripeness on the finish for twenty-eight quid. Fifteen selected stores.

Hardys Bankside Shiraz 1997 14 D

Juicy and tobacco tinged. Expensive, gently tannic and tense to finish. Not at all stores.

Hardys Cabernet Shiraz Merlot 1996 16.5 D

Hugely meaty construct of immense and tannic furriness. The texture and richness make it exceptional. 155 stores.

Hardys Coonawarra Cabernet Sauvignon 1995 15 E

Impressive caressing fruit which has lovely tannic bite on the finish. Meaty and mouthwatering. Selected stores.

Leasingham Cabernet Sauvignon Malbec 1996 14.5 E

Leasingham Domaine Shiraz 1996 15 E

Some character and rich fruit here. Soupy yes, but there is a hint of backbone to the flesh. 70 selected stores.

Lindemans Bin 45 Cabernet Sauvignon 1997 14.5 D

More correct than exciting but well-formed and rich to finish. Good with food.

Lindemans Cawarra Homestead Shiraz Cabernet 1998 14 C

Smooth, untroubled, fruity and unpretentious. Not at all stores.

Lindemans Limestone Coast Shiraz 1997  15 D

Hints of earth to the cherry/plum softness. All fruit mostly. Selected stores.

Lindemans Padthaway Pinot Noir 1997 15 E

Mount Hurtle Cabernet Merlot 1996 14 D

Mount Hurtle Grenache Shiraz 1997 15.5 C

Soupy, rich, very soft and cherry/plum on the finish and simply grand, modern glugging, Not at all stores.

Oxford Landing Cabernet Sauvignon Shiraz 1998 15 D

Martian: 'This wine is made from grapes?'

Winewriter: 'Yes.'
Martian: 'It defies belief. How can alcohol taste so yummy?'
Winewriter: 'They don't have palates on Mars?'

Penfolds Bin 389 Cabernet Shiraz 1995 15 F

Expensive muscle here. It's a bouncer of a wine: you don't get in without a hassle. Highly drinkable with food – spicy, rich, deep. Eighty selected stores.

Penfolds Organic Merlot Shiraz Cabernet 1998 15.5 E

Delicious, if a while in getting the point of its soft fruitiness. It begins monosyllabically; ends with loghorrea. Selected stores.

Rosemount Diamond Label Shiraz 1997 15 D

Rosemount Estate Grenache/Shiraz 1998 15 D

Yes, it's immensely juicy but fine tannins interrupt the flood – well in time. Selected stores.

Rosemount Estate Shiraz 1997 16.5 E

Massively mouth-filling and rampant. Almost an alien construct compared to similar graped Rhone reds.

Rosemount Estate Shiraz Cabernet 1998 15.5 D

So deliciously sweet and fruity: soft and full yet delicate on the finish. Deliciously approachable and warm.

Stowells Australian Red Mataro/Shiraz NV (3-litre box) 15.5 C

Price bracket has been adjusted to the 75cl equivalent.

Tyrrells Old Winery Cabernet Merlot 1997 13 D

115 selected stores.

Wolf Blass Shiraz/Grenache 1998 15 D

Lovely rich softie for Indian food. Oh yes! Selected stores.

Wolf Blass Yellow Label Cabernet Sauvignon 1997 16 E

Fabulous rich fruit which would be wonderful with Indian food. Ripe and rampant. Selected stores.

Wynns Coonawarra Shiraz 1996 16.5 D

Superbly classy and rich. Hints of mint cling to the deeply textured (denim and corduroy) fruit (plums, cherries and blackcurrants) and the sheer cheek of the fruit, its bounce yet gravitas, is terrific – the finish is syrup of figs.

AUSTRALIAN WINE WHITE

Australian Chardonnay NV, Sainsbury's 16 C

Superb value for money. Great richness and acidic balance here. Remarkable value.

Australian Semillon Chardonnay NV, Sainsbury's (3-litre box) 15 B

Price bracket has been adjusted to the 75cl equivalent.

Australian White Wine NV, Sainsbury's (3-litre box) 14 B

Price bracket has been adjusted to the 75cl equivalent.

Brown Brothers Late Harvested Orange Muscat and Flora 1998 (half bottle) 14.5 D

Sweet and floral, it goes best with fresh fruits. Ninety selected stores.

Hardys Banrock Station Chenin Blanc/Chardonnay 1998 12.5 C

Very blowsy, fat and sticky rich. Odd fruit. Is it wine? Or jam?

Hardys Chardonnay Sauvignon Blanc 1998 14.5 D

Nutty, soft, rich, deftly double-whammied and most unhesitant to please. Not at all stores.

Hardys Padthaway Chardonnay 1997 15.5 E

Hints of wood and dry lemon overcoating with rich and elegant fruit. Fifty selected stores.

Hardys Stamp of Australia Chardonnay Semillon 1998 15.5 C

Delicious! Unusually complex yet modern and fresh. Has layers of melon (not overripe) and what seems like a hint of raspberry. Good acidity buffers this fruity attack.

Hardys Stamp of Australia Riesling Gewurztraminer 1998 15.5 C

The perfect Thai dish wine. It has spice and freshness, pace and plump, roseate fruit. Selected stores.

Jacobs Creek Semillon/Chardonnay 1998 

Old warhorse still good value and richly fruity (but balanced).

Lindemans Bin 65 Chardonnay 1998 

A hugely elegant vintage, this, for a classic Aussie chardonnay. It has purpose, stealth, wit and warmth, and invites comparison with chardonnays daring to cost a lot more.

Lindemans Cawarra Homestead Unoaked Chardonnay 1998 

Lovely rich edge to the fresh, never over-baked fruit.

Lindemans Limestone Coast Chardonnay 1997 

Full of personality, polish, plumpness and poise. Lovely stuff. Selected stores.

Mount Hurtle Grenache Rosé 1998 

Very jammy and toast-spreadable. Not at all stores.

Ninth Island Chardonnay 1998 16 E

An expensive treat with its creamy depth and complex finish. Has a suggestion of old world vegetality but it is a triumph of cold fermentation and full fruit-retaining winemaking techniques. 150 stores.

Penfolds Koonunga Hill Chardonnay 1998 

What a great brand! Stunning richness and balanced, classy finish. If only white burgundians at three times the price could be this good.

Penfolds Organic Chardonnay/Sauvignon Blanc, Clare Valley 1997 14 E

Curious over-ripe touches here. Great with rich fish dishes. Selected stores.

Penfolds Rawsons Retreat Bin 21 Semillon/Chardonnay/Colombard 1998 15 C

Fat and full of fun. Great striding style of behaviour over the taste buds.

Penfolds The Valleys Chardonnay 1998 16.5 D

Delicate yet potent, rich yet unshowy, balanced yet full-frontal and unashamedly hedonistic. A lovely wine. 125 stores.

Rosemount Estate Diamond Label Chardonnay 1998 16 D

Has a very sure sense of itself, this mature, beautifully textured, warmly fruity wine. Delicious. At most stores.

Tyrrells Old Winery Chardonnay 1997 12 D

Selected stores.

Wolf Blass Chardonnay 1998 16 D

Unusually elegant and restrained for old Wolfie. Has a lovely buttery afterglow, very subtle, and firm delivery. Selected stores.

Wynns Coonawarra Riesling 1997 17 C

Stunning classic style of riesling with forward lemon fruit plus a hint of paraffin. A superb thirst-and-thought quenching wine. Not at all stores.

BULGARIAN WINE RED

Bulgarian Cabernet Sauvignon, Sainsbury's (3-litre box) 13.5 C

Price bracket has been adjusted to the 75cl equivalent.

Bulgarian Country Dry Red, Russe, Sainsbury's (1.5 litre) 14.5 B

Price bracket has been adjusted to the 75cl equivalent.

Czar Simeon Bulgarian Cabernet Sauvignon 1990 13.5 D

Domaine Boyar Premium Oak Barrel Aged Merlot 1997 14 C

Sweet but very dry. Good for curries and what not.

JS Bulgarian Merlot, Oak Aged, Russe 13.5 B

BULGARIAN WINE WHITE

Bulgarian Chardonnay NV, Sainsbury's 12 B

Very raw fruit. At most stores.

CHILEAN WINE RED

35 Sur Cabernet Sauvignon 1998 16.5 C

Superb cabernet of wit, warmth, character, concentration, softness yet dryness, approachability yet seriousness and a great potency of flavour on the finish. A vivacious cabernet of punch and pertinacity.

Caliterra Cabernet Sauvignon 1998 16 C

A lovely dry, chewy (yet chocolatey) cabernet of richness, savour and svelte texture.

Canepa Zinfandel 1997 15.5 C

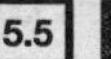

Jammy, hint of spice, rich and lingering on the finish. The finish is a real climax of hedgerow fruit and tannins.

Chilean Cabernet Merlot, Sainsbury's 15 C

So slurpable and romantic it brings tears to the drinker's eyes and a blush to the cheeks.

Chilean Cabernet Sauvignon/Merlot NV, Sainsbury's 16 C

Volatile on the nostrils and slightly overripe but the fruit is brilliant: dry, rich, flavourful and character packed. Real class runs through it. Wonderful rich, dry, textured stuff. Also available in a 3-litre box.

Chilean Merlot, Sainsbury's 16.5 C

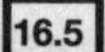

Wonderful richness of tone, texture, and even a touch of soulfulness. A gorgeous, savoury, smooth wine of lingering depth.

Chilean Red, Sainsbury's 

La Palma Merlot Gran Reserva 1998 

Vividly coloured, vivaciously fruity, this magnificently perfumed and very poshly polished merlot is simply world class. The texture is awesomely delightful. Sixty stores.

Mont Gras Cabernet Sauvignon Reserva 1997 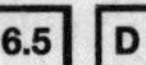

It descends by devious means. The first step is sheer fruity fun then it gets deeper, dryer and richer and finally the echo is sheer classic cabernet. Around 100 selected stores.

Mont Gras Carmenere Reserva 1998 

Lots of delicious, rippling muscle here – touch jammy, but the tannins are deep and very classy. 120 stores.

Mont Gras Merlot Reserva 1997 

Very juicy. 105 selected stores.

Terra Mater Zinfandel Syrah, Maipo 1998 

Fruit juice with real street-cred attitude – i.e. it's sassy and confident, dry yet rounded. Not at all stores.

Valdivieso Malbec 1998 

Malbec as smooth and plump as it comes picked. Selected stores.

Valdivieso Merlot, Lontue 1998 

More perfumed than previous vintages and with more chewy richness on the finish.

Valdivieso Reserve Cabernet Sauvignon 1997 17 D

Has the lot (except an obscene price tag). But the fruit is forbidden and x-certificate: dark, dry, mysterious, touch spicy, highly aromatic and heady and finally it's so damned delicious. Hellish good drinking here. 185 selected stores.

Villa Montes Gran Reserva Cabernet Sauvignon 1996 16 D

Nicely warmly composed, leathery, savoury, crumpled-velvet textured and classy. 150 selected stores.

Vina San Pedro Cabo de Hornos Special Reserve 1995 17 F

It pours out from the bottle in a flood of dark crimson glints. It impinges on the nose as tobacco-scented, faintly ripe, subtly-spiced plum with a touch of leather. The fruit is controlled, rich, leathery, chocolate touched with cassis – plus tannins, ripe yet firm and in perfect alliance with the fruit, the acidity, and the gently vegetal, oily fruit which can be glucoid rich and flowing because the overall sense of the wine is dry but richly fruity. The texture is the finest ruffled velvet. Elegant, haughty, polished – it is ineffably Chilean. It has warmth in its blood, strength in its sinews, a pulse, a heart and a soul. Etc. Eighty selected stores.

CHILEAN WINE WHITE

35 Sur Sauvignon Blanc 1998  C

Superb! The grassiness of the acidity and the richness of fruit, still classic dry sauvignon, make for a wonderful crisp mouthful. Selected stores.

Canepa Gewurztraminer 1998 

Needs a year to blossom – then it might rate 15/16 points for its spicy fruit. Selected stores.

Casablanca Sauvignon Blanc 1998 

Chewy, edgy richness with faraway hints of meadow and brook. Selected stores.

Chilean Cabernet Sauvignon Rosé NV, Sainsbury's 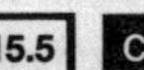

The essence of what fine rosé should be: utterly quaffable and fruity, yet dry and food friendly. Selected stores.

Chilean Chardonnay NV, Sainsbury's 

Touch of grass, almond, spinach and rich melon fruit. Motley crew but great with food.

Chilean Sauvignon Blanc, Sainsbury's 

Beautiful balance and fruity attack. Rivetingly crisp, fresh, modish fruit.

Chilean Semillon Sauvignon NV, Sainsbury's (3-litre box) 

Price bracket has been adjusted to the 75cl equivalent.

Santa Carolina Chardonnay 1998 15 C

Not as rich as the '97 but has a lovely nuttiness on the finish. Selected stores.

Stowells Chilean Sauvignon Blanc NV (3-litre box) 13 B

Almost good enough, but not quite. Price bracket is the 75cl equivalent.

ENGLISH WINE — WHITE

Denbies Estate English Table Wine NV

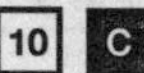

Duller than watching paint dry. Like chewing on a sweater. Selected stores.

Lamberhurst Sovereign Medium Dry NV

The worst label on Sainsbury's shelves fronting an ineffably boring wine.

FRENCH WINE — RED

Abbotts Cumulus Shiraz 1997

The impressive fruit of the '96 is not quite so powerfully in evidence in the '97. Abbotts is herby, rich, dry and characterful and with a deft balance of elements providing class and substance. This is more playful and soft than the '96. 190 selected stores.

Bankside Gallery Merlot, VdP d'Oc 1997

Warm and soft, ripe but dry. Selected stores.

Bankside Gallery Syrah, VdP d'Oc 1997 16 C

Tutti-frutti juicy yet the tannins give it richness and rampancy plus structure. Selected stores.

Beaujolais NV, Sainsbury's 13.5 C

Simple glugging pleasure.

Beaujolais Villages Les Roches Grillees 1998, Sainsbury's 13 C

Has a tang of old rubber boots coated in soft fruits.

Bordeaux Rouge, Sainsbury's 13 B

Cabernet Sauvignon d'Oc NV, Sainsbury's 15.5 C

Cabernet Sauvignon VdP d'Oc, Caroline Beaulieu 1997 17 C

Superb, tobacco-edged richness, ripeness and depth and a tannic-edged finish. Fantastic class for the money.

Cahors, Sainsbury's 13.5 C

Chartreuse de la Garde, Pessac-Leognan 1995

Lovely alert fruit vigilantly unbowed by the strident tannins. A most stylish claret of aplomb and alacrity. 165 stores.

Chasse du Pape Cotes du Rhone 1997

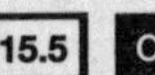

Bulky yet lithe. Great hints of vegetality and spice to some warm, rich, soupy/dry wine. Selected stores.

Chateau Barreyres, Haut-Medoc 1996 14 E

Chateau Beaumont Cru Bourgeois, Haut Medoc 1995

Very classy and bold with a mass of crunchy cassis-and-tannin-coated fruit. Selected stores.

Chateau Carsin, Premieres Cotes de Bordeaux 1996 17 D

Magnificent texture, ripeness, with an initial perfume of great charm, an immediate lushness which then turns seriously oily and fat in the mouth buttressed by perfectly precise tannins. A fabulous modern claret of superb depth and elegance. 150 selected stores.

Chateau Clement-Pichon, Haut-Medoc 1995 13 F

Chateau Coufran Cru Bourgeois, Haut Medoc 1996 13 F

Selected stores.

Chateau de Chamirey Rouge, Mercurey 1996 14 F

Wickedly French and rich with hints of rustic real estate. Selected stores.

Chateau de la Grande Gandiole Chateauneuf-du-Pape 1997 16.5 F

Rolling fruit which unfurls like a complex carpet of tufted fruits and dry, woody richness. Lovely toe-tingling finish. 100 selected stores.

Chateau de la Tour Bordeaux Rouge 1997 13.5 D

Well, it's claret. So it's dry and a touch growly and slightly unfulfilled. Thirty stores.

Chateau de Mercey, Mercurey Rouge 1995 13.5 E

A lot of dry fruit. Tenner's worth? Not quite. Selected stores.

Chateau Fourcas Dumont, Listrac 1996 14 F

Intense tannins and woody fruit. A roast beef wine. Selected stores.

Chateau Grand Bourdieu, Bordeaux Superieure 1995 13 D

Chateau Haut de la Pierriere Cotes de Castillon 1997 16 D

The essence of what minor league but bonny claret is all about: cigar boxes, bell pepper, spice, tannins, blackcurrants. True, it's very dry but it's classy and terrific value.

Chateau la Cardonne, Medoc 1995 16 E

Hugely gripping fruit which will choke the incautious quaffer. Has Falstaffian robustness and dryness of wit. Selected stores.

Chateau la Vieille Cure, Fronsac 1995 16.5 F

Better than ever this vintage. Wonderful classic cigar-rich finish. Selected stores.

Chateau le Noble, Bordeaux Rouge 1996 14.5 C

Crushed blackberry fruit with a chewy edge. Terrific little claret. Thirty selected stores.

Chateau les Alberts, Lussac St Emilion 1997 15 D

Nice plump fruit, with some polish to the dry, cracked leather interior.

Chateau Memoires, Bordeaux 1996 14 D

Very dark, dry merlot with a rich middle palate of flavours, but rests on the finish. Selected stores.

Chateau Semeillan Mazeau Cru Bourgeois, Listrac 1996 14 G

Bit pricey but the fruit needs some swallowing too. It's tannicity personified. Selected stores.

Chateau Verdignan Haut-Medoc 1996 15.5 F

A most accomplished, polished claret of some style. Not yet completely as ready to drink as it will be in four or five years, it has great tannin and no mean degree of blackcurrant fruit. Sixty selected stores.

Chateauneuf-du-Pape, Domaine Michel Bernard 1997 13 F

Chinon Domaine du Colombier 1997 14 C

Very dry and a touch austere. But some of us like cabernet franc that rustic way. Not at all stores.

Claret Cuvee Prestige, Sainsbury's 14 C

Richer and smoother than the cheaper, straightforward Claret. A rich cousin.

Claret, Sainsbury's 14.5 C

Good tobacco-edged fruit of typical dryness here. Really drinkable.

Classic Selection Brouilly 1997, Sainsbury's 14 D

Classic Selection Chateauneuf-du-Pape 1997, Sainsbury's 15 E

Beautiful clods of earthy plums and subtle strawberries, a hint of pepper. Touch rustic? Perhaps – but it's very characterful. 165 stores.

Clos Magne Figeac, St Emilion 1994 16 E

Gorgeous rich texture, high class fruit – rich and dry – and a broad, multifaceted finish. Good now, very good, but will develop for five to seven years. Selected stores.

Clos Rene, Pomerol 1994 16.5 H

If one must spend £25 on a claret this is worth every penny. It drips with developed tannins, has huge complexity of fruit, will age for seven or eight years and it's all roaring now. Eighteen selected stores.

Cornas Les Serres Delas Freres 1992 14 G

Cotes du Rhone NV, Sainsbury's 14.5 B

Fantastic value: rich, soft, bright and bonny. Selected stores.

Cotes du Rhone Villages Domaine Michel Bernard 1997 14 C

Very soft and approachable. Selected stores.

Crozes Hermitage Petite Ruche 1997 15.5 E

Old cheroots and spice jars plus a hint of charcoal. Selected stores.

Fitou Chateau de Segure 1997 14 D

Juicy but dry to finish and highly flavoured dishes will mar its freshness. Not at all stores.

Hautes Cotes de Nuits Les Dames Huguettes, Domaine Bertagna 1997 15 D

Excellent texture here and huge seriousness of purpose. Classier than many examples at three times the price. Selected stores.

Kressman Monopole Bordeaux Rouge 1996 12 D

Dead boring claret. Suit an old field-marshal on his death bed facing his maker (having, in his lifetime, sent a quarter of a million men to their deaths). Such a warrior will find some hellish charm here. So do I – in part. Selected stores.

La Baume Cabernet Sauvignon, VdP d'Oc 1997 17 C

Cherries, earth, ripeness, balance, a subtle herbiness and wonderful deep savoury beefy tannins. What a broth! Selected stores.

La Demoiselle de Sociando Mallet, Haut Medoc 1996 10 G

Great overture, poor symphonic finale. 105 stores.

LPA Cotes de St Mont 1996 14 C

More like a stingy claret than a roustabout rustic red. Great with food. Selected stores.

Merlot VdP d'Oc NV, Sainsbury's (1.5 litre) 15.5 D

Price bracket has been adjusted to the 75cl equivalent.

Merlot VdP de la Cite de Carcassonne, Caroline de Beaulieu 1998 17 C

Fantastic leathery tannins, rich ripe fruit (cherries/plums/blackberries), and wonderful dry-edged finish. Hugely elegant and compelling. Selected stores.

Minervois, Sainsbury's 15 B

Pauillac Bouvoyre 1995 13.5 G

Very polished and demurely tannic. Touch arrogant. 105 stores.

Philippe de Rothschild Cabernet Sauvignon d'Oc 1997 12 C

Philippe de Rothschild Merlot VdP d'Oc 1997 13 C

Prieure de Cenac, Cahors 1995 15.5 D

Old style/new style. Interesting clash of styles providing ripeness and raunchiness. Selected stores.

Red Burgundy NV, Sainsbury's 12 D

Savigny-les-Beaune, Paul Dugenais 1996 13.5 E

Nice firm tannins. A tenner for tannins? Not on, is it! Selected stores.

Stowells Claret NV (3-litre box) 10 C

Price bracket has been adjusted to the 75cl equivalent.

Syrah VdP d'Oc NV, Sainsbury's 13.5 B

A simple party wine with a parting shot of earth and plums.

Trilogie VdP d'Oc, Maurel Vedeau 1996 16.5 C

Fabulous subtle spiciness, meatiness, richness, tannicity and texture. Selected stores.

Valreas Domaine de la Grande Bellane 1998 16.5 D

Wonderful damson-coloured fruit which stretches, as a flavoured artefact, over the taste buds with huge softness and richness. Hugely civilised, svelte and well tailored. Not at all stores.

Vieux Chateau Landon, Medoc 1996 13 E

Eighty selected stores.

Vin de Pays de l'Aude Rouge, Sainsbury's 16 B

Tremendous richness and savoury depth here. Hint of leather, hedgerow fruit, tannin. Fantastic. Selected stores.

Vin de Pays des Bouches du Rhone NV, Sainsbury's 14.5 B

Good controlled earthiness, tannins, and a rich, warm finish.

Vougeot Domaine Bertagna 1995 13 G

FRENCH WINE WHITE

Bankside Gallery Chardonnay, VdP d'Oc 1997 16 C

Gently burnt-rubbery and off-handedly rich and nutty. Selected stores.

Blanc Anjou, Medium Dry, Sainsbury's 12 B

Blason de Maucaillou Sauvignon, Bordeaux 1997 16 C

Terrific melon and lemon, rich and ripe. Great with all sorts of fish. Unusually good value Bordeaux blanc.

Bordeaux Blanc, Sainsbury's 14.5 B

Utterly simple but delightfully charming. Terrific fresh, clean, gently fruity value.

Bourgogne Chardonnay Domaine Laroche 1996 13.5 D

Selected stores.

Cabernet Rosé de Loire, Lurton 1998

Very dry. Selected stores.

Chardonnay VdP d'Oc, Sainsbury's (3-litre box) 15 C

Price bracket has been adjusted to the 75cl equivalent.

Chateau Carsin, Cadillac 1996 (half bottle)

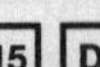

Chateau de Cerons 1990 (half bottle) 13 E

Chateau de Valmer Vouvray 1997 13.5 D

Young, as yet, and the minerals embedded in the soft, honeyed edge need more aging. In five or six years it will be terrific and great with Chinese food.

Chateau Liot Sauternes 1996 (half bottle) 15 E

Gorgeous marmalade thick waxy texture. Selected stores.

Classic Selection Pouilly Fuisse 1997, Sainsbury's 13.5 D

Classic Selection Sancerre 1998, Sainsbury's 14.5 E

Has the classy mineral bite, and the dry concentrated freshness, of classic Sancerre.

Classic Selection Vouvray 1998, Sainsbury's 14.5 D

Lovely honeyed-edged aperitif. Delicious and will age well for years. Selected stores.

Domaine Belle-Croix, Coteaux de St Bris 1996 13.5 D

Sharp and clean, but picky – good with shellfish. Eighty-four selected stores.

Domaine Leonce Cuisset, Saussignac 1996 15 E

Sweet and chewy and simply wonderful with pastry/fruit desserts. Sixty selected stores.

Hermitage Blanc, Cave de Tain l'Hermitage 1996 15.5 F

Acquired taste and an expensive lesson in white Rhones which, in this exemplary specimen, achieve a great dryness and pebbly richness. Eighteen selected stores.

La Baume Sauvignon Blanc, VdP d'Oc 1998 15.5 C

Very crisp and cos-lettuce fresh. Classy and cool. Selected stores.

LPA Cotes de St Mont Blanc 1998 

Very biting and fresh. Terrific shellfish mate. Has real incisiveness as it finishes. Not at all stores.

Moulin des Groyes, Cotes de Duras Blanc 1997 

Muscadet de Sevre et Maine sur Lie NV, Sainsbury's (3-litre box) 

Price bracket has been adjusted to the 75cl equivalent.

Muscadet Sevre et Maine Sur Lie, La Goelette 1998 

Fresh and clean, not mucky as Muscadet used to be, and a faint earthy/mineral edge on the finish.

Orchid Vale Medium French Chardonnay, VdP d'Oc 1998 

For people, life drying out, who are on their way up from Liebfraumilch. Not at all stores.

Pernand-Vergelesses Domaine Laleure Piot 1996 

Pouilly Fume, Cuvee Pierre Louis 1996 

Expensive, if typically crisp-edged. Selected stores.

Reserve Saint-Marc Sauvignon Blanc, VdP d'Oc 1998 

One of the most compelling sauvignons at JS. Lovely subtly rich edge and mineralised purposefulness. A very elegant, satisfying wine. Not at all stores.

Rosé d'Anjou, Lurton 1998

Touch sweet on the finish.

Sancerre Domaine la Croix Canat 1998

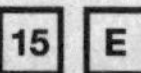

Too expensive to rate higher – though it's clean enough – since other JS sauvignons, which are as good, cost less. Not at all stores.

Touraine Sauvignon Le Chalutier 1998

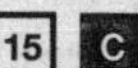

Deliciously gooseberryish and fresh edged. A cheerful, dry, highly accomplished wine. At most stores.

Vin Blanc de France Dry White Wine, Sainsbury's (3-litre box)

Price bracket has been adjusted to the 75cl equivalent.

Vin de Pays de l'Aude Blanc, Sainsbury's

Chipper with healthy fruit. Remarkably clean and fresh, delightfully impishly fruity wine. 265 selected stores.

Vin de Pays des Cotes de Gascogne NV, Sainsbury's 15 B

Vouvray la Couronne des Plantagenets 1998

Superb dry honey and richly mineralised fruit. A wonderful aperitif. Not remotely sweet.

White Burgundy NV, Sainsbury's 14 D

Not bad, for a bourgogne blanc. Has some classic hints. Touch expensive.

GERMAN WINE WHITE

Bereich Bernkastel Riesling 1997 12 B

Makes an adequate spritzer.

Dalsheimer Berg Rodenstein Kabinett, Rheinhessen 1997, Sainsbury's 

Don't think of it as German. Think of a glass of it, chilled, with a good book. It has real charm, this wine.

Fire Mountain Riesling 1997 

Graacher Himmelreich Riesling Spatlese von Kesselstatt 1997 

Keep it for five or six years yet and watch it blossom into a 17.5 point masterpiece of dry-sided honeyed fruit and rich mineralised acids. Sixty-two selected stores.

Hock NV, Sainsbury's 11.5 B

Mosel, Sainsbury's 14 B

Piesporter Michelsberg, Sainsbury's 12 B

Sancta Clara Morio-Muskat, Pfalz 1997 13.5 B

Makes an amusing warm-weather aperitif. Selected stores.

GREEK WINE RED

Kourtakis Vin de Crete Red 1997 13 B

HUNGARIAN WINE WHITE

Hilltop Chardonnay Bin 058 1997 16 C

Classy, restrained, dry yet fruity, double-layered, nutty, not remotely overdone or smug. Selected stores.

Hungarian Cabernet Sauvignon Rosé NV, Sainsbury's 15.5 B

Always a firm favourite with this rosé-hater, this continues to offer wit and style.

ITALIAN WINE RED

Classic Selection Chianti Classico 1997, Sainsbury's 15.5 D

115 stores.

D'Istinto Sangiovese Merlot 1998 (Sicily) 14 C

One of the best examples of this curate's egg of a wine range. Has fruit, tannins and acidity in good order. At most stores.

L'Arco Cabernet Franc, Friuli 1997 16.5 C

Fabulous cabernet franc fruit of classically exquisite wild raspberry and slate tannins. Selected stores.

Lambrusco Rosso, Sainsbury's 10 B

Merlot Corvina 1998, Sainsbury's 13 B

Light and simply cherried. As undemanding as a peck on the cheek.

Merlot delle Venezie 1997, Sainsbury's 14 C

Merlot delle Venezie, Connubio 1998 16 C

Dark and blackcurranty, nary a hint of leather (merlot's trademark) and lots of dry tannins. A wonderful glug for serious quaffers. Selected stores.

Montepulciano d'Abruzzo 1997, Sainsbury's 16 C

Terrific, dry, earthy fruit combining herbs, baked earth and ripe plums.

Montepulciano d'Abruzzo, Connubio 1997 15.5 C

The essence of Italian food-friendly yet utterly rich – though oddly dry – glugging.

Rosso di Provincia di Verona NV, Sainsbury's 15 B

Try it chilled. It's the perfect wine for grilled meat, veg and fish. Dry earthy cherries, light and lissom.

Sangiovese dell'Umbria, Tenuta di Corbara 1998 16.5 C

Brilliant! The new vintage has slower tannins and more marzipan and spiced fruit. A superb wine under a fiver, it oozes richness and charm – and it works with loads of different foods from complex partners to exotic stuffed lamb roasts. Not at all stores.

Sangiovese di Toscana, Cecchi 1998 15.5 C

Delicious earthy cherries impinge on the palate to refreshing and satisfying effect.

Stowells Montepulciano del Molise NV (3-litre box) 12 C

Price bracket has been adjusted to the 75cl equivalent.

Teuzzo Chianti Classico, Cecchi 1995 15 D

Valpantena Ripasso Valpolicella, Connubio 1997 14 D

Needs a couple more years to show its vast syncopated repertoire. If you drink it now, let it breathe out of the bottle for two or three hours. Selected stores.

Valpolicella NV, Sainsbury's 13.5 B

ITALIAN WINE WHITE

Anselmi Soave 1997 15 D

Bianco di Custoza, Geoff Merrill 1998 13.5 C

Very dry and a touch ungenerous.

Bianco di Provincia di Verona NV, Sainsbury's 14 B

Delicious, soft and gently fruity, hint of raspberry and lime but finishes crisply.

Cecchi Tuscan White NV 13.5 C

Unusual hint of almond to the fruit. 280 selected stores.

Classic Selection Frascati Superiore 1997, Sainsbury's 13 D

Bit expensive! Selected stores.

Connubio Pinot Grigio delle Venezie 1998 12.5 C

D'Istinto Chardonnay 1998 (Sicily) 13 C

Finishes a touch crudely. Not at all stores.

Lambrusco dell'Emilia Bianco. Sainsbury's 12 C

Lambrusco Rosato, Sainsbury's 13 B

Lambrusco Secco, Sainsbury's 11 B

Pinot Bianco delle Venezie 1998, Sainsbury's 13 B

Selected stores.

Pinot Grigio Collio 1996 15.5 D

Sicilian White, Sainsbury's 13.5 B

Perfect party wine. Strong enough to withstand acid conversation.

Soave, Sainsbury's 15.5 B

Tenuta di Corbara Orvieto Classico Superiore 1997 15.5 C

Has that delicious warmth of fruit melded with typically Italianate nuttiness and crispness. 115 selected stores.

MACEDONIAN WINE RED

Macedonian Cabernet Sauvignon 1996 13 B

MACEDONIAN WINE WHITE

Macedonian Chardonnay 1997 8 B

NEW ZEALAND WINE WHITE

Cooks Sauvignon Blanc, Marlborough 1998 13.5 C

Always a bit too raw and grassy for me to rate it higher. Selected stores.

Montana Reserve Barrique Fermented Chardonnay 1998 16 E

Compelling style here of great class. Combines an impish directness of freshness with a suggestion of rich maturity. Selected stores.

Montana Sauvignon Blanc 1998 16 D

A rich vintage – fewer cold nights to build up acids – has resulted in Marlborough's sauvignons for '98 being fatter than normal, but there is good balancing acidity. A very elegant wine.

Shingle Peak Chardonnay, Marlborough 1998 16.5 D

Superb richness and depth of gentle smoky melon fruit. Really stylish and fine. Fifty-two selected stores.

Shingle Peak Pinot Gris, Marlborough 1998 16.5 D

Superb apricot/peach/orange edged fruit – very fine, very pinot gris – a minor classic of a wine. Ninety-five selected stores.

Shingle Peak Sauvignon Blanc, Marlborough 1998 16 D

Gorgeous concentration of fruit here, with a lovely zippy finish. 123 selected stores.

Stoneleigh Vineyard Chardonnay, Marlborough 1997 15.5 D

Always one of the more reliably fruity Kiwis, in this vintage there is fatness yet fitness. Selected stores.

The Sanctuary Chardonnay, Marlborough 1997 16 D

Gorgeous, luscious, full of finesse yet flavoursome and exhibits both polish and depth. How can Chablis compete with it? Selected stores.

Villa Maria Private Bin Sauvignon, Marlborough 1998 — 17 D

Back to the form of a few years back when it was the least grassy style of NZ sauvignon yet the most elegant.

PORTUGUESE WINE — RED

Bela Fonte Baga 1998 — 15.5 C

A vigorously fresh-edged and keenly tannic specimen, which has hugely food-friendly cherry/plum fruit, textured and taut. A lot of tension between the elements, this wine. Not at all stores.

Bright Brothers Atlantic Vines Baga 1997

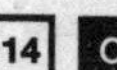

C

Ripe, touch cheesy, good chilled with fish and chorizo stew.

Tinto da Anfora 1994 — 16 D

Very complete, mature and ready for immediate consumption. The ripe plums are already turning pruny and the tannins slowing down. But a classy specimen of texture, tension and tractability (with lots of foods).

PORTUGUESE WINE — WHITE

Do Campo Branco, Sainsbury's — 14 B

Portuguese Rosé, Sainsbury's 13.5 B

Vinho Verde, Sainsbury's 13.5 B

ROMANIAN WINE — RED

Idle Rock Merlot Reserve 1997 14 C

Idle Rock Pinot Noir Reserve 1997 13 C

River Route Limited Edition Merlot 1997 15 C

Rather claret-like in its dryness but it has a hint of Romanian sun and a hint of spice. Great food wine.

ROMANIAN WINE — WHITE

Romanian Merlot Rosé NV, Sainsbury's 14 B

Deliciously dry and food friendly.

SOUTH AFRICAN WINE — RED

Bellingham Merlot 1997 14 D

A sweet merlot. Very slurpable. Not complex. Touch expensive for the style. Selected stores.

Bellingham Shiraz 1997 14 D

Fairview Cabernet Sauvignon 1997 16 D

The sheer class and unruffled texture of this cabernet strike the thoughtful drinker with compelling richness. Selected stores.

Fairview Pinotage 1998 16.5 D

One of my favourite pinotages. It comes across like a real old Richebourg in a ripe, warm year. The texture and the tannins are rich, deep and lingering. Selected stores.

Kumala Cabernet Sauvignon Shiraz 1998 16 C

Delicious as both a throat charmer and food companion. It has layers of textured fruit, warm, touch spicy, hint of pepper, good tannins. Lush, luxurious, lissom, lovely to down!

Neil Ellis Cabernet Sauvignon Merlot 1996 14 D

Australia meets Chile with a hint of South African sun and spiciness. Selected stores.

Reserve Selection Merlot 1996, Sainsbury's 15.5 D

South African Merlot NV, Sainsbury's 13 C

Very light and so easy to drink you forget it's in your throat let alone your glass. Selected stores.

South African Pinotage, Sainsbury's 15 C

South African Red, Sainsbury's 14.5 B

South African Reserve Selection Cabernet Sauvignon 1996, Sainsbury's 14 D

Ripe, juicy and altogether up for it. Selected stores.

South African Reserve Selection Merlot 1996, Sainsbury's 16.5 D

Lovely aroma of old E-type Jags, ripe debs and warm cashmere. Selected stores.

South African Reserve Selection Pinotage 1998, Sainsbury's 16.5 D

A high class pinotage which manages to put a brave face on burnt rubber, cassis, pepper, blackberries and dry earthy tannins. 155 selected stores.

Spice Route Cabernet Merlot 1998 17 E

Sheer unadulterated richness of such texture and finesse, yet power and depth, the drinker waits as each act unfolds. A dramatic wine of huge class. Thirty selected stores.

Spice Route Pinotage 1998 16.5 E

Is the Spice Route trademark lush texture and compelling, savoury tannins? It seems so. This example simply cudgels the taste buds with riches. Thirty selected stores.

Spice Route Shiraz 1998 16.5 E

The spiciest and most lushly fulfilling of the JS Spice Route reds. The fruit is soft and ripe and the texture is alive, composite and very sunny. Thirty selected stores.

SOUTH AFRICAN WINE WHITE

De Wetshof Estate Lesca Chardonnay 1998 15 D

One of the Cape's most committed chardonnays. Danie de Wet

never makes a bad one, or one wholly unreconciled with charm, and though, like this example, the result is often low key it always provokes the palate.

Mont Rochelle de Villiers Oak Matured Chardonnay 1997 16 D

Lots of wood but not would-be. It is itself, not a copy (of white burgundy) and has lovely warmth and well-tailored fruit. Sixty-five selected stores.

South African Chenin Blanc NV, Sainsbury's (3-litre box) 14.5 B

Price bracket has been adjusted to the 75cl equivalent.

South African Colombard NV, Sainsbury's 

Good firm fruit. Needs food, I feel.

South African Medium Wine, Sainsbury's 11 B

South African Reserve Selection Chardonnay 1998, Sainsbury's 15.5 D

Very rich and warm with a hint of spicy lime. A lovely quaffable chardonnay. Selected stores.

South African Reserve Selection Sauvignon Blanc 1998, Sainsbury's 16 D

Sauvignon as eager, filthy rich and full of flavour. Selected stores.

South African Sauvignon Blanc, Sainsbury's 15 B

Springfield Estate Methode Ancienne Chardonnay 1997 11 F

Fails to grip on the finish. Fatal – for a wine costing £13.

Springfield Estate Special Cuvee Sauvignon Blanc 1998 16 D

A very classy Sancerre in style, but not price. It's superb.

Vergelegen Chardonnay Reserve 1997 16.5 E

Has that great luxury of flavour of the armpit of a massive lottery winner. Sixty selected stores.

Vergelegen Sauvignon Blanc 1998 15.5 D

Elegance and understatement. Selected stores.

SPANISH WINE RED

Agapito Rico Jumilla Reserva 1995 16 C

Intense fruit which clumps deliciously across the taste buds at first in a big wave of textured ripeness, then more sedately as the tannins grip.

Alteza 600 Old Vines Garnacha NV 16 C

Burnt leaves and ripe plums, dry tannins, vivid acidity and fruit balance. Superb for food or mood. Selected stores.

Alteza 750 Tempranillo NV 15.5 C

Beaujolais meets Cotes du Rhone stylistically. A lovely rolling quaffing wine, this. Selected stores.

Alteza 775 Tempranillo Cabernet Sauvignon NV 15.5 C

Fully fleshed out tempranillo meets spicy, vegetal cabernet and the result is a superb food wine. Loads of personality and pertinacity. Selected stores.

Bodegas Castano Yecla Crianza 1997

Ripe yet dry and dusty on the finish. Selected stores.

Dama de Toro 1998

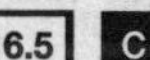

Rampant, wild, uncultivated, hairy – yes. Yet: polished, plump, animated and, yes, gently feral. The texture carries the day. It's quite spreadable. Selected stores.

El Conde Oak Aged Vinho de Mesa, Sainsbury's

A gorgeously flavoured, cherry-and-vanilla-undertoned wine of soupy warmth.

Jumilla NV, Sainsbury's

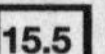

Very soft and sticky but so unabashedly luxurious and flavour-some. Great with food.

La Mancha Castillo de Alhambra 1997, Sainsbury's

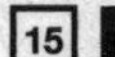

Bargain fruity tippling here: soft, sweet, deep yet dry. Selected stores.

Marques de Grinon Valdepusa Syrah 1996

One of the classiest under-a-tenner reds in Spain. It's dry, spicy, savoury, balanced, rich and very deep. Hugely lingering flavours.

Mota del Cuervo Premium Tempranillo 1997 16 C

Ripe spiced damsons, a hint of cheroot (cheap) but the overall effect is full of charm and makes for compulsive quaffing. Selected stores.

Navarra Tempranillo/Cabernet Sauvignon Crianza 1995, Sainsbury's

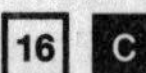

Wonderful mature fruit here: tobaccoey, ripe, rich, deep, woody, balanced and very eager to please. Loads of class.

Old Vines Garnacha, Navarra NV

Stowells Tempranillo La Mancha NV (3-litre box)

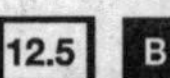

Price bracket has been adjusted to the 75cl equivalent.

Valencia Oak Aged NV, Sainsbury's

Very plump, ripe and softly rich. Bit emulsion-like but very engaging.

Vina Albali Gran Reserva 1991

Vanillary, spicy, nicely warmly textured and softly, savourily tannic. Has an almost yoghurt touch on the finish. Not at all stores.

Vina Ardanza Rioja Reserva, La Rioja Alta 1990

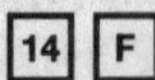

A special occasion treat with its dry woodiness and rich tannins. 105 stores.

SPANISH WINE — WHITE

Navarra Rosado NV, Sainsbury's

Handsome fleshy edge – not overdone, pleasantly and curvaceously sculpted. Selected stores.

Oaked Viura, Alteza 640 NV

Interesting range of dry flavours here, from almonds to under-ripe melon and a hint of apple, but the texture is very polished and gently plump. Selected stores.

URUGUAYAN WINE — RED

Bright Brothers Merlot/Tannat 1998

Interesting. Tastes like tobacco juice spat out by a dry-mouthed angel.

USA WINE — RED

Bonterra Cabernet Sauvignon 1995 (organic)

Sweetly ravishing fruit of such richness and tannic brilliance! Selected stores.

Coastal Pinot Noir, Robert Mondavi 1996

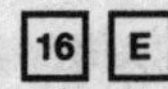

To be preferred to a hundred Volnays. Superb texture, with raspberry and truffle fruit, hint of plum jam, great tannins and big, beetle-browed length of finish. Selected stores.

Eagle Peak Merlot, Fetzer Vineyards 1997

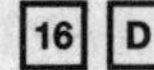

Decidedly chewy yet very soft and warm. Curious paradox of styles: seems composty and ripe then goes dry and tannin-teasing, blackcurrant beneath its feet. Delicious stuff. 139 selected stores.

Gallo Turning Leaf Vintners Collection Cabernet Sauvignon 1995

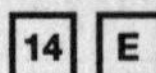

Drinkable enough. Bit waspish on the finish. And eight quid is a lot.

McDowell Syrah, Mendocino 1997

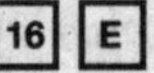

A briar soup of old bones, ripe damsons and blackberries, and great gobbets of earth. Real quaffing here. Top thirty stores.

Old Vines Estate Zinfandel, California 1996

Pour it into a jug and let it then pour itself. It has sufficient fruity volition to make the journey to the glass unaided. Not at all stores.

Stonybrook Vineyard Cabernet Sauvignon 1997

14.5 D

Friendly beyond criticism. Even the tannins wipe their feet first. Selected stores.

Stonybrook Vineyard Merlot 1997

16 D

Massively gluggable, gorgeous, textured, ripe, stylish and beautifully tailored, soft, leather fruit. Thirty selected stores.

Sutter Home Merlot 1997 

Touch sweet on the finish. Selected stores.

Sutter Home Pinot Noir 1997 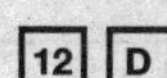

Thirty selected stores.

USA WINE — WHITE

Fetzer Bonterra Chardonnay 1996 (organic) 

Rivetingly rich, rampant, creamy, woody, balanced and flamboyant – but so elegant with it! It's like a Vivienne Westwood man's shirt – only subtly outrageous. Selected stores.

Fetzer Sundial Chardonnay 1997 

Smoky, melon-rich fruit with a hint of tropicality . . . intense composition but ineffably Californian: warm and giving and very delicious. Seventy selected stores.

Gallo Colombard NV 

Gallo Turning Leaf Chardonnay 1997 

Bit blowsy on the finish.

Garnet Point Chardonnay Chenin Blanc 1997 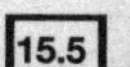

Very warm and fruity, hint of muskiness to the ripe melon. As easy to drink as breathing.

Stonybrook Vineyards Chardonnay 1997 16 C

Staggeringly good value here. Loads of richness and flavour without being remotely overbaked or clumsy. Selected stores.

FORTIFIED WINE

Aged Amontillado, Sainsbury's (half bottle) 16 B

Superbly thick, nutty fruit with tea leaves, almonds and dry treacle fruit. At most stores.

Blandy's Duke of Clarence Madeira 15.5 E

Gonzales Byass Matusalem Old Oloroso (half bottle) 14 E

Medium Dry Montilla, Sainsbury's 13.5 B

Old Oloroso, Sainsbury's (half bottle) 16 B

Has a faint pruney tang. A wonderful winter warmer and fire-side aperitif. At most stores.

Pale Cream Montilla, Sainsbury's 14 B

Pale Cream Sherry, Sainsbury's 15.5 C

Pale Dry Amontillado, Sainsbury's 15 C

Pale Dry Fino Sherry, Sainsbury's 15 D

Pale Dry Manzanilla, Sainsbury's 15 C

Pale Dry Montilla, Sainsbury's 14 B

Palo Cortado, Sainsbury's (half bottle) 16 B

Be different. A winter warmer of quirkily nutty richness yet not sweetness. Not at all stores.

Ruby Port, Sainsbury's 13 D

Sainsbury's LBV Port 1992 15.5 E

Wonderful sweet fruit here. Superb value for money.

Tawny Port, Sainsbury's 13.5 D

Ten Year Old Tawny Port, Sainsbury's 15 E

A brilliant start to a winter's evening.

SPARKLING WINE/CHAMPAGNE

Asti, Sainsbury's (Italy) 13 C

Australian Chardonnay/Pinot Noir Brut 1992, Sainsbury's 14 D

Some lean elegance here. Ninety selected stores.

Blanc de Noirs Champagne NV, Sainsbury's 16 F

One of the best value champagnes around. Really elegant.

Cava Brut NV, Sainsbury's

Still a flagship sparkling wine: crisp, clean, fresh, classic. Better than hundreds of champagnes.

Cava Rosado Brut, Sainsbury's 15 C

Lovely touch of ripely rosy fruit.

Champagne Canard Duchene NV 14 G

Has the tell-tale Duchene fruit yet dryness. Has real character. Selected stores.

Champagne Chanoine 1990 15.5 G

If you must spend twenty pounds on a vintage champagne, this has more complexity than most. It runs a delicious gamut through plump fruit to a dry, classic finish. Selected stores.

Champagne Charles Heidsieck Mis en Cave 1995 14.5 H

Has an almost buttery edge to it. Very plump and firm with a rousing finish. But a lot of money. Selected stores.

Champagne Demi-Sec NV, Sainsbury's 14 F

Lot of fruit for a bubbly but it works! Try it well chilled as an aperitif. It's better than many a rosé. Selected stores.

Champagne Jeanmaire Brut 1990 14 G

Dry, hints of fruit, finishes well but not too warmly. Selected stores.

Champagne Krug Grande Cuvee 10 H

Unbelievably po-faced and straight-laced. Not complex or grand. Ten selected stores.

Champagne Laurent Perrier NV 13.5 H

Signs of finesse. But the most notable sign is the £ one – times twenty-two. Selected stores.

Champagne Louis Roederer NV 13 H

Very rich and almost cloying on the finish. Fifty selected stores.

Champagne Nicolas Feuillate Premier Cru NV 14 G

Very appley and crisp. Real orchard-fresh fruit here. Selected stores.

Champagne Perrier-Jouet NV 14 G

Nice fatness on the finish. Squats on the tongue. Selected stores.

Champagne Pol Roger 1990 13 H

Far too much money! £35! Simply not impactful enough for the money. Selected stores.

Champagne Pommery Brut Royal NV 13 H

Too expensive for the money. Twenty-one quid!!!! Cava rather. Selected stores.

Champagne Premier Cru Extra Dry, Sainsbury's 16 G

One of the lushest tasting yet very dry chardonnay champagnes at a decent price around.

Champagne Veuve Clicquot Grande Dame 1990 12 H

Too fat and flouncy for me. Grips on the finish, but it's sudsy not firm. Ten selected stores.

Champagne Veuve Clicquot Rosé 1990 11 H

I cannot believe anyone but an idiot would spend £38 on this marginally exciting bubbly. Seventy selected stores.

Chardonnay Brut, Methode Traditionelle, Sainsbury's (France) 15 D

Crisp and clean as a whistle. Great value.

Freixenet Cava Rosada NV 13.5 D

Very dry. Doesn't seem to this palate to justify the rosé tag (or price).

Graham Beck Brut NV (South Africa) 14 D

Crisp and gently fruity.

Grand Cru Millennium Champagne NV, Sainsbury's 13 G

Lot of hype, the millennium. What makes it grand cru? Only the price, as far as I can tell. Selected stores.

Jacobs Creek Chardonnay/Pinot Noir Brut NV (Australia) 13 D

Light and fruity. Selected stores.

Lindauer Special Reserve NV (New Zealand) 14.5 E

Has finesse and dryness. Class, too.

Millennium Vintage Cava 1997, Sainsbury's 13 D

I prefer the non-vintage. Touch soapy, this vintage specimen.

Pelorus 1994 (New Zealand) 14 G

Curious ripe richness makes this vintage less classically dry and witty than it has been in the past. Fifty selected stores.

Seaview Brut NV (Australia) 14 D

Lithe and light. Delicious simplicity.

Seaview Brut Rosé NV (Australia) 14 D

Delicate little rosé.

Sekt, Medium Dry, Sainsbury's (Germany) 13 C

Vin Mousseux Brut, Sainsbury's (France) 13 C

SOMERFIELD/ KWIK SAVE

Official supermarket of New Labour?

Even though we will still be seeing the Kwik Save name for a little while longer, its days are numbered. Having acquired Kwik Save in March 1998, Somerfield has taken the decision to kill it off in its prime. When I was writing last year's guide, the fate of the Kwik Save name was still unsure but it subsequently emerged that Somerfield planned to convert the 800 stores to the Somerfield format. The good news for customers of both Somerfield and Kwik Save was that the retailer also intended to upgrade all its 1,400 stores in a £1 billion programme.

This news came at a time when the wine range of Kwik Save was reportedly moving upmarket. *Off Licence News* reported in June 1998 that Kwik Save was introducing more upmarket wines following successful trials. The new additions brought the number of wines on the list to 122.

Further evidence that Somerfield was still investing in Kwik Save came when it announced a major advertising campaign for Kwik Save even after it had decided that the name had to go. In September 1998, *The Times* wrote that Somerfield planned a £7 million ad campaign for Kwik Save, with adverts featuring Michael Barrymore no less. The strapline, which could end up haunting Michael Barrymore, was the pithy legend 'We're cheap so you're cheerful'.

More details of Kwik Save's euthanasia emerged in early 1999. In March, it was reported in *The Times* that Somerfield planned to convert 200 Kwik Save stores by April 2000. One can perhaps not blame the retailer for going ahead with this course of action. Somerfield said that in eight out of the 10 stores where the conversion had been carried out sales had risen by 24%. It said the conversions would cost £10 million in 1999 and £20 million in 2000.

All in all, this was not proving a particularly happy time for Kwik Save. In March, *The Grocer* reported that a County Court had awarded damages of nearly £70,000 against Kwik Save after a customer had fallen in its Newtown store and subsequently died back in 1995. The customer, Mrs Jean Thomas, 60 years of age, broke her hip and died from a bi-lateral pulmonary thrombo-embolism 22 days later. It was alleged that water on the floor had caused the fall though Kwik Save denied negligence.

The next month, Kwik Save was back in court. The store in Darlington had its alcohol licence revoked after it was found guilty of selling alcohol to teenagers, some as young as 13. The company did not oppose the order banning it from selling alcohol and had earlier admitted that it had sacked seven members of staff following a police crackdown on underage drinking in the area. Kwik Save lodged an appeal but said that following the Darlington case it had introduced new procedures nationwide. Perhaps Somerfield was at this stage considering speeding up the conversions or certainly putting the Darlington store to the top of the list.

On a cheerier note, my researcher, the eagle-eyed Ben Cooper, spotted in *Supermarketing* magazine in May that the Kwik Save store in Wisbech had come up with an innovative way of raising money for charity. The store was hoping to sell 1,000 copies of a calendar it had produced in which 11 staff members appeared in various states of undress including even the store manager, Mr Phil Wait. A very commendable effort I am sure, but isn't May a rather odd time to be trying to sell a calendar? The photographs must have been phenomenally good to compensate.

Meanwhile, Somerfield have clearly caught the acquisition bug. In August 1998, it was reported that the retailer was in talks to acquire the food distribution company, Booker, which was also at one stage on Budgens' shopping list. It was reported in the *FT* on 29 August 1998 that Somerfield had pulled out as indeed did Budgens.

Now that supermarkets sell almost anything and, with regard to wine at least, can often provide excellent quality and value for money, the principal bane in the life of a supermarket shopper would have to be queues at the checkout. Tesco has its one-in-front policy of opening checkouts if too many customers are queuing but Somerfield was apparently considering an alternative and rather less satisfactory solution to the problem. It was reported in *The Sunday Times* in June last year that the retailer was considering introducing a fast-track check-out system whereby consumers paid a premium for getting through the checkout more quickly. The report said that The Henley Centre, the business analysis people, had found that up to a quarter of full-time workers would be prepared to pay the extra.

Among those who could afford to bow to such extortion would be a number of former Somerfield/Kwik Save directors who following the merger received generous golden handshakes. Of course one might suppose that they now have plenty of time to hang around in a check-out queue as well. In August 1998, *The Times* reported that the former Somerfield property director, Philip Coates, was paid £194,800 in compensation and was entitled to exercise share options worth £958,000. David Coles, former marketing director, may have collected up to £1.84 million, while Derek Pretty, formerly finance director at Kwik Save, received compensation of £356,800 plus share options.

Somerfield was also throwing its money about in the hope of political patronage. The retailer's sponsorship of the Labour Party Conference in 1998 was reputed to cost about £25,000, according to an article in *Marketing* magazine in October 1998. The deal involved sponsoring delegates' name tags and having a stall in the conference centre, which was visited by none other than T. Blair himself, where staff could give delegates samples of food and drink.

Somerfield said that the sponsorship was a good opportunity to get its voice heard regarding matters such as out-of-town development. The retailer is firmly committed to the redevelopment of the high street, not surprisingly given its store profile. Some Labour MPs boycotted the Somerfield-branded tags preferring to wear their own including some bearing the slogan 'Support the UK workers'. Somerfield was I expect just as pleased with this as it probably generated more publicity than anything else.

The *Marketing* article went on to say that Somerfield was not alone in sponsoring the conference, Thomas Cook paid for the Party's champagne reception. Now there are two ways of interpreting this. Was this a reception for Champagne Socialists? In which case it would have been heavily attended, a big affair costing a fortune. If, however, it was a reception for socialists which just happened to serve champagne, it would have been an altogether smaller and lower profile gathering if not, with regard to the centrist politics of New Labour, a non-event altogether.

Somerfield like most of the major retailers has made strides over the last year in the home shopping market and like M&S singled out wine for special attention. In December, *The Grocer* magazine reported that Somerfield had launched a Wines Direct Service. Shoppers use a freephone number to order wines which are delivered within two working days; the delivery charge of £5 is waived if more than two cases are ordered. All the wines offered had, apparently, won awards in a wine competition. (Such things as wine competitions are meaningless theatricals as far as I am concerned but retailers have persuaded themselves that they carry significance.)

In February, *The Grocer* further reported that Somerfield had signed up with BIB (British Interactive Broadcasting) to offer a home shopping service via the channel which will be open to 1 million Sky subscribers from the autumn. The next month, it was reported in *Marketing* that Somerfield had bought a

London-based home shopping company, Flanagans, for £3.25 million which was to be the base for its launch into the home shopping sector. At that stage Flanagans already had a base of 10,000 customers and sales of £4 million.

Also in common with a number of other major retailers, the company has plans to expand its forecourt retailing activities. Somerfield said in *The Times* in January that it planned to open up to 50 stores at Elf petrol stations during the next 18 months. In January it had five Elf stores operating. The £25 million investment is being shared between Elf and Somerfield.

Buoyed by its acquisition of Kwik Save in March 1998, which helped to double its pre-tax profits in January 1999 to £111.5 million, beating City forecasts, we are now seeing a more confident, assertive Somerfield. It is not afraid to mix it with the big boys. In April, the retailer took Tesco to task over the price of turkeys. Somerfield complained to the Advertising Standards Authority about Tesco's advertising of the UK's cheapest turkeys. It said most chains were selling birds for 39p per pound over Easter, the same as Tesco's price.

In May, it was Sainsbury's turn to feel the rough edge of Somerfield's tongue when it threatened the retailer with legal action over its use of a slogan marketing a holiday discount scheme. Somerfield said Sainsbury's use of the line 'What will you do with yours?' plagiarised a line they have been using since August 1997. Sainsbury's dismissed Somerfield's claim as a cheap PR stunt. If plagiarism was an indictably illegal offence in the world of advertising, there would be no advertising industry whatsoever.

Similarly, certain other supermarkets also dismiss wine buyer Angela Mount's regular price cutting policy. Hardly a month goes by that wines under £3, one even at £1.95, are announced and I know for a fact that there are a great many readers out there who find such offers irresistible – especially as some of the wines are terrific. This has led to a huge increase in the numbers of wine drinkers prepared to browse Somerfield's shelves and it must be counted as amongst the great successes at this retailer. There are now 32 million wine drinkers in the UK, a figure which will not significantly increase for some time, so the task for a retailer like Somerfield is to take a decent and growing percentage of a statically populated market. You can only persuade existing customers to drink more by selling cheaper wines and this is the same token which also brings customers from competitors to Somerfield's door. Mrs Mount knows how to finesse both these situations perfectly.

Somerfield
Somerfield House
Hawkfield Business Park
Whitchurch Lane
Bristol BS14 OTJ
Tel: 0117 935 9359
Fax: 0117 978 0629

Kwik-Save Stores Limited
Warren Drive
Prestatyn
Clwyd LL19 7HU
Tel: 01745 887111
Fax: 01745 882504

SEE STOP PRESS SECTION AT END OF BOOK FOR LAST-MINUTE ADDITIONS OR UPDATES TO THIS RETAILER'S RANGE.

ARGENTINIAN WINE RED

Bright Brothers San Juan Reserve Cabernet Sauvignon 1998

16 B

Huge surge of flavour – like a full frontal attack. The fruit is very savoury, hugely deep and dangerous, and it takes no prisoners. Great vein of chutzpah running through it like spice.

Argentine Country Red NV, Somerfield

14.5 B

Soupy yet far from simply all-fruit-not-for-the-squeamish. It has a dry, rich edge of some charm. More gauche than gaucho, perhaps, but entertaining.

Bright Brothers Argentine Tempranillo 1997

15 C

Bright Brothers San Juan Cabernet Sauvignon 1998

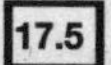

17.5 C

Utterly magically alive and alert wine which opens up such rich savoury depths as it lingers on the taste buds. It's exotic yet classic, beautifully textured and compellingly well finished off. A fantastic fiver's worth.

Santa Julia Bonarda Reserva Sangiovese 1998

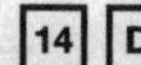

14 D

Juicy and jammy and very joyful.

Santa Julia Sangiovese 1997

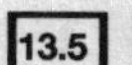

13.5 C

Very ripe.

Santa Julia Tempranillo 1998 

What utter chutzpah! It's simply wonderful! It makes a billion riojas seem like antique crones.

Trivento Syrah 1998 

Absolutely fantastic texture and savoury richness here. Superb tannins and tenacity.

ARGENTINIAN WINE — WHITE

Argentine White NV, Somerfield 

Terrific value quaffing: has style, flavour, modernity and crispness.

Bright Brothers Argentine Chardonnay 1998 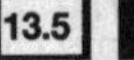

Bright Brothers San Juan Chardonnay Reserve 1998 

Santa Julia Syrah Rosé 1998 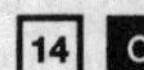

A big rich rosé – richer than many red wines.

AUSTRALIAN WINE — RED

Australian Cabernet Sauvignon 1998, Somerfield  

Reeks of and resounds with the Aussie sun, saddles, flair,

inventiveness and sullen richness of demeanour. A hugely soft yet dry-sided wine of consummate quaffability.

Australian Cabernet Shiraz 1998, Somerfield 14.5 C

Rollingly rich and frolicsome.

Australian Dry Red, Somerfield 

Delicious! Delicious! Delicious! Did you get that? I said . . . oh, never mind.

Banrock Station Mataro/Grenache/Shiraz 1998 

From the very over-ripe sticky Banrock '98 stable.

Basedow Barossa Shiraz 1996 

Minty cherries and plum, soft tannin, rich deep finish. A hugely drinkable wine of substance and style.

Hardys Nottage Hill Cabernet Sauvignon/ Shiraz 1998 

Loads of savoury plums and blackberries with lovely earthy tannins. Scrumptious drinking here.

Hardys Stamp Shiraz Cabernet 1998 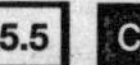

Lovely rich and bright and a touch emulsion-like in texture. But it has balance and savoury ripeness. It's a great food wine.

Penfolds Bin 28 Shiraz 1996 15 E

Intensely savoury and warm. Needs food, I think, as a glass is enough on its own. An enthusiastic specimen of softness and huge eagerness to please.

Penfolds Coonawarra Bin 128 Shiraz 1994 13 E

Getting a bit ragged now that the tannins have overtaken the sugars. Very dry and sulky.

Penfolds Koonunga Hill Shiraz Cabernet Sauvignon 1997 16 D

Most elegant, with a lively varnish to the soft fruit which is not normally as high gloss as this. Terrific style here – it purrs across the taste buds on padded feet.

Rosemount Estate Shiraz 1997 16.5 E

Massively mouth-filling and rampant. Almost an alien construct compared to similar graped Rhone reds. Top 150 stores.

Rosemount Estate Shiraz Cabernet 1998 15.5 D

So deliciously sweet and fruity: soft and full yet delicate on the finish. Deliciously approachable and warm.

AUSTRALIAN WINE WHITE

Australian Chardonnay 1998, Somerfield 16.5 C

Rich, smoky, developed, full and rich – hints of nut. Ripe but not too rampant. A lovely wine of great flavour.

Australian Dry White 1998, Somerfield 16 B

Superb value for money here, indeed astonishing: rich, fresh, classy, plump yet lissom, this is lovely wine of style and decisiveness.

Australian Semillon/Chardonnay 1998, Somerfield 14 C

Very sticky and ripe – needs Thai food or roasted chillied chicken wings.

Banrock Station Chardonnay 1998 12 C

Very sticky and uncomfortable.

Basedow Barossa Chardonnay 1997 16.5 D

Chardonnay in the rich, buttery, oily, baked yet balanced Aussie style. Utterly wonderful tippling here.

Hardys Banrock Station Chenin Blanc/Chardonnay 1998 12.5 C

Very blowsy, fat and sticky rich. Odd fruit. Is it wine? Or jam?

Hardys Chardonnay Sauvignon Blanc 1997 15 D

A very assertive companion of gently sticky fruit. Wonderful wine for shellfish dishes with rich sauces. Top 150 stores.

Hardys Padthaway Chardonnay 1996 16 E

Do you like Meursault? You'll like this, then. This kind of woody, hay-rich, vegetal fruitiness is a miracle under eight quid. Top 200 stores.

Hardys Stamp of Australia Chardonnay Semillon 1998 15.5 C

Delicious! Unusually complex yet modern and fresh. Has layers of melon (not overripe) and what seems like a hint of raspberry. Good acidity buffers this fruity attack.

Hardys Stamp of Australia Riesling Gewurztraminer 1998 15.5 C

The perfect Thai dish wine. It has spice and freshness, pace and plump, roseate fruit.

Hardys Stamp Semillon/Chardonnay 1998 16 C

Superb medley of fruits in firm adult display. Loads of richness and runaway depth but not remotely over-the-top.

Jacobs Creek Semillon/Chardonnay 1998 

Old warhorse still good value and richly fruity (but balanced).

Lindemans Bin 65 Chardonnay 1998 16 C

Supremely sure of itself, this well-established brand showing, in its '98 manifestation, what a great year this is for Aussie whites from the region (Hunter Valley). This has great hints of warm fruit balanced by complex crispness and acidity. A lovely under-a-fiver bobby dazzler.

Lindemans Padthaway Chardonnay 1997 15 E

A most accomplished, subtle Aussie chardonnay of sensitivity and charm. Very good manners: hint of wood, delicate melon and lemon.

Loxton Lunchtime Light Chardonnay (4% vol) 12 B

Very light for a miserable lunchtime.

Penfolds Bin 202 Riesling 1998

Will rapidly improve over the next year and should achieve a high level of complexity. Already in swaddling clothes it's deliciously mineral-tinged and elegantly fruity.

Penfolds Koonunga Hill Chardonnay 1998

What a great brand! Stunning richness and balanced, classy finish. If only white burgundians at three times the price could be this good.

Penfolds Rawsons Retreat Semillon/ Chardonnay/Colombard 1998

Has lovely deft balance: the fruit holds the acidity in a gorgeous embrace.

Penfolds The Valleys Chardonnay 1998

Delicate yet potent, rich yet unshowy, balanced yet full-frontal and unashamedly hedonistic. A lovely wine.

St Hilary Padthaway Chardonnay 1997 15 E

Not the most elegant expression of the '97 chardonnay harvest but it has character and a subtly chewy texture. Top 150 stores.

BULGARIAN WINE RED

Bulgarian Cabernet Sauvignon 1996, Somerfield

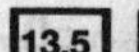

Basic dry blackcurrant.

Bulgarian Country Wine Merlot & Pinot Noir NV, Somerfield 15 B

When I first offered a Frenchman a Bulgar marriage of these two grapes he dismissed the wine as an absurd 'marriage of Bordeaux and Burgundy'. His loss is our gain. This wine is dry, cherry-ripe and simply charming and well-mannered.

Domaine Boyar Special Reserve Cabernet Sauvignon, Oriachovitza 1994 15.5 C

Plummy, ripe, dry, balanced – you can spend lots more and get lots less.

Iambol Bulgarian Merlot 1997 15.5 B

Superb value – real hints of merlot's classic leatheriness but in a fresh, new, polished form.

BULGARIAN WINE WHITE

Barrel Fermented Chardonnay, Pomorie 1997 14 C

Chewy and lemony. Top 150 stores.

Bulgarian Chardonnay 1998, Somerfield 14 B

An all-lemon performance of scant classicism but modern refreshment.

Bulgarian Country White, Somerfield 14 B

Fresh and lemony, simply appealing. Great with smoked fish.

Domaine Boyar Barrel Fermented Chardonnay 1996 14.5 C

Suhindol Aligote Chardonnay Country White, Somerfield 14 B

Bit fresh: but fish will love its bony features.

CHILEAN WINE RED

Chilean Cabernet Sauvignon 1997, Somerfield 16.5 C

Oh what nerve! It offers all of a great Bordeaux's tannins but none of the austere fruit. It's simply terrific.

Chilean Cabernet Sauvignon Vina La Rosa 1997, Somerfield 16.5 C

A gorgeous bargain of not only consummate drinkability but also food matching possibilities. It is not only chocolate-rich with prime fruit but has a judicious dusting of fine tannins. The best red wine under a fiver in the UK? Well, I've not tasted anything better.

Chilean Merlot 1998, Somerfield 16.5 C

Lovely rich warmth to the texture, ripeness to the fruit and a whiplash clean fruity finish of elegant leather.

Chilean Red 1998, Somerfield 15.5 B

Compulsively slurpworthy softness and lovely dry lingering fruit.

Cono Sur Pinot Noir 1998

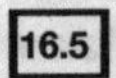

Very rich and ripe, not classic, but feral raspberries and truffles are detectable and the texture is superdeep. But it elevates itself over ten thousand red burgundies asking five times more.

Isla Negra Merlot 1998

Terrific leathery richness here: textured, taut, dry (yet full and deep), lovely layers of fruit, and a resounding finish.

La Palmeria Cabernet Sauvignon Merlot Reserve 1998

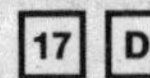

So accomplished and unshowy yet demonstratively brilliant, textured, balanced, very smooth and hugely drinkable. It literally purrs with stylishness.

Terra Noble Merlot 1997

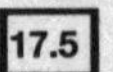

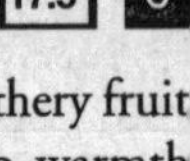

What a tremendous price for such wonderfully soft leathery fruit (cherries, blackcurrants and plums) and such superb warmth and texture to it. It's a wonderful wine of huge class and depth. It'll manage either food or mood magnificently. Top 100 stores.

CHILEAN WINE — WHITE

Chilean Chardonnay 1998, Somerfield

Woody complexity, hint of vegetality, persistence of rich fruit and clean acids – is this a bargain or what?

Chilean Sauvignon Blanc 1998, Somerfield 15 C

A lovely hint of dry, grassy, fresh gooseberry fruit.

Chilean Semillon Chardonnay 1998, Somerfield 13.5 C

Curious inelegance on the finish spoils the performance a touch.

Chilean White 1998, Somerfield 15.5 B

Thunderingly tasty bargain on all fronts: fruit, balance with acidity, class and fresh finish.

Cono Sur Viognier 1998 15 C

Lovely apricot aroma but the fruit is more in the lemon line. I'd be inclined to cellar this wine for three or four years to develop and become an 18-pointer and possibly in the Condrieu class. Top 150 stores.

Isla Negra Chardonnay 1998 

Fresh and fulfilling.

FRENCH WINE RED

Beaumes de Venise Carte Noire, Cotes du Rhone Villages 1997 

C

Brilliant earthy fruit. Loads of hedgerow personality and purposeful finishing power.

Bourgogne, Hautes-Cotes de Bourgogne Rouge 1997 10 D

Brouilly Les Celliers de Bellevue 1998 12.5 D

Dull for the money. Beaujolais mostly is.

Brouilly, Selles 1998 11 D

Buzet Cuvee 44 1997 14.5 C

Cabernet Sauvignon VdP d'Oc NV, Somerfield 16 B

Wonderful classy clods of earth, herbs, hedgerow fruits and all wrapped in a texture of crumpled velvet. Terrific character and class here.

Chateau Blanca, Bordeaux 1997 14 C

Chateau Cazal-Viel Cuvee des Fees Vieilles Vignes, St Chinian 1997 16 D

Wonderful! Drenched in tobacco and herbs which slowly resonate on the taste buds like a sustained bass chord.

Chateau de Caraghuiles, Corbieres 1996 14 C

One of the best value organic reds around – in this vintage, riper and a touch sweeter.

Chateau la Rose d'Orion, Bordeaux 1997 12 E

Curious composty aroma I find off-putting.

Chateau Pierredon, Bordeaux Superieur 1995 14 D

Chateau Plaisance, Montagne St Emilion 1996 15.5 D

Chateau Saint Robert, Graves 1996 15 D

Chateau Talence, Premieres Cotes de Bordeaux 1997 13.5 D

Chateau Valoussiere, Coteaux du Languedoc 1996 16 C

Like a minor claret of a great year (plus a herby undertone of savoury richness).

Claret 1998, Somerfield 12.5 B

Very austere.

Corbieres Rouge Val d'Orbieu, Somerfield 15.5 B

Terrific! Tasty, taut, tangy, tantalising! (Price suits to a T, too.)

Cotes de Gascogne Rouge 1998, Somerfield 13.5 B

Cotes de Roussillon NV, Somerfield 13.5 B

Cotes du Rhone Villages Lucien de Nobleus 1998 16 C

Terrific ripeness yet herby dryness here. Savoury, plump, layered, good rich tannins, this has lovely lingering texture and depth.

Crozes Hermitage 1998 12 C

Extremely juicy.

Domaine de Bisconte, Cotes du Roussillon 1996 14 C

Very very ripe – super-ripe, and as such it needs food to embrace it.

Domaine Haut St George Corbieres Rouge 1995 14 C

Very soft and ripe but the gentle tannins keep the whole in great shape.

Domaine la Tuque Bel Air, Cotes de Castillon 1997 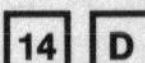

Handsome little claret. Good with grilled lamb chops.

Fitou Rocher d'Ambree 1998, Somerfield 

Gigondas Chateau St Andre 1997 

Big bonny bouncing fruit of lushly controlled meaty depth.

Gouts et Couleurs Cabernet Sauvignon 1998 

If only claret could be this warmly textured, soft, dry yet fruity as this!

Gouts et Couleurs Syrah Mourvedre 1997 

Urgency to please disguises some layers of complexity here. A dry, herby, sunny, aromatic wine of texture and charm.

Hautes Cotes de Beaune, Georges Desire 1996 12 D

James Herrick Cuvee Simone VdP d'Oc 1997 16.5 C

Gorgeous, tobacco and plum aroma, invigoratingly rich, dry fruit as the palate is struck, and a fine fulfilling finish. Classy and full of wit, this wine. Fantastic price, too.

Laperouse Syrah Cabernet, VdP d'Oc 1995 13 C

Touch raw on the finish.

Medoc, Somerfield 10 C

Merlot VdP d'Oc 1998, Somerfield 14.5 B

Most accomplished sense of balance between acid/fruit/tannins. Boring description? Yes, sorry.

Oak Aged Claret, Somerfield 13 C

Red Burgundy 1997, Somerfield 11 D

Sirius Bordeaux Rouge 1996 14 D

Getting more personality as it ages. Not a bad little claret now.

Vacqueyras Domaine de la Soleiade 1998 15 C

Soft, bruised-fruit texture, hint of thyme and a big fruity finish. Highly drinkable.

Vacqueyras Domaine le Brussiere 1998 14 C

Ripely forward into the breach.

Vin de Pays de l'Ardeche Red 1998, Somerfield 13 B

Dry and rustic.

Vin de Pays des Bouches du Rhone Red 1998, Somerfield 13.5 B

Sticky, rich and ripe. Bit too much for me. (It's like emulsion.)

Winter Hill VdP de l'Aude Rouge 1998 15 B

Gorgeous dry cherry/plum ripe fruit.

FRENCH WINE WHITE

Alsace Blanc de Blancs, Caves de Turckheim NV 14 C

Lovely aperitif and grilled fish wine. Has class and hauteur.

Anjou Blanc 1998, Somerfield 12 B

Touch sweetish.

Bordeaux Clairet 1998 13 C

Bordeneuve Blanc VdP des Cotes de Gascogne 1998, Somerfield 13 C

Bourgogne Haute Cotes de Beaune, Cottin Blanc 1997 13 D

Chablis 1997, Somerfield 12.5 E

Chablis Premier Cru 1997 10 F

Absurd price.

Chardonnay VdP d'Oc 1998, Somerfield 13.5 C

Chardonnay VdP du Jardin de la France 1998 14 C

Very fresh and knife-edge keen to finish. A wine for shellfish.

Domaine d' Arain Muscat de Frontignan (50cl) 16 C

Wonderful honeyed, strawberry/peach-edged sweetness here. Great with pastry tarts and creme brulee and ice cream. Terrific price and the size makes it perfect for a loveable pair of meal-ending hedonists.

Domaine du Bois Viognier, VdP d'Oc 1998 

Terrific apricot (yet subtle) fruit. A class act from nose to throat to soul.

Domaine Ste Agathe Chardonnay 1997, Somerfield 

Elegant and unencumbered by any concession to provinciality, earthiness, Midi herbiness or warmth.

Domaine Ste Agathe Oak Aged Chardonnay, VdP d'Oc Maurel Vedeau 1998 16 D

Oozes class and subtle fruit flavours – a lovely welcoming wine.

Entre Deux Mers 1998, Somerfield 13 C

Bit flabby on the finish.

Gewurztraminer Alsace, Caves de Turckheim 1998 15 D

Superb spicy, crushed rose-petal fruit, but this specimen will also age well for two or three years *and* improve greatly.

Gouts et Couleurs Chardonnay Viognier 1998 16 C

Delightfully complicated yet un-neurotic fruit. Great texture, fruit (peaches and nuts) yet dry and delicate.

Gouts et Couleurs Cinsault Rosé 1998 14.5 C

A dry, cherry-edged rosé, good with food.

James Herrick Chardonnay 1997 15 C

One of southern France's most accomplished, classically styled, bargain chardonnays.

Laperouse Chardonnay VdP d'Oc 1996 15.5 C

Lovely woody undertones of a mature chardonnay – bit white Burgundy-like and rather a snip at this price. Top 150 stores.

Les Marionettes Marsanne, VdP d'Oc 1997 15.5 C

Rich and ripe, warm and food-friendly.

Muscat de Frontignan NV (50 cl) 17 C

Fantastic accompaniment to pastry desserts: it's creamy, toffeed, caramel-edged, hugely honeyed and husky and it tastes like a drink you could offer to a goddess (before you ask her to live with you).

Rivers Meet Sauvignon/Semillon, Bordeaux 1998 13 C

Very grassy undertone.

Sancerre Domaine les Grands Groux 1998 13 E

Youthful mineral aroma is promising, but the fruit seems adolescently fruity and less than classic.

Vin de Pays Comte Tolosan 1998, Somerfield 13.5 B

Vin de Pays des Bouches du Rhone Blanc 1998, Somerfield 10 B

Rustic isn't the word.

Vin de Pays des Coteaux de l'Ardeche White 1998, Somerfield 13.5 B

Vouvray 1998, Somerfield 13.5 C

Medium sweet aperitif.

White Burgundy 1997, Somerfield 13 C

Winter Hill White 1998 14 B

Some dry, lemony fruit in good form.

GERMAN WINE — WHITE

Baden Dry NV, Somerfield 13 C

Plain and simple.

Baden Gewurztraminer NV 14 C

Good Chinese food wine. Great with duck, rice, noodles etc.

Hock, Somerfield 12 B

Mix with Perrier and ice for a lovely spritzer (15.5 points).

Morio Muskat 1997 14 B

A bargain off-dry aperitif smelling and tasting of dried rose petals (subtle but not unattractive).

Mosel Riesling Halbtrocken NV 14 B

Niersteiner Spiegelberg, Riesling Kabinett Rudolph Muller, Somerfield

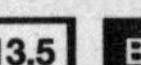

Needs spritzering to kill the sugar.

Rheingau Riesling 1996

Rheinhessen Auslese NV, Somerfield

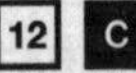

Laughable as an auslese (which is a designation of the ripeness of the picked grapes) but will perk up if frozen, a stick stuck up its middle, and licked during hot weather.

Rudesheimer Rosengarten NV, Somerfield

Brilliant value aperitif – try it well chilled.

Schloss Schonborn Riesling Kabinett 1987 15.5 D

St Johanner Abtey Kabinett 1998

Miserable offering which requires the addition of sparkling water to turn it into a 13.5-point acceptable spritzer.

St Ursula Devils Rock Riesling 1998

Go on – give it a try. Won't kill you. Though the Germans

are killing themselves trying to make more dry, modern wines like this.

St Ursula Dry Riesling 1997 12 C

GREEK WINE WHITE

Samos Greek Muscat NV (half bottle) 15.5 B

HUNGARIAN WINE WHITE

Castle Ridge Pinot Grigio, Neszmely 1997 13 C

Top 150 stores.

Castle Ridge Sauvignon Blanc 1998 15.5 C

Superb dry sauvignon of class and finely woven fruit and acid. Classic style here.

Tolna Region Chardonnay 1998 13.5 B

Meaty wine which turns a touch sour on the finish.

ITALIAN WINE RED

Barbera d'Asti 1997 12.5 C

Bright Brothers Nero di Troia Primitivo 1996 14 C

Civilised rusticity in one gulp.

Cabernet Sauvignon delle Venezie 1998, Somerfield 14 C

Ripe and cherry-bright, soft and a touch sullen on the finish.

Caramia Primitivo del Salento 1996 16 D

Terrific buzz about this wine: mature yet saucy, spicy yet seriously dry and savoury, textured and characterful yet chummy and mood-friendly.

Chianti Classico Montecchio 1996 14 D

Cherries and plums and nice dollops of earth. Good food wine.

Conti Serristori Chianti 1997 15.5 C

Lovely rich fruit, not typically Chianti-like (very hard baked) at first, but then the tannins cruise in. Excellent texture.

D'Istinto Sangiovese/Merlot 1997 (Sicily) 15.5 C

I Grilli di Thalia 1997 (Sicily) 14 C

Juicier than previous vintages.

L'Arco Cabernet Franc, Friuli 1996 15.5 C

Marano Amarone Boscaini della Valpolicella Classico 1995 16.5 F

Luscious, licorice-bar rich red with hints of wild strawberry, spicy cherry and prunes – plus a hint of tobacco and coffee. A glorious Italian contribution to civilised quaffing.

Mimosa Maremma Sangiovese 1997 15.5 C

Juicy undertone controlled by good assertive tannins. Modern yet traditional. Lovely stuff.

Monrubio Sangiovese, Umbria 1997 

Not remotely like the Tuscan example of this grape, this has richness, gripping tannins, and subdued hedgerow fruit. Top 150 stores.

Montepulciano d'Abruzzo 1998, Somerfield 

Piccini Chianti Classico 1996 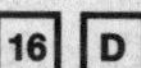

Real maturity of earthy cherries and spicy plums. Gruff voiced but avuncular, this wine is grand quaffing and great with robust food.

Riparosso Montepulciano d'Abruzzo 1997 

Lovely baked fruit, textured and though ripe handsomely balanced and dry. Has gorgeous richness, dry, complex layers of soft fruits and a resounding finish. A bargain by any standards.

Soltero Rosso, Settesoli 1995 (Sicily) 14 C

Terrale, Primitivo di Puglia 1998, Somerfield 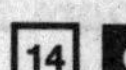

Very earthy, dry and with some strident tannins. A real foodie's bottle.

Terralle, Primitivo di Puglia 1997, Somerfield 16.5 C

Oh, what wonderfully chewy, savoury, soft, rich, dry, very classy and highly individual fruit. Marvellous mouthful.

Tre Uve Ultima 1997 14 E

Rich, ready, rampant, very juicy and up for food.

Trulli Primitivo 1997 15.5 C

Spicy, warm, herbal, rich, yet has a stealth-of-foot deftness as it quits the throat. Generous quaffing here and food-friendliness.

Valpolicella Classico, Vigneti Casterna 1996 14 C

Good grilled food wine – has hedgerow ripeness plus dry tannins. Top 150 stores.

ITALIAN WINE WHITE

Bianco di Puglia 1998, Somerfield 13.5 B

Bright Brothers Barrel Fermented Chardonnay 1998 15.5 C

Chewy, dry yet with restrained nutty richness, and an elegance on the finish which belies its price.

Bright Brothers Greganico/Chardonnay 1998 15.5 C

Delightfully crisp and clear-headed wine of charm and consummate drinkability.

Chardonnay delle Venezie 1998, Somerfield 14 C

Needs to be well-chilled to balance out the rich lemon fruit. Good party wine.

D'Istinto Insolia Trebbiano 1998 13 B

Four Corners Pinot Grigio 1998 13.5 D

Too underfruited to carry the weight of a six quid price tag.

Le Vele Verdicchio di Castello di Jesi Classico 1998 13 C

Marc Xero Chardonnay, Salento 1997 13 C

Has a screwcap! Delicious innovation. The fruit is somewhat less innovative.

Marche Bianco 1998, Somerfield 14 B

Hints of raspberry to the gentle citricity. A grand little thirst-quencher.

Salice Salentino Cantele 1998 16 C

Lovely balance of warm fruit and crisp, subtly lemonic acids. Real class and style here. Great with mood or food.

Sicilian White 1998, Somerfield 14 B

Richly flavoured and thickly knitted in texture. A grilled fish wine.

Soave 1998, Somerfield 14 B

Pity about the sad label but the fruit's in fine form. A dry wine of balance and food friendliness.

Trulli Chardonnay Salento 1998 

Delicate progression of richness yet delicacy courses over the taste buds here, leaving one refreshed and panting for more. It would be easy to quaff this wine too quickly and miss its abundant charms as it trips, with variegated steps, down the throat.

NEW ZEALAND WINE WHITE

Coopers Creek Chardonnay, Gisborne 1998 

Consummate class in a glass here: dry, fruity, calm, elegant, ripe, balanced, precise and total, utter quaffing quality of the highest order. Top 150 stores.

Coopers Creek Sauvignon Blanc, Marlborough 1998 

Shows the fatness of finish of the Marlborough '98s and as such lacks elegance and value. But make no mistake, it is still highly drinkable. Top 150 stores.

Montana Sauvignon Blanc 1998 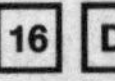

A rich vintage – fewer cold nights to build up acids – has resulted in Marlborough's sauvignons for '98 being fatter than normal but there is good balancing acidity. A very elegant wine.

Timara Dry White 1998 

One of the few Kiwis I am less than over-the-moon about.

PORTUGUESE WINE RED

Alta Mesa Red, Ribatejo 1997 14.5 B

Terrific posture! Sits up straight and true – muscled, lithe, fleshy.

Alta Mesa Vinho Regional Estremadura 1998 13 B

Begins like cough syrup, ends sweetly. Some throats will love it.

Atlantic Vines Bright Brothers Baga 1997 14 C

Ripe, touch cheesy, good chilled with fish and chorizo stew.

Bright Brothers Trincadeira Preta, Ribatejo 1997 14 C

Fiuza Bright Cabernet Sauvignon 1996 16 C

Classic green pepper aroma and hint of black pepper and this edginess is carried through to the rich, rippling fruit. Lovely wine. Top 150 stores.

Portada 1997 15 B

Ripe cherries, crisp apple, mature plums – about do for you? (Does for me.)

Portuguese Red 1998, Somerfield 14 B

A light, tobacco-tinged cherry wine – best chilled.

Ramada Red 1998 12.5 C

Very ripe and pruney.

PORTUGUESE WINE — WHITE

Fiuza Bright Chardonnay, Ribatejo 1998 15.5 C

Starts full and rich, then gets mellow and discrete, but it has finesse, class and persistence and is a bargain bottle. Top 150 stores.

Portuguese White 1998, Somerfield 15 B

A proud fish and chips wine.

ROMANIAN WINE — RED

Pietrossa Young Vatted Cabernet Sauvignon 1997 15 C

Romanian Special Reserve Pinot Noir 1995 15 B

Old raspberries and a hint of farmyard fowls. Classic? Not quite but so well priced and fruity it's reminiscent of the great stuff. Great with gentle Indian dishes.

SOUTH AFRICAN WINE — RED

Bellingham Pinotage 1997 15 D

Sweet and lush, hint of wild strawberry. Top 150 stores.

Bush Vines Pinotage 1998

Big pinotage richness and tobacco-edged fruit with lovely texture and savoury finishing tannins.

Cape Red 1998, Somerfield

What a wonderful house red! It may bring the house down but you will be protected. This wine is an elixir – it wards off evil.

Kumala Cinsault Pinotage 1998

Chewy, ripe, wonderfully fruity and hedgerow sweet.

Kumala Reserve Cabernet Sauvignon 1997

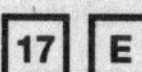

Wonderful one-off marvel of sublime cabernet class: pepper, cheroots, blackberries, tannins – it's got the lot. Plus superb textured richness. Top 150 stores.

South African Cabernet Sauvignon NV, Somerfield

Classic peppery edge to some ripe and very deep wine of great charm and concentration. It has a sense of being an old-fashioned claret but cloaking this respectability is some real, rampant, new world richness.

South African Cinsault Ruby Cabernet 1998, Somerfield

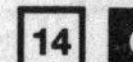

Very soft and juicy but hugely quaffable (chilled, too).

South African Pinotage 1998, Somerfield

Baked rubber, cheroots, plum – a classic dry pinotage!!! Drink it all before Christmas! It's too wonderfully youthful to appreciate middle age – except with the throat it will pour down. A terrific pinotage of depth and deftness.

Winds of Change Pinotage 1998 13.5 C

Very warm, soft, pliable, rich, gently toffeed fruit. Quaffability runs through every drop of it.

SOUTH AFRICAN WINE WHITE

Bellingham Sauvignon Blanc 1998 14.5 C

Fresh and frisky to finish – good rich fruit opens up this attractive display. Top 150 stores.

Bush Vines Colombard 1998, Somerfield 13.5 C

Very chewy and dry.

Hercules Paragon Chardonnay 1998 14 D

Chewy and woody and rather straining for effect, but with food it purrs very nicely.

Kleinbosch Chenin Blanc Chardonnay 1998 15.5 C

Delicious, gently spicy gooseberry and peach fruited wine.

Kumala Sauvignon Blanc/Colombard 1998 14 C

Has a hint of plumpness (but it's not cellulite) and overall it's crisp and clean and enjoyably quaffable.

South African Chardonnay 1998, Somerfield 13.5 C

Improving slightly in bottle.

South African Colombard 1998, Somerfield 14 C

Ripe melon and green lemon. A great fish wine is the result.

South African Dry White 1998, Somerfield

SPANISH WINE RED

Berberana Rioja Tempranillo 1997 15.5 C

Classic vanilla edge (American wood) but it's not too dry or sulky but silken and fresh.

Bright Brothers Navarra Garnacha 1997 15.5 C

Terrific throughput of fruit here: style, depth, richness and a measure of cool class.

Castano Monastrell Merlot 1998 15.5 C

Terrifically tasty tannins and richness here. Great with all sorts of cheese and vegetable dishes.

Don Darias Red NV 15 C

Good with curries.

Med Red Merlot/Tempranillo 1998 15.5 B

Very sunny and ripe but the tannins are excellent, well-shaped and properly mature and integrated. The result is, unusually, exactly what the label claims: a Med red. Real quaffing pleasure to be had here. It has character and wit.

Pergola Tempranillo, Manchuela 1998, Somerfield 15 C

Lovely dryness to what are some layers of savoury, rich fruit. Great pasta plonk.

Rioja Tinto Almaraz NV, Somerfield 15.5 C

Terrific value Rioja! Handsome fruit here.

Sierra Alta Cabernet Sauvignon 1998 16.5 C

High indeed! Proof that Spain can take on Chile. A wonderful wine of great class and style, huge depth and richness, and superb tannins. It's fresh, seriously complex and delightfully unfussy!

Valencia Red, Somerfield 15.5 B

Stunningly rich value for money. Baked plum, hint of apple skin, good non-nonsense tannins.

SPANISH WINE WHITE

Castillo Imperial Blanco 1998, Somerfield 14.5 B

Terrific fresh fruit here.

Don Darias White NV 13 C

Ed's White 1998 14.5 B

Very dry and fresh and terrific with fish. A bargain.

Moscatel de Valencia, Somerfield 16 B

Superb, rich fruit here, great with dessert, of cloying texture, candied melon, honeyed fruit. And a screw-cap too! No filthy tree bark!

Muscatel de Valencia, Somerfield 16 B

Hint of marmalade, lashings of honey and hint of strawberry jam. What a bargain pud wine this is. And its screw cap ensures it stays fresh and frisky.

Pergola Oaked Viura 1997 15 B

Delicious layered fruit which commences with a rich melon-ness and then rises to encompass lemons and a hint of mineralised pineapple.

Pergola Viura 1998, Somerfield 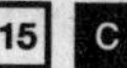

Has a nutty, dry aspect but it's immensely charming as it smiles with fruit as it finishes.

Santa Catalina Sauvignon Blanc/Rueda 1997, Somerfield 

Nice nutty crispness here.

Santa Catalina Verdejo/Sauvignon 1998, Somerfield 15 C

Excellent richness and flavour, touch less impactful on the finish but overall it deserves its rating because of its class.

Vina Cana Rioja Blanco 1998, Somerfield 

A lovely balance, this wine, combining crispness and good, vanilla-tinged richness which is very much the sane side of OTT. It has precision and delicacy.

URUGUAYAN WINE RED

Bright Brothers Tannat Cabernet Franc 1998

14 C

Very spry and fruity with not a coarse note struck anywhere.

URUGUAYAN WINE WHITE

Bright Brothers Uruguayan Sauvignon/ Semillon 1998

15 C

Vegetal elegance aromatically and on the finish. Surprising charmer of a specimen.

USA WINE RED

Californian Dry Red, Somerfield

16 C

Astonishing level of complexity given the bargain basement price. It's warm and rich, all-envelopingly textured, ripe yet dry, full of flavour and fully fit fruit.

Gallo Turning Leaf Cabernet Sauvignon 1995

15 D

Laguna Canyon Zinfandel 1997

15 C

USA WINE — WHITE

Californian Colombard/Chardonnay, Somerfield 13.5 C

Garnet Point Chenin Chardonnay 1997 15.5 C

Wonderful plump fruit here. As easy to drink as breathing.

Redwood Chardonnay 1996 15 D

Talus Chardonnay 1997 16.5 D

Terrific racy fruit, semi-opulent in its lazy richness, creamy smoothness, layers of fruits and posh acids, and final flourish. Lovely stuff.

FORTIFIED WINE

Amontillado Sherry, Somerfield 15 C

Lovely off-dry attack of fruit and tea-leaves, then it goes bone dry, then the warm fruit returns. A lovely complex mouthful. Brilliant aperitif.

Cream Sherry, Somerfield 14 C

Not remotely so simplistic that it can be described as sweet, this multi-layered wine has dry molasses, caramel and dry cob nuts in the background. Overall it's rich and forward. Delicious winter warmer.

Fino Luis Caballero, Somerfield 

Gorgeous bone-dry fruit: saline, almondy, tea-leafy – it's sheer classic Spanish tippling. Great with grilled prawns fresh from the sea.

Manzanilla Sherry, Somerfield 

Subtle, nutty and very dry – but immensely toothsome with olives. Or as a serious tippler's early evening drink.

SPARKLING WINE/CHAMPAGNE

Asti Dolce, Somerfield 

Sweet as toffee. Much easier, though, to chew.

Australian Quality Sparkling NV, Somerfield 

Fat and fruity on the finish, and I guess off-dry is its category, but a glass is not unpleasant if the company's congenial.

Australian Sparkling Chardonnay 1996, Somerfield 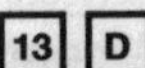

Finishes a touch abruptly.

Cava Brut 1996 

Has extra weight and concentration and the finish is enhanced as a result. Certainly bears comparison with much pricier bubblies.

Cava NV, Somerfield 

Fantastic price! The best bubbly in the UK for the money!

Cava Rosé NV, Somerfield 15 C

Dry but a lovely hint of cherry to it which justifies the intrusion of red grape skins to give it colour and more fruit for those who relish such things.

Cremant de Bourgogne, Caves de Bailly 1995 16 D

What a bargain! As dryly, wryly expressive as many a Champagne at four times the price.

Devauzelle Champagne NV 13.5 F

Huguenot Hills Sparkling (South Africa) 14 D

Lindauer Brut NV (New Zealand) 14.5 E

Expressive of nothing but great value for money and utterly charming sipping.

Millennium Champagne 1990, Somerfield 13 G

Don't buy it unless you are certifiably unbalanced in the pocket. Yes, it's drinkable but Somerfield has better bubblies for a lot less dosh.

Moscato Fizz, Somerfield 14.5 C

Mumm Cuvee Napa Brut (California) 16 E

So much more assertive, refined, tasty and sanely priced than its French cousins I'm surprised there aren't serious riots in Rheims.

Nicolas Feuillate Brut Premier Cru NV 14 G

Difficult to rate such insouciance and style any lower. Top 150 stores.

Nottage Hill Sparkling Chardonnay 14.5 D

Nottage Hill Sparkling Chardonnay 1997 (Australia) 15.5 D

Perfumed and stylish with a lovely undercurrent of fruit.

Pierre Larousse Chardonnay Brut NV (France) 16 C

Superb value for money. Has good rich fruit but it's serious and dry and not remotely tart or blowsy. Real bargain elegance here.

Prince William Blanc de Blancs Champagne NV, Somerfield 13.5 G

Nice fat chardonnay fruit continuing to be dry.

Prince William Champagne 1er Cru, Somerfield 14 G

Justifies its price tag by the evident elegance of its charms. It pulls off the great trick of good bubbly: dryness and fruitiness, refreshment with complexity.

Prince William Champagne Rosé NV, Somerfield 13 G

Prince William Millennium Champagne 1990, Somerfield 13 G

A lot of money for what it parades on the palate: dry bubbles of straightforward appeal.

Seaview Brut Rosé 14 D

Delicate little rosé.

Seaview Pinot Noir/Chardonnay 1995 (Australia) 15 E

Expands in the mouth on the finish with sesame seeds and some uncategorised fruit. It is dry, very classy and works well from nose to throat.

South African Sparkling Sauvignon, Somerfield 16 D

Gorgeous, just gorgeous! Loads of personality and flavour – yet it's stylish withal.

Vintage Cava 1992, Somerfield 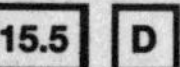

Better than many a vintage champagne at three times the price. Real class and elegance here.

TESCO

Scoots to the top.

The main story at Tesco in the past few years has been its ascent to the top of the UK retail heap at the expense of arch-rivals, Sainsbury's. However, over the past year Tesco has also scaled the top of the European retail ladder. In September 1998, the *Financial Times* reported that Tesco had become Europe's biggest retailer in terms of sales, knocking the German discount group, Aldi, off the top-spot. Expansion in Ireland, Scotland and central Europe had contributed to Tesco's rise, as had the strength of sterling particularly against the D-mark and the Franc.

Looking at events at Tesco over the past year or so, one can see why the retailer is consolidating its presence as the number one player, with announcements about expansion, entry into new markets and moving into new areas of business coming thick and fast.

For instance, in June 1998 the *FT* reported that Tesco was planning to expand its presence in the petrol/forecourt retailing market. It aims eventually to build a chain of 100 Tesco Express petrol stations. In August, it was reported in both the *Independent* and the *FT* that Tesco and Esso were discussing the feasibility of locating Tesco Express convenience stores at selected Esso forecourts. In fact, in April this year when Tesco announced a 7.8% rise in annual pre-tax profits to £881 million, the *FT* commented that the retailer was not resting on its laurels. Its market share had risen to 15.8%, stretching its lead over Sainsbury's. Tesco is developing hypermarkets in South Korea in collaboration with the Samsung Corporation. Tesco's initial investment is around £80 million with two hypermarkets planned. It already owns stores in Thailand.

In April 1999, it was reported that Tesco was to open four hypermarkets in Hungary later in the year. It already has five hypermarkets, five Tesco outlets and 27 S-markets in Hungary. Tesco will open five more hypermarkets in 2000 and five more in 2001. The group is also reported to have its eyes on Malaysia and Taiwan. By the end of the year, Tesco said that 30% of its selling space will be overseas. It even announced that it was to develop a 40,000 sq ft store in Douglas, Isle of Man, its first store on the island.

Meanwhile, 25 new store openings are planned for the UK during the current financial year bringing the total to around 600 and creating 10,000 jobs. However, the retailer's store-opening programme ran into one unexpected snag. The Council for the Protection of Rural England had opposed the development of a Tesco supermarket in Hadleigh in Suffolk. It probably would not be anything to worry about were it not for the fact that the president of the Council for the Protection of Rural England is none other than Prunella Scales, star of Tesco's very successful ad campaign. A conflict of interest possibly and certainly the potential for quite a few column inches for the CPRE (not to mention *Private Eye*).

Not only is Tesco opening more stores but it wants to keep those it has open for longer. In *The Times* in August 1998, Tesco revealed that it planned to more than double the number of its stores trading 24 hours a day to 63, creating 600 jobs. Round-the-clock opening had certainly helped the retailer over the Christmas period. Tesco said in *The Times* in early-1999 that 24-hour opening and strong sales of mobile phones and computers, which it had added to its range, were to thank for strong Christmas sales. Like-for-like sales rose by 4.1% in the six weeks to Jan 2. Some 84 stores were open 24 hours a day over the Christmas period, against 24 a year earlier. About 100 are expected to open 24 hours a day during the 1999 Christmas period.

Tesco said in May 1999 that it was also planning to introduce 24-hour opening at its Irish shops despite protests from Irish trade unions. In the UK too, unions have been concerned about initiatives like 24-hour and Sunday opening but even in its relationship with the unions, Tesco seems to be one step ahead of the game. *Retail Week* in September 1998 reported that Tesco was backing a major recruitment drive for the shopworkers union, USDAW, in its stores following an innovative partnership agreement struck between retailer and union earlier in the year. USDAW aimed to boost its membership among Tesco employees by a third to 120,000. Under the deal, Tesco agreed to give USDAW access to staff for recruiting purposes. But Tesco does at least have some claim to be an inclusive employer. *Retail Week* reported in December that the retailer was drawing staff from all the company's operations into a resource pool to review seven key areas of the business, the latest phase in its Future analysis and review programme.

The question of whether staff in the modern day supermarket are obliged to work longer hours is not the only thorny political question which Tesco and its like (is there its like?) have to field. The damage caused by the growth of one-stop shopping also provokes considerable debate. With Tesco gaining extra growth from selling mobile phones and computers, *The Times* in January commented on the cost of one-stop shopping. Tesco's good news about its financial results risked alienating most of the high street *The Times* said. The truth is that for Tesco to continue notching up sales growth at these levels, some stores will inevitably be sacrificed.

Tesco certainly has broadened its product repertoire over the past year or so. In advance of the World Cup last year, it was selling cut-price televisions at £99, but its electrical goods range has now expanded well beyond the cathode ray tube. In July, *Marketing* reported that Tesco was entering the own label electronics market, commissioning Amstrad to build budget CD players for sale in its stores. At the same time, Tesco became an internet service provider. TescoNet offers unlimited internet access for £8.99 a month. In February this year, *Supermarketing* reported that Tesco was offering free internet access to 10 million Clubcard holders. In November 1998, it formed a partnership with Vodaphone offering cheaper phones. The deal followed a link-up between Cellnet and Asda.

While most of the more outlandish new product developments have been in non-food, Tesco has enlarged its organic range over the past year. In late-1998, it launched 200 new own label organic products in more than 50 of its stores and said it wanted all of its top selling conventional lines to have organic counterparts by the end of 1999. But wine was not mentioned specifically. Tesco's new flagship store in Kensington (an interesting territorial claim since if it was 150 yards further south it would be in much less fashionable Earls Court and a few hundred yards further west and it would be in Hammersmith) which opened in 1998 boasts a sushi bar, takeaway Chinese and Indian counters, an antipasto and olive counter and an espresso bar. As much as 45% of the store is given over to fresh food, 10% more than other stores. Tesco refused to comment in March this year on speculation that it was about to launch a 25-product range of premium groceries targeted at upmarket shoppers. I can confirm this trend has reached fruition since on the several occasions I have shopped there the car park has been full of four-wheel drive vehicles and ex-debs shopping for exotic pastas.

Personal finance has been another area where retailers have looked to develop and Tesco is no exception. In June 1998, *The Grocer* magazine reported that Tesco was selling personal pension plans in 20 of its stores in collaboration with Scottish Widows. Meanwhile, the *FT* reported in May that home insurance had been added to the range of financial products on offer from Tesco. However, the retailer had to admit defeat with its video booths initiative for selling pensions. In December, so *Marketing* magazine told us, Tesco scrapped plans to extend the trial of in-store video booths giving advice on its personal finance products after disappointing trial results. In six months, fewer than 10 people had used the eight booths. Tesco attributed this to consumers' shyness. But no-one could call Tesco shy. It really tries out ideas which certain of its competitors would find utterly alien and this is an aspect of this retailer I admire and warm to. Of all supermarkets, it responds fastest to innovations and fresh ways to excite customers.

In April 1999, Tesco launched the Tescooter, a motor scooter selling for £1,200. The 50cc scooter is sourced from the Far East grey market and is about £300 cheaper than equivalent products in the conventional market. It went on sale in June at 100 of the larger outlets. Tesco's commercial director, the splendidly named John Gildersleeve, commented in *The Times* that scooters were the shopper's choice in Europe because they are easy to buy but that in the UK customers consider the situation complicated and expensive and that Tesco 'wants this to change'. This immediately inspired a defensive and frosty response from the Motor Cycle Industry Association. Tesco loves stirring it up (to the advantage of customers).

It was also rumoured that Tesco was looking at the feasibility of selling cars on the Internet. Some analysts were sceptical, however, as Asda had tried this in the 80s and it had been a flop. (Typical of leaden-brained analysts to assume the sceptical posture because something has been tried before and failed. What's new about it is the fact that it's Tesco trying it, dummies.) No doubt the Society of Motor Manufacturers and Traders, which has had to face up to some underhand price-fixing tricks from members (Volvo springs to mind), is already bracing itself and briefing a spin-doctor.

In October 1998, the *Bookseller* magazine revealed Tesco's plans to launch its first series of own-branded books beginning with 27 children's titles and 16 cookery books. Just over half of Tesco's 600 stores sell books. *The Grocer* added that Tesco began to sell books in 1985; the retailer commenting that the market had really opened up following the collapse of the NBA in 1995.

It is when supermarkets discount these additional peripheral items, selling them effectively as loss leaders, that other retailers and politicians become particularly concerned. One report in December 1998 suggested that Tesco was discounting some electrical goods sourced from abroad by up to 46%. Nowhere has this been more controversial than in the area of branded fashion goods, with the major retailers being chastised by the European Court for sourcing such goods from the grey market. The so-called Silhouette ruling last year outlawed the practice of buying goods from the grey market outside the EU and selling them cheaply in the UK. This legal argument – much to the lawyers' glee – looks set to run and run because just as brands like Ralph Lauren and Levi Strauss were poised to bring cases against UK retailers the British High Court issued a ruling which may undermine the European judgement.

One accusation the brands have sometimes made is that the products sourced via the grey market are not always genuine. This is precisely what happened to Tesco in May 1998 when the ludicrously overhyped and over-expensive fashion company, Tommy Hilfiger, issued a writ against Tesco for allegedly selling counterfeit Hilfiger merchandise obtained via the grey market – believed to be the first legal action of its kind in this country. Tesco was quoted in the *FT* as saying that the accusations were outrageous and close to defamatory and it was confident that the items in question were not counterfeit.

Tesco's pricing policy was news for another reason when *The Times* reported in August 1998 that the Tesco board had approved a dual pricing policy. This meant that customers would pay less for everyday items in 300 stores where till receipts and social profiling showed shoppers to be particularly price sensitive. The initiative was likely to cost the retailer around £15 to £20 million. Other dual pricing trials have included Asda's 10% price reduction to customers shopping at particular quiet times and Safeway's mother-with-baby discount.

Dual pricing, which many believe has been common in UK retailing for years and which analysts reckon could become increasingly so in years to come, is likely to be fostered by technical advances. *The Grocer* in March 1999 reported that

Tesco may be planning to introduce state-of-the-art electronic shelf-edge labelling which would facilitate the local pricing policy. The system would allow the retailer at the touch of a button to vary prices of products depending on the area or the time of day. Tesco Metro stores incidentally are said to carry a price difference of about 2%.

According to some reports, Tesco had been conducting a dual pricing trial of a different type in six of its stores in Dublin. In March the stores were accused of persistent over-charging by Irish independent retailers association, the RGDATA, following a survey. The association suggested customers were being over-charged by an average of 3% per trip. According to the report in *The Grocer*, Tesco had accepted that regular discrepancies did occur. The following month, *The Grocer* reported that the RGDATA had said the overcharging could account for as much as £133 million of the retailer's Irish turnover. Ireland's deputy Prime Minister called for Tesco to reimburse customers; other politicians demanded prosecutions. Tesco said there had been some procedural weaknesses but the overcharging did not involve anything like £133 million.

Accusations of such nefarious activity lead on to a snippet about Tesco's enlightened approach to recruitment. In March, *The Grocer* reported that the retailer was backing a scheme aimed at re-integrating offenders into society. The Going Straight Back to Work campaign launched by the National Association for the Care and Resettlement of Offenders (NACRO) is aimed at eliminating prejudice against ex-offenders. Tesco retail director, Michael Wemms, said Tesco was working with NACRO in reviewing its recruitment policies. Meanwhile, *Retail Week* magazine published the findings of a survey by property company, Healey & Baker, in which Tesco topped the poll as consumers' favourite place to shop. Some 18% nominated Tesco as their top shop. Sainsbury's and Asda were equal second with 11%, while 10% of interviewees nominated M&S.

Healey & Baker did not say what the split was between men and women in its sample but I would hazard a guess that

Tesco's stock with men has risen markedly over the past year. In February, Tesco announced that it planned to introduce creches for men. These are rooms with TV, pinball machines, sports magazines and the like where women can leave troublesome husbands while they shop. The first such area will open at the Tesco Extra store in Peterborough. Research showed that three quarters of men would prefer to stay at home watching sport than do grocery shopping; they only go to help load the car and to avoid feelings of guilt.

From personal experience, I query some of the underlying assumptions of these findings. It may be true of younger men, who might prefer beer, but wine drinking husbands, maturer and with the patience to browse, will surely find Tesco's wine aisles a source of endless fascination. Not only is Tesco's range vast, and the bargains abundant, but there are plenty of initiatives to keep the alert browser intrigued. (Thus suggesting, if nothing else, that all Tesco creches should be positioned with easy access to the wine shelves.)

Tesco experiments with wines as it does with so many other things. It introduced a range of screwcapped wines last year (not as successful as expected), it has introduced ranges which match food with the wines, its annual spring wine fair offers some terrific bargains specially purchased and, best of all this spring, it introduced wines which blatantly announced their styles on the label. Tesco Crisp Elegant White 1998 lived up to its name (15.5 points, £4.99), as did Tesco Smooth Voluptuous White (15 points, £4.99), Tesco Huge Juice Red 1998 (16 points, £4.99), and Tesco Monster Spicy Red 1998 (16 points, £4.99) – though I did think on first tasting that the nomenclature of the last two wines should be swapped over.

On my last visit to the Kensington (sic) Tesco I saw an ex-deb, her trolley already groaning with exotic meats and spices, enthusiastically loading up with Smooth Voluptuous White. I suspect the wine reminded her of her husband (they are now amicably separated) who, as far as I know, never set foot in a supermarket in his life and is too old now to attempt the experiment.

Five years ago such a trim and tremulous individual would not have been seen dead, let alone decked out in her Calvin Klein jeans, at any branch of Tesco. How times have changed and, of all retailers, Tesco has had the wit and the energy to change with them.

Tesco
Tesco House
P O Box 18
Delaware Road
Cheshunt
Herts EN8 9SL
Tel: 01992 632222
Fax: 01992 644235
website www.tesco.co.uk

SEE STOP PRESS SECTION AT END OF BOOK FOR LAST-MINUTE ADDITIONS OR UPDATES TO THIS RETAILER'S RANGE.

ARGENTINIAN WINE RED

Bright Brothers San Juan Reserve Cabernet/Shiraz 1998

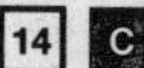

Very juicy and ripe but excellent food wine. Top 200 stores.

Bright Brothers San Juan Reserve Shiraz 1998

Bright and breezy, ripe yet dry, hint of minestrone as it finishes. Top 200 stores.

Chimango Tempranillo Malbec NV

Fruity and rich, that's about it. Not at all stores.

Familia Zuccardi 'Q' Tempranillo 1997

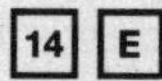

A 16.5-point opening turns clotted and overbaked. Smells of a lively cheroot, then delivers more rich, leafy flavours with ripe damsons, a suggestion of yoghurt and old leather. There's subtle cassis coating to the tannins and an odd, highly individual double cream finish. Tempranillo never tasted this rampant in Spain. A glass is enough for most palates, I would have thought.

Monster Spicy Red Syrah 1998, Tesco

Fabulous! And it's spicy and deep and intense. A lovely rip-roaring, juicy wine with a dry underbelly of insistent richness and classiness. Great stuff.

Picajuan Peak Bonarda NV 14.5 C

Picajuan Peak Malbec NV 15 C

Picajuan Peak Sangiovese NV 14.5 C

'Q' Tempranillo 1997 16 E

Astonishing level of juicy, creamy, ripe richness here. Hint of vanilla, touch of plum and wild strawberry – utterly yummy. Top eighty stores.

Santa Julia Cabernet Sauvignon Oak Reserve 1996 17 D

Wonderful layers of juicy richness and dry tannins beautifully intermingled. Immediacy, class, concentration and sheer velvet deliciousness. Top 200 stores.

Santa Julia Malbec Oak Reserve 1996 16 D

Leathery and very tannic. Deep, rich, and hugely nose-filling. You really do feel here that you've bitten off more than you can chew – but you chew it. Top eighty-five stores.

Santa Julia Montepulciano Oak Reserve 1998 16.5 D

So deliciously meaty and ripe, dry and dangerous – it's sheer crumpled velvet and vivacious fruit. Top eighty stores.

ARGENTINIAN WINE WHITE

Picajuan Peak Chardonnay NV 12 C

Not as exciting as in previous non-vintage blends.

Picajuan Peak Viognier NV 15.5 C

AUSTRALIAN WINE RED

Australian Cabernet/Merlot NV, Tesco 14 C

Australian Red, Tesco 14.5 B

Australian Ruby Cabernet, Tesco 14 C

Australian Shiraz NV, Tesco 13 C

Australian Shiraz/Cabernet NV, Tesco 14 C

Baileys Shiraz 1996 16 D

Daintier than I remember, and fresher on the finish, but the sense of rugged vines, each grape polished in the calloused palm of a leathery Aussie vigneron, still prevails. 200 stores.

Barramundi Shiraz/Merlot NV 15.5 C

Unusually tobacco-edged fruit here, very savoury and ripe, and there's a hint of woodsmoke to the plummy depths of what is a hugely entertaining wine.

Brown Brothers Tarrango 1998 13 D

They should put it on a lolly stick.

Chapel Hill Coonawarra Cabernet Sauvignon 1996 15.5 E

Coonawarra Cabernet Sauvignon 1997, Tesco 16 D

Demonstrates two wonderful things: Coonawarra is a unique region which can turn out finely textured, gently minty/spicy, very fine red, and second, Tesco is a dab hand at negotiating great prices for anything on earth. In Coonawarra's case, this earth is so-called Terra Rossa and I, for one, feel greatly heartened by this.

Cornerstone Grenache, Clare Valley 1997 17 E

Magnificently aromatic plummy richness and softness and gorgeous Aussie sweaty warmth. A great treat for the Christmas fowl. Offensively modern, brash, full-frontal and unashamedly luscious. Top eighty-five stores.

Cranswick Estate Dry Country Cabernet Sauvignon 1996 16 D

Terrific value here: a mature Aussie in prime condition. It's rich, dry, stylish, has fully integrated elements and motors like ruffled denim across the taste buds. Top eighty stores.

Geoff Merrill Cabernet Sauvignon Reserve 1994 16 E

Lafite – eat your heart out. Grow cabbages – this wine is so delicious, woodily elegant, warm yet serious cabernet you wonder if pigs can fly after all. Top eighty stores.

Geoff Merrill Shiraz Reserve 1994 18 F

A stunningly concentrated, smooth yet spicy shiraz of such depth, persistence and richness it puts many a Hermitage at four times the price to shame. A lovely fruity wine of great class. Very limited stock remaining as this book went to press. Top eighty stores.

Hardys Nottage Hill Cabernet Sauvignon/ Shiraz 1998 16 D

Loads of savoury plums and blackberries with lovely earthy tannins. Scrumptious drinking here.

Leasingham Domaine Cabernet/Malbec 1995 15.5 E

Very ripe and raisiny. Must be drunk at Christmas with the celebratory fowl. It'll love the spicy fruit stuffing, this wine. 200 stores.

Lindemans Bin 50 Shiraz 1998 15 D

So Australian in richness, texture and sheer smooth fruit, it's surprising the wine doesn't wear a hat with corks instead of a boring single cork and no hat.

McLaren Vale Shiraz 1997, Tesco 16 D

Ditto everything I said about the Coonawarra cabernet except there's no minty subtleties. McLaren Vale is a great region for red wine of substance, staying power ad potency. At most stores.

Ninth Island Pinot Noir 1998 13 E

Oxford Landing Cabernet/Shiraz 1998 15 D

Juicy and rich, wery wery (sic!) soft and sibilant tannins and altogether once in a glass the glass is drained. And you feel the opposite. Not at all stores.

Penfold Koonunga Hill Shiraz/Cabernet Sauvignon 1997 16 D

Most elegant, with a lively varnish to the soft fruit which is not normally as high gloss as this. Terrific style here – it purrs across the taste buds on padded feet. At most stores.

Rosemount Estate Shiraz/Cabernet 1998 15.5 D

So deliciously sweet and fruity: soft and full yet delicate on the finish. Deliciously approachable and warm.

Rosemount Shiraz 1998 14.5 E

Very juicy and ripe and the tannins come late into it. With food? My choice would be lamb pasanda or imam biyaldi. At most stores.

St Hallett Cabernet Merlot 1996 14 E

Bit juicy on the finish but jolly drinkable. Tannins have little grip, though. Top eighty-five stores.

St Hallett Faith Shiraz 1996 13.5 E

Very gooey and adult-Ribena-ish for me. And at this price, shouldn't we expect more complexity, subtlety and guile? Top 200 stores.

Stonyfell Metala, Shiraz/Cabernet Sauvignon 1996 11 E

I have never been able to enthuse about this medicinally labelled and quite ghoulishly juicy – rampantly so! – wine. It does indeed seem like a brew to restore iron deficient nonagenarians. Top eighty-five stores.

Temple Bruer Cornucopia Grenache 1997 14 D

Lovely spicy undertone. Not at all stores.

Tim Adams Shiraz 1997 14.5 E

Very juicy and integrating and the tannins are now fully melded with the fruit. Touch expensive, I feel, but this may be harsh considering the level of craftsmanship the wine conveys. 200 stores.

AUSTRALIAN WINE — WHITE

Australian Chardonnay, Tesco 16 C

Terrific value here, fully represented by the exuberance of the blue rollers on the label as much as by the tidal wave of flavour in the fruit. Lush, loving, warm, delicious.

Australian Colombard/Chardonnay, Tesco 13.5 C

Australian Semillon/Chardonnay, Tesco 15 C

Very incisive as it strikes the taste bud, fresh with a hint of fuller depths to come, but these never quite arrive as fat as you might expect. The result, then, is a terrific smoked fish and cold meats wine.

Australian White NV, Tesco 14 B

Barramundi Semillon/Chardonnay NV 16 C

Lovely oily fruit, hint of bellpepper and mango, and the whole thing is altogether more serious than the playful label suggests. A great wine to quaff or to match with oriental, European or South American meat and fish dishes. At most stores.

Blues Point Semillon/Chardonnay 1998 12.5 D

Not at all stores.

Brown Brothers Late Harvest Muscat 1998 15 D

Not as sweet as you might expect, it makes an interesting glass before dinner or, after, with grapes and goat's cheese. 200 stores.

Chapel Hill Reserve Chardonnay 1996 15.5 E

Starts with a trumpeting richness, finishes clean with a high piccolo-like note of freshness. Top eighty-five stores.

Clare Valley Riesling 1998, Tesco 16 C

Brilliant apple/pear/lime and spicy melon fruit. All subtle touches, these, true, and time will concentrate them but it presents a powerful case for immediate consumption. A wine of vivacity yet restraint. At most stores.

De Bortoli Noble One 1994 (half bottle) 17.5 F

Quite gorgeous sweet wine which somehow contrives to offer honey, nuts and hard fruit in such off-burnt harmony that it surprises by its complexity and breadth of flavour rather than a full-frontal sweetness.

Geoff Merrill Chardonnay Reserve 1995 17 E

Delicious Le Montrachet style Aussie with all the thrilling vegetality that implies but no sullenness on the finish. A brilliant wine of great class and world-class winemaking. Top eighty stores.

Hardys Grenache/Shiraz Rosé 1999 14 C

Charming cherry fruit, hints at sweetness but is undercut by good acidity. Not at all stores.

Hardys Stamp of Australia Chardonnay Semillon 1998 15.5 C

Delicious! Unusually complex yet modern and fresh. Has layers of melon (not overripe) and what seems like a hint of raspberry. Good acidity buffers this fruity attack.

Hunter Valley Semillon 1998, Tesco 13.5 D

Touch sour for six quid. At most stores.

Jacobs Creek Dry Riesling 1998 14 C

Great with Chinese food, though this is not a spicy riesling at all so don't go barmy with the chillies. At most stores.

Lindemans Bin 65 Chardonnay 1998 16 C

Supremely sure of itself, this well-established brand showing, in its '98 manifestation, what a great year this is for Aussie whites from the region (Hunter Valley). This has great hints of warm fruit balanced by complex crispness and acidity. A lovely under-a-fiver bobby dazzler. Top 205 stores.

Lindemans Padthaway Chardonnay 1997 15 E

A most accomplished, subtle Aussie chardonnay of sensitivity and charm. Very good manners: hint of wood, delicate melon and lemon. Top 205 stores.

Mount Pleasant Elizabeth Semillon 1994 15.5 E

Seems to be a rich beast as the aroma deliciously assaults the nostrils but then it strikes clean and fresh on the palate. Elegant and restrained – touch haughty even. Top eighty stores.

Ninth Island Chardonnay 1998 16 E

An expensive treat with its creamy depth and complex finish. Has a suggestion of old world vegetality but it is a triumph of cold fermentation and full fruit-retaining winemaking techniques.

Normans Unwooded Chardonnay 1998 16 D

It's as green and gracious as any Chablis from a great vintage and a beautiful vineyard.

Oxford Landing Sauvignon Blanc 1998

Amazingly fresh and cheeky for a warm climate sauvignon.

Penfolds Koonunga Hill Chardonnay 1998

What a great brand! Stunning richness and balanced, classy finish. If only white burgundians at three times the price could be this good. Not at all stores.

Pewsey Vale Rhine Riesling 1998

Something to drink now, with its rich mineralised edge, or to cellar to anything up to five or seven years whereupon the real classic riesling attributes of petroleum and under-ripe melon will be more concentrated. It could rate 17 or 18 by the year 2005. Top 205 stores.

Rosemount Chardonnay 1998

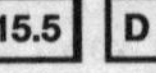

Always one of Australia's most accomplished chardonnays. Class and composure, fluency and flavour. Available at most stores.

Rosemount Semillon/Sauvignon 1998

A wine for complex fish dishes because it combines the fruity richness to combat the food plus the incisive edge of fine acids to refresh the palate and enhance the experience of food and wine between mouthfuls. Available at most stores.

Smooth Voluptuous White NV, Tesco

Curiously the reverse of smooth and voluptuous. But this only adds to the tension. This is a charming, direct, gently fruity and very even-tempered wine.

St Hallett Poachers Blend 1997

Delicious little treat to enjoy with the same retailer's lunchtime snack offerings and sandwiches. Top 200 stores.

Tasmanian Chardonnay 1998, Tesco 16 D

A rich, very rich, melon-edged chardonnay of impressive layered fruit but with a nice leavening of pert, pineapple acidity – very subtle but significant.

Tim Adams Riesling 1998 16 E

Very classy and very advanced acidically (limey and mineral-tinged) and it has years of development ahead of it. But it is striking now – and superb with smoked fish. 200 stores.

AUSTRIAN WINE RED

Blauer Zweigelt Lenz Moser 1997 

Brilliant! The best vintage yet for this Beaujolais of the Danube. Has more texture and soft richness but that unique smoked rubber and baked plum fruit is intact. Get it chilled!

AUSTRIAN WINE WHITE

Lenz Moser's Prestige Beerenauslese 1995 (half bottle) 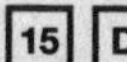

Delicious ripe honey, lemon peel, orange zest and melony ripeness as a subtle undertone. Great with fresh fruit or a creme brulee.

BULGARIAN WINE RED

Bulgarian Merlot Reserve 1994, Tesco 14 C

Very dry and arthritic-edged. Needs charcoal-grilled boar – bristles, tusks and all. At most stores.

Reka Valley Bulgarian Cabernet Sauvignon, Tesco

CHILEAN WINE RED

Altum Terra Mater Cabernet Sauvignon Reserve 1997

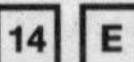

Terrific sweet-natured red for Indian food!! Not typical of Chile, and it's pricey. True, it has tannin, but the cherry and blackcurrant fruit is rich and glucoid.

Altum Terra Mater Merlot Reserve 1997

Very rich and earthy, pricey, untypical-of-Chile merlot. Wonderful with rich exotic food – like Balti stew – but the price? Difficult to swallow. Not at all stores.

Canepa Zinfandel 1998

Zingy and a touch exotic, spicy and saucy. Food-slurping style and great with mild curries. Top twenty-five stores.

Chilean Cabernet Sauvignon NV, Tesco

Chilean Cabernet Sauvignon Reserve 1998, Tesco 17 C

Brilliant layered richness and brightness of fruit. Goes from juicy ripeness through rich fat tongue-lashing chocolate edginess, then turns on a subtle cocoa-and cassis edge. Fantastic drinking here.

Chilean Merlot 1998, Tesco 16 C

Wonderful warmth of givingness to this richly textured wine. It has piles of carpet-thick fruit (hint of soft leather and blackberries) and the balance is lovely. It strikes softly, true, but it strikes true, softly.

Chilean Merlot Reserve 1998, Tesco 16 D

Shows the lovely subtle sweetness of young merlot, gentle yet gripping tannins, and well developed balanced fruit of some wit. Not at all stores.

Chilean Red NV, Tesco 

Earthy and rich, it comes across more like a Tuscan red than one from Chile. As such, with the dryness and food versatility, this implies this wine is a highly drinkable bargain. At most stores.

Cono Sur Pinot Noir 1998 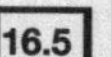 C

Very rich and ripe, not classic, but feral raspberries and truffles are detectable and the texture is superdeep. But it elevates itself over ten thousand red burgundies asking five times more. Top 200 stores.

Errazuriz Cabernet Sauvignon Reserve 1996 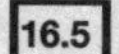 E

Finishes like a Pauillac, a Lynch-Bages say, of twelve years vintage (and a ripe warm vintage to boot). But this slight criticism (joke) is one's reward for permitting the taste buds to be so beautifully battered by the thick, rich, dark, savourily-tannic fruit. Like a Bordeaux, really. Archer is like Tolstoy by analogy but who would compare them in truth? Indulge me in my little extravagances. Top 200 stores.

Errazuriz Merlot El Descanso Vineyard 1998 15 D

Classic leather aroma, thick fruit with hints of cassis and plum, very soft, hardly intrusive tannin, and a touch of coffee on the finish. At most stores.

Errazuriz Syrah Reserva 1997 17.5 E

Ah! The poor Aussies . . . they knock the Frogs for six, then along come the Chileans with this opening bat. Life's a bitch isn't it guys?

Isla Negra Cabernet Sauvignon 1997 16.5 C

With its plastic cork guaranteeing no taint, this is a perfect wine for the finely palated, for it is in perfect cabernet shape: rich, clinging, dry yet cassis-edged, very swirling and dark and all-engulfingly slurpable.

Montgras Merlot 1998 16 C

Staggering good value here. The fruit is bold, leathery, hint of spice, firm and all in order from nose to throat. It energises the corpuscles and caresses the palate. At most stores.

Santa Ines Carmenere 1998 16 C

Massively dry and warmly textured fruit, reminiscent of hot saddles and dried plums at first, then a surge of hedgerow richness strikes. A perfumed, lingering, elegantly tannic wine of substance and style. Not at all stores.

Santa Ines Legado de Armida Carmenere Reserva 1998 15.5 D

Less quirky than its non-reserva brother and admittedly more temperate and calm in attitude. Loads of tannins to cheer the blood, however, and lots of dry fruit. 200 stores.

Santa Ines Legado de Armida Malbec Reserva 1998 15.5 D

Very soft and accommodating, restrained spiciness and thick blackcurrant/plum fruit. 200 stores.

Undurraga Familia Cabernet Sauvignon 1995 14 E

Very expensive and impressively rich and warmly textured. The tannins are impressive but I wish it were cheaper.

Undurraga Pinot Noir 1998 14.5 D

Not classic pinot but immensely drinkable as a representative of dry, cherry/plum/blackberry ripe fruit with no hint of farmyard, true, but loads of personality.

Valdivieso Chilean Cabernet Franc Reserve 1997 16 E

Can a wine be hugely elegant? This one continues to be. It's very smooth, polished, yet a yawning chasm of fruit is suggested as it coddles the taste buds. What does it taste of? Life. Life lived lovingly. Top eighty-five stores.

CHILEAN WINE WHITE

Chilean Chardonnay Reserve 1997, Tesco 16 C

Lovely depth of sophisticated unsnottiness here: dry, rich and deliciously melon and lemon ripe. Subtle yet forceful, calm yet enthusiastic.

Chilean Chardonnay, Tesco 14 C

Bit nervous on the finish, and only subtly suggestive of chardonnay in its rich and melon form, but drinkable enough.

Chilean Sauvignon Blanc NV, Tesco 14.5 C

Hints of grass to some fairly chewy fruit. Good for fish dishes, soups and salads.

Chilean White NV, Tesco 14.5 C

Great value tippling here. Not complex or intensely dry but has charming sotto-voce fruit.

Errazuriz Chardonnay 1997 16 D

I love the nutty, baked fruit aroma and the gentle fumaceous edge to the fruit as it descends, plump, ripe yet elegant, down the throat. Utterly delicious. About 400 selected stores.

Errazuriz Chardonnay Reserva 1997 16 E

Deep and richly resounding, it has hauteur and highly developed manners. Very classy and cool. Not at all stores.

Undurraga Gewurztraminer 1998 13.5 C

Interesting up front, but the finish seems to miss the mark

and the elegance of the well-tailored materials finishes slightly raggedly. Top eighty-five stores.

ENGLISH WINE — WHITE

Chapel Down Bacchus 1997 

Bit raw and appley. Top eighty-five stores.

Chapel Down Summerhill Oaked NV 

FRENCH WINE — RED

Baron de la Tour Fitou 1997 

Seems to be a conventional dry, herby, sunny Fitou as it lashes the buds but the throat gets a real fresh edge of peeled plum. Not at all stores.

Beaujolais, Tesco 

Nope, I'm just not a Beaujolais lover.

Buzet Cuvee 44 1997 

Chateau Clement Pichon, Cru Bourgeois Haut Medoc 1996 13 G

Classic cigar box aroma falls away into dryness and austerity on the finish. Probably needs five or six years yet. Top thirty stores.

Chateau de Cote de Montpezat, Cotes de Castillon 1996 15.5 D

Chateau Ginestiere Coteaux du Languedoc 1997 15.5 C

A juicy modern wine but also full of character and dryness. A terrific price for such a gluggable wine.

Chateau Haut-Chaigneau Lalande de Pomerol 1996 14 G

Again, a '96 claret which needs years to come really good. In this case, three or four. Top thirty stores.

Chateau La Raze Beauvalet Haut Medoc 1997 14 D

A smooth operator, clean shaven and unbristly of manner. Good with light vegetable risottos (including chucking a glass in the stock). Not at all stores.

Chateau la Tour de Mons Bordeaux 1996 13.5 G

An expensive treat which will deepen in appeal if cellared for another five years. Top thirty stores.

Chateau Lafarque Pessac Leognan 1996 12 G

Needs another seven or eight years. Top thirty stores.

Chateau Liliane-Ladouys Cru Bourgeois Superieur Saint-Estephe 1996 12 G

The most immediately drinkable of Tesco's '96 clarets. But what dodgy value. Yes it's classy but Tesco has wines with more exciting fruit at a quarter of the price. Top thirty stores.

Chateau Maucaillou, Cru Bourgeois Moulis en Medoc 1996 12 H

A nice £6's worth of fruit. Top thirty stores.

Chateau Maurel Fonsalade, St Chinian 1997 14.5 C

An edge of sweet hedgerow fruit. Untypically Minervois and charmingly unrustic.

Chateau Tour de l'Esperance Bordeaux Superieur 1997 16 C

Classic claret at an astonishing price. Has smoky richness, developed charcoal tannin, and the fruit, brave and battling, shines through. Top 200 stores.

Claret, Tesco 12.5 B

It cannot be possible to produce amusing claret for £2.99. Actually, that's not quite true; this example is amusing – it's absurdly presumptuously dry and ungenerous where it should be just tannically teasing.

Corbieres, Tesco 14.5 B

Cotes du Rhone NV, Tesco 13.5 B

As simple a construct as Rhone red gets – can be chilled well – where the earthiness is gentle and the fruit tender.

Cotes du Rhone Villages 1998, Tesco 15 C

Full of berries and rich baked fruit, not a hint of soil or horny-handed sons of it, and the finish is all dry fruit. An exemplary unadulterated Cotes du Rhone red.

Dark Horse Barrique Aged Cahors 1998 14 C

Brisk, businesslike, gets it over quick, leaves a faint tang of savoury tannins. Not at all stores.

Domaine de la Grande Bellane Valreas Cotes du Rhone Villages 1997 16 D

Ragged yet dainty on its feet, this richly finishing, very dry wine combines a fair spread of hedgerow fruit and delicious tannin. It is classic Rhone Villages red. Great drunk out of a Viking horn or sipped with lievre a la royale. Top 200 stores.

Domaine du Soleil Syrah/Malbec VdP d'Oc NV 14.5 C

Delicious! Who would have thought an old rustic bumpkin like this would come across as dainty? Not at all stores.

Domaine Marguerite Carillon Volnay 1er Cru, Les Santenots 1996 12 G

Top eighty stores.

Four Corners Fine Merlot 1997 13.5 E

Top eighty stores.

French Cabernet Sauvignon Reserve, Tesco 14 C

French Cabernet Sauvignon, Tesco 15.5 B

French Grenache Prestige, Tesco 14.5 C

Smells cabbagey but gets into terrific gear on the taste buds with food.

French Grenache, Tesco 14 B

French Merlot Reserve, Tesco 14.5 C

French Merlot VdP de la Haut de l'Aude, Tesco 15 B

Gamay, Tesco 10 B

Gevrey Chambertin 1997 12 G

Top 200 stores.

La Bareille Beaujolais 1998 12 D

200 stores.

Les Etoiles French Organic Red Wine NV 13 C

Earthiness is its most significant feature. Bit, though, like Cyrano's hooter – it tends to overshadow other aspects. Top 200 stores.

Les Fiefs de Lagrange, St Julian 1995 16 G

Big and tannic and hugely chewy. A brilliant posh wine for the roast Christmas fowl. Top eighty-five stores only.

Minervois, Tesco 14 B

Montirius Sigondas Cotes du Rhone 1998 15 F

This is a satisfying construct combining several layers of berried fruit, tannins, acidity and that ineffable warmth and vegetal richness of southern Cotes du Rhone. It is expensive, though, and will develop over the next couple of years.

Montirius Vacqueyras Cotes du Rhone 1998 14 E

Svelte, plump, gently ripe and softly herby, it does have its textured charms but the tenner it costs is not one of them.

Moulin Houchant Cotes de Provence 1997 14 C

Will it remind you of that holiday in Saint Raphael? Only if you chill it, sit in a deckchair, bung on Ambre Solaire and have Debussy on your Walkman. Top eighty-five stores.

Nuits St Georges, Les Chezeaux 1996 13 G

Has some tannins to the juice. Top eighty stores.

Oak Aged Cotes du Rhone NV 13.5 C

Don't catch the oak (except on the price tag). Not at all stores.

Oak Barrique Syrah 1995 15 D

Pauillac 1994, Tesco 13 D

Pommard 1er Cru, Clos des Verger 1996 13.5 G

Top 200 stores.

Raison d'Etre, Rhone Valley 1998 14 C

Get the pun? If not, the wine may be beyond your interest as well – it's not hugely earthy but it has some echo of that kind of Rhone red. 200 stores.

St Emilion, Tesco 13 D

Syrah VdP d'Oc, Tesco 13.5 B

Terroir de Tuchan Fitou 1995 14 D

Totally tastes of vinified hedgerow: sweet, earthy, brambly, delicious. Not as pricey as it was.

Trilogie, VdP d'Oc 1997 16 C

Wonderful couth fruit for £4.50! Lithe tannins, lissom fruit and light acidity – it all adds up to a subtly rich, soft, compelling, slurpable wine. It's also a versatile food wine. I drank a bottle with a spicy fish stew.

FRENCH WINE WHITE

Alsace Gewurztraminer 1998, Tesco 16 D

Lovely rich, rosy fruit, hint of ripe lychee and a touch of pear, and the whole construct is designed to soothe the troubled mind or lubricate Thai food. At most stores.

Alsace Reserve La Pagode 1998 12 C

Alsace Riesling Graffenreben 1996 14 D

Interesting and spirited. Sourer than its German cousin, it has a sullen edge, great with food. Top thirty stores.

Barrique Aged Marsanne Roussane 1997 15.5 C

Seriously nutty, gently rich wine with a gooseberry heart, subtle but clinging, with a fruit and lemon finish. It provides an elegant and firmly fruity rebuke to the idea that the Languedoc is no producer of charming, uncluttered whites.

Cabernet de Saumur Rosé, Tesco 13.5 C

Chablis 1997, Tesco 13 D

At the risk of boring you, isn't too much Chablis underfruited and overpriced? (Written for the umpteenth time.)

Chenin Blanc, VdP du Jardin de la France, Tesco 15 B

Cotes du Rhone Blanc NV 14 C

Domaine de la Jalousie Late Harvest 1998 14 C

A deliciously different, if sweetish, aperitif or wine for light fruit tarts. Not at all stores.

Domaine de la Jalousie VdP des Cotes de Gascogne 1998, Tesco 14.5 C

Nervous edge of chewy pineapple and overall a real thirst-quencher.

Domaine de Montauberon Marsanne 1998 12 C

Not at all stores.

Domaine du Soleil Chardonnay VdP d'Oc NV (vegetarian & vegan) 15.5 C

Domaine du Soleil Sauvignon/Chardonnay NV (suitable for vegetarians & vegans) 14 C

Domaine Saubagnere, VdP des Cotes de Gascogne, Tesco 13.5 C

Entre Deux Mers, Tesco 13 C

French Chardonnay NV, Tesco 12 C

Touch raggedy on the finish.

French Viognier VdP d'Oc 1998, Tesco 14.5 C

Lovely apricot-edged fruit. Delicious with food or to raise the eyebrows of pre-prandial tipplers. At most stores.

Gaston d'Orleans Vouvray Demi Sec 1998 12 D

Not at all stores.

James Herrick Chardonnay VdP d'Oc 1998 16.5 C

Cracking performer: elegant toasty fruit, firm balance of fresh acid (lemon-edged) and an overall politeness of manner and form. Has well-established credentials which the '98 vintage only amplifies. Not at all stores.

La Cote Chery Condrieu 1996 13 G

Les Estoiles Organic Chardonnay/Chenin VdP d'Oc NV 13.5 C

Sticky rich yet appley. Has echoes, indeed, of Cox's Orange Pippin apple crumble.

Macon Blanc Villages 1998, Tesco 11 C

Not at all stores.

Montagny Oak Aged 1997 13.5 E

Too pricey for my blood. Not at all stores.

Muscadet de Sevre et Maine Sur Lie 1998, Tesco 14 C

Some decent mineral acids bite the back of the tongue here – exactly where shellfish taste best. Not at all stores.

Muscadet NV, Tesco 13.5 B

Good price for a Muscadet (the price it should be) but the fruit is not as gripping, as biting as it might be. (A function of the price, says the snob? No, a matter of winemaking.)

Muscat de Rivesalte, Tesco (half bottle) 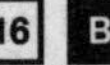

Excellent size for two gourmands' end-of-meal pudding (spotted dick and custard, perhaps). The fruit here is thick, sweet, hints at candied orange, and finishes with elegant honey. At most stores.

Oak Aged White Burgundy 1997, Tesco 

Touch ordinaire for a fiver. At most stores.

Pouilly Fuisse Louis Jadot 1997 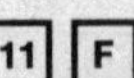

Frankly, I wouldn't give you four quid for it. Not at all stores.

Pouilly Fume Cuvee Jules 1998 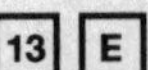

Lot of money for such straightforward fruit. Top eighty-five stores.

Premieres Cotes de Bordeaux, Tesco 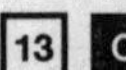

Puligny Montrachet Premier Cru 'La Mouchere' 1996 

Sancerre 1998, Tesco 12 E

Saumur Blanc, Tesco 13 C

Vouvray, Tesco 13 C

White Burgundy 1998, Tesco 10 C

GERMAN WINE WHITE

Devil's Rock Riesling 1998 14 C

The best vintage yet of one of the German wine revolution's pioneer names? Certainly you can catch it while it's young. The fruit is less likely to mature to any great advantage and the finish is positive.

Fire Mountain Riesling 1997 13.5 C

Almost very good . . . but. Well, it should be £3.49 and there needs to be a touch more fruit as the wine crisply attacks the taste buds.

Liebfraumilch, Tesco 12 B

Nierstein 1997, Tesco 13.5 B

Nierstein Kabinett 1997, Tesco 12.5 B

Steinweiler Kloster Liebfrauenberg Kabinett, Tesco 13.5 C

Steinweiler Kloster Liebfrauenberg Spatlese, Tesco 12.5 C

Villa Baden Chasselas 1998 12 C

I find it as difficult to comprehend the ululating beast on the label as I do the howling fruit in the bottle. At most stores.

HUNGARIAN WINE RED

Reka Valley Hungarian Merlot, Tesco 13.5 B

HUNGARIAN WINE WHITE

Chapel Hill Pinot Noir Rosé 1998 15 B

A lovely cherry-edged but crisply finishing rose of commendable elegance. Top 200 stores.

Hungarian Oak Aged Chardonnay, Tesco 13 C

Reka Valley Hungarian Chardonnay, Tesco 12 B

Tokaiji Aszu 1990 16 E

Will age for ten to twelve years (and more) but it will go well with goose liver – which I drank it with. It lacks conventional sweetness but has a rich acidic vein like marmalade and lime. It has been bought in specially for Christmas at the top eighty-five stores, so please be aware that stocks may be limited.

ITALIAN WINE RED

Allora Sangiovese 1997 15 C

Delicious earthy cherries here, not elegantly bound together, but richly interwoven with warm tannin. Has a good perfume and a firm finish. At most stores.

Barbera d'Asti Calissano 1997 15.5 C

Chianti 1998, Tesco 13 B

Very juicy.

Chianti Rufina 1996, Tesco 15.5 C

Terrific positive fruit here – from the underrated Rufina zone – and it repays its purchasers with a bargain classico ripeness and terracotta richness of fruit. Great with food. At most stores.

L'Arco Cabernet Franc, Friuli 1996 15.5 C

Merlot del Piave, Tesco 14 B

Merlot del Trentino, Tesco 15.5 C

Morellino di Scansano 1996 15 D

Pinot Noir del Veneto, Tesco 14 C

Sicilian Red, Tesco 13.5 B

Taruso Ripassato Valpolicella Valpentena 1997 16.5 D

Wild strawberries, cherries, licorice, almonds and sweet lushness overall. A wonderfully fruity wine of immense charm. It also has smooth tannins which will permit it to be aged for five or six years and become even lovelier (and perhaps reach 18/19 points). A superb food wine with such plumpness and depth it overrides the most robust dishes. Top eighty stores.

Trulli Negroamaro 1997 14.5 C

Warm, savoury, very polished and almost sedate, it packs a punch of gentility, yet style. Hint of leather to it.

Trulli Primitivo 1997 15.5 C

Spicy, warm, herbal, rich, yet has a stealth-of-foot deftness as it quits the throat. Generous quaffing here and food-friendliness.

Tuscan Red 1998, Tesco 14 C

Great chilled with cheese dishes. Not at all stores.

Villa Pigna Rosso Piceno 14 C

Seems light but it isn't. The tannins coat the teeth, snag morsels of spiced rice, and altogether make for the perfect wine for risottos (I eat a lot of risottos, sorry). At most stores.

ITALIAN WINE WHITE

Asti NV, Tesco 13 C

A real sweetie. Great-Great-Grandma, if she's remotely human, will lap it up.

Elegant Crisp White 1998, Tesco 15.5 C

A wine which lives up to its label billing! Great to sip, terrific with fish.

Frascati 1998, Tesco 13 C

La Gioiosa Pinot Grigio 1998 15 C

Comes in a patented thermic glass bottle which keeps the wine cooler once removed from the fridge, for several hours. And the wine inside this modern marvel is well worth keeping. It's dry and deliciously apricot-edged.

Marc Xero Chardonnay, Salento 1997 13 C

Has a screwcap! Delicious innovation. The fruit is somewhat less innovative. At most stores.

Orvieto Classico Abbocato 1998, Tesco 

Solid fruit, crisp on the finish, which would be perfect, for example, with spaghetti a la vongole.

Trulli Chardonnay Salento 1998 

Delicate progression of richness yet delicacy courses over the taste buds here, leaving one refreshed and panting for more. It would be easy to quaff this wine too quickly and miss its abundant charms as it trips, with variegated steps, down the throat.

Trulli Dry Muscat 1998 

Lovely floral edge, dry as you like it, and not a sissy side in sight. A sophisticated aperitif or to go with minted fish dishes and tomato tarts. Due to move to the '99 vintage at the end of December (not tasted at time of going to press).

Tuscan White 1998, Tesco 13 C

Touch of earth on the finish slightly clogs the style. At most stores.

Verdicchio Classico 1998, Tesco 13.5 C

It's the price. Should be £3.29.

NEW ZEALAND WINE RED

Montana Cabernet Sauvignon/Merlot 1998 16.5 D

This is more like it! A humdinger of a lump of rich meat here – full of blood and guts – and the texture is perfectly cooked and utterly compelling. It strikes me that the '98 vintage of Marlborough reds was the best ever. A concentrated wine of class and passion. Top eighty-five stores.

New Zealand Cabernet Sauvignon NV, Tesco 13.5 C

Waimanu New Zealand Red 1996 13 C

Tastes like a whacky pinot noir. Not at all stores.

NEW ZEALAND WINE WHITE

Azure Bay Chardonnay/Semillon 1998 14 C

Great with a Chinese takeaway. Not at all stores.

Cooks Chardonnay, Gisborne 1998 13 D

Not at all stores.

Jackson Estate Sauvignon Blanc, Marlborough 1998 15.5 E

Ripe, fresh and plumply purposeful.

Kim Crawford Marlborough Sauvignon Blanc 1998 15.5 E

Very elegant and stylish. Dry but decisively fruity. Top eighty-five stores.

Montana Marlborough Riesling 1998 16 C

Interesting question: do you drink it now or keep it? Both are possible options. It has a lovely drinkable crispness and gentility of steely fruit but it will also age, over three or four years, with distinction and deepen in richness and complexity. Not at all stores.

Montana Sauvignon Blanc 1998 16 D

A rich vintage – fewer cold nights to build up acids – has resulted in Marlborough's sauvignons for '98 being fatter than normal, but there is good balancing acidity. A very elegant wine. Not at all stores.

New Zealand Chardonnay, Tesco 15 C

New Zealand Dry White, Tesco 13.5 C

New Zealand Sauvignon Blanc 1997, Tesco 14 C

Rongopai Chardonnay Reserve 1996 16.5 E

A superbly wood chardonnay in the Montrachet mould. It only falls from the high standard, impeccable aroma and frontal fruit on the finish, which is quicker than a great wine would exhibit. This is, I feel, a function of its youth. But then if the acidity loses its grip – if one aged the wine for two more years – would the essential clean bite of the wine lessen? A conundrum – it is worth a tenner to try to solve it. Top eighty-five stores.

Stoneleigh Chardonnay 1997 15.5 D

Always one of the more reliably fruity Kiwis, in this vintage there is fatness yet fitness. Top 200 stores.

Villa Maria Private Bin Sauvignon Blanc 1998 14.5 D

Quiet, reserved and very dainty. A thought-provocative wine which needs no food. Not at all stores.

PORTUGUESE WINE RED

Alianca Particular Palmela 1995 17 D

Such sweetness and emulsion-thick texture yet it's dry, herby, very rich and classy on the finish. A terrific wine. Top eighty-five stores.

Bela Fonte Baga 1998 15.5 C

A vigorously fresh-edged and keenly tannic specimen, which has hugely food-friendly cherry/plum fruit, textured and taut. A lot of tension between the elements, this wine. Not at all stores.

Bright Brothers Douro 1996 16 C

Very juicy and ripe yet, astonishingly, dry and tannic to finish. Lovely trick to pull off here – great with food and for quaffing with serious company. Not at all stores.

Bright Brothers Old Vines 1996

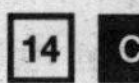

Lush fruity charms – deep and delicious. Can be chilled and drunk with fish. Top eighty stores.

Dao, Tesco

Very juicy and ripe.

Dom Ferraz Bairrada 1997

Old Dom's back on form and sprightlier than ever! Terrific juice here – and serious underlying tannin. A tenacious wine of substance and style. Top eighty stores.

Dom Ferraz Dao 1997

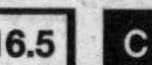

Fabulous tufted texture and soft, ripe, curvaceous fruit. It really wraps itself round the taste buds. Quite gorgeously quaffable and delicious.

Vinha Nove Tras-os-Montes 1998

Terrific fruit here: dry yet fruity (raisins, plums, cherries and a hint of fig), good assertive tannins, and an overall structure, for the money, of surprising detail and daring inventiveness. At most stores.

PORTUGUESE WINE WHITE

Bela Fonte Bical 1998

Terrific pace to the gooseberry fruit here (hint of raspberry also). The style is not forward, but modern and fresh and it finishes with style. 200 stores.

Dry Vinho Verde, Tesco 13.5 C

Teasing aperitif. Not at all stores.

ROMANIAN WINE RED

Four Corners Romanian Merlot 1998 13.5 C

Some dry fruit here which lacks a bit of punch on the finish.

Reka Valley Romanian Pinot Noir, Tesco 15.5 B

SOUTH AFRICAN WINE RED

Beyers Truter Pinotage NV, Tesco 16 C

Pinotage in its Sunday best. The tannins give it presence and persistence but there's none of the burnt rubber juiciness of the grape. Instead, we get well pressed and neatly pleated fruit of style and flavour.

Cape Cinsaut NV, Tesco 15.5 B

Cape Cinsaut/Pinotage NV, Tesco 15.5 C

Diemersdal Merlot 1998 15.5 D

Rich, ripe, rivetingly well-packed with lush fruity flavours and it goes all squashy and meaty on the finish. Not at all stores.

Diemersdal Shiraz 1998 15 D

Interesting shiraz, at this price, more tobacco-scented, tannic complexity and ruffled-denim fruit than many an Aussie example of this grape for the same money. It finishes less sweetly than an Oz example, but its mid-palate performance, that is to say in the mouth and on the buds, is good and rich. Not at all stores.

Four Corners Fine Cabernet/Merlot 1997 13.5 E

Top eighty stores.

Goiya Glaan 1998 15.5 C

So much more exuberant, lively and charmingly fruity than any Beaujolais nouveau. Drink it for the sheer unpretentiousness of its immediate charm.

International Winemaker Cabernet Sauvignon/Merlot, Tesco 13 C

Long Mountain Cabernet Sauvignon 1998 13.5 C

Very juicy and dry to finish. Not at all stores.

Pinnacle Cabernet Sauvignon 1997 16 D

A deliciously tobacco-edged cabernet, not remotely shy, which turns in a serious smile of grim tannicity on the finish.

Pinnacle Merlot 1998 16 D

Yes, it's jammy and ripe but it has some lovely herby dryness underneath. Terrific quaffing here. Top eighty stores.

Pinnacle Shiraz/Cabernet 1997 14.5 D

Very spry and energetic on the taste buds. Great chilled with oriental meat dishes. Not at all stores.

South African Red, Tesco 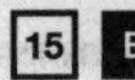

South African Reserve Cabernet Sauvignon, Tesco 

South African Shiraz/Cabernet Sauvignon 1998, Tesco 

Warm and winsome. More Aussie than perhaps its makers would care for it to be thought. At most stores.

Spice Route Andrew's Hope Merlot/ Cabernet, Malmesbury 1998 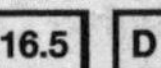

The essence of new world cheekiness – it dares to be utterly unashamedly immediate and all-embracing. It's got so much jammy richness, which never goes gooey or blowsy. It's great, gorgeous and grandly underpriced. Top eighty stores.

Stellenbosch Merlot, Tesco 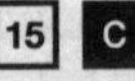

Thandi Pinot Noir 1998 

Rather ramshackle, though gamy, pinot, of fair cherryish fruit. Too expensive for the style.

Woodlands Cabernet Sauvignon 1997 15.5 E

SOUTH AFRICAN WINE WHITE

Barrel Fermented Franschoek Semillon 1998, Tesco 

Less rich than any Aussie semillon, here it's more nervous, chewier, and leaner. Not at all stores.

Boschendal Grande Cuvee Sauvignon Blanc 1998 13.5 D

Seem a lot, seven quid, for a four pound fifty construct in a pretentious bottle and with a pretentious appellation.

Cape Chenin Blanc, Tesco 14 B

Cape Colombar/Chardonnay, Tesco 13.5 C

Fairview Chardonnay 1998 16 D

The richness and class is superb.

Goiya Kgeisje 1999 14 C

Eager, more fruit than previous vintages, but still keeps its dainty charms.

Oak Village Sauvignon Blanc 1998 15 C

Delicious persistence of gentle melon and nutty fruit. Will go well with loads of fish dishes.

Paul Cluver Sauvignon Blanc 1997 16 E

Steely, with a hint of crisp lettuce leaf but this is well coated with some textured fruit so the final effect is very, very classy. Top eighty-five stores.

Pinnacle Chenin Blanc 1997  16 C

What an improvement since I first tasted it last autumn! Brilliant rich fruit hinting at dryness but so thick that the fruit, vegetal and nutty with a lush edge, is very stylish, very high class, and of an impactful generosity.

Ryland's Grove Barrel Fermented Chenin Blanc 1998

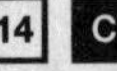

Brilliant chewy fruit here, undercut by a freshness yet fullness which the Cape with this grape variety has made its distinct style. Has loads of charm and meaningful manners and it even throws in a touch of elegance. A bargain. At most stores.

Ryland's Grove Chenin/Colombard 1997

Has some gummy fruit to its edge, essentially fresh, and it is very keen to quench. Not at all stores.

Rylands Grove Sauvignon Blanc 1998

Softly rich and ripe, rather classy and structured. Not hugely dry but nice gooseberry fruit and excellent refreshing qualities. Neat finish.

South African Chardonnay/Colombard, Tesco

South African Reserve Chardonnay 1998, Tesco

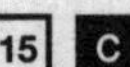

Delicious richness lapped by ripples of peaches/pineapple acidity.

South African White, Tesco

Spice Route Long Walk Sauvignon Blanc 1998

Hint of earthy minerals and concentrated gooseberries. Excellent structure and depth.

Thandi Chardonnay 1998

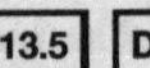

An attempt to make serious chardonnay. But I find the creamy woodiness a touch crude and fruit-masking. With tandoori fish or chicken, though, this wine would be marvellous.

SOUTH AMERICAN WINE RED

Two Tribes Red 13.5 C

SOUTH AMERICAN WINE WHITE

Two Tribes White 13.5 C

SPANISH WINE RED

Don Darias NV 15 C

Still keeping his nose in shape, this gent, and the Don has, in this latest blend, more tannins and ripe plummy fruit. He'll take you through a mild curry most charmingly.

Espiral Moristel Tempranillo/Cabernet Sauvignon 1998  16 C

It's the blackcurrant jam richness which startles – but it's dry and herby. Tannins and tenacity, style and utter drinkability – a lovely wine.

Huge Juicy Red 1998, Tesco

Wonderful stuff! It is hugely dry and juicy but this fruit is classy and bouncy, like a young cru Beaujolais in a great year, but there's the added tonic of rich tannins. A very versatile wine – chilled with fish or meat or veg or cheese.

Marques de Chive Reserva 1994, Tesco

Can't imagine anything nicer with grilled lamb chops or Toulouse sausages. At most stores.

Marques de Grinon Rioja 1997

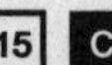

Not remotely typical. And this refreshing virtue makes it a Rioja which can be both pleasurably gulped and drunk with all sorts of food from risottos to grilled vegetables. Not at all stores.

Muruve Crianza 1996

Expensive but classy, ripe, rich and rivetingly fruity on the taste buds. Top eighty stores.

Orobio Tempranillo Rioja 1998

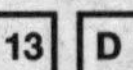

Finishes a touch wanly for a wine at this price level. Not at all stores.

Perdido Navarra Cabernet Sauvignon Crianza 1995

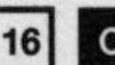

Brilliant value here. The rich, textured, warmly tannic fruit has depth and weight and the polish has not obscured the character.

Piedmonte Merlot Tempranillo 1998

Beaujolais lovers will lap it up!

Spanish Tempranillo 1996, Tesco 13.5 C

Lovely rich beginning, bit of a sweet and soppy ending.

Valduero Ribera del Duero Crianza 1995 15 E

A real treat – though a touch sweet on the finish – for it has lush tannins and forceful fruit.

Vina Mara Gran Reserva Rioja 1989, Tesco 13.5 E

Too sweet for a tenner. Not at all stores.

Vina Mara Rioja Alavesa 1998, Tesco 16 D

A simply terrific rioja. It just bounces with ripe, plump, dark fruit with lovely attendant tannins of savoury richness.

Vina Mara Rioja Reserva 1994, Tesco 15.5 E

Hint of coconut here, and deeply textured plummy fruit, but it's all good natured and friendly. The texture is the thing, though, it's like crushed denim with patches of satin. At most stores.

Vina Mara Rioja, Tesco 14 C

Earthy, no hint of vanilla or coconut, just good honest fruit.

SPANISH WINE WHITE

Agramont Cabernet Sauvignon Rosado 1998 14 C

One of the crispest and cleverest of rosés. Top 200 stores.

Moscatel de Valencia, Tesco 15.5 C

URUGUAYAN WINE RED

Four Corners Tannat/Merlot 1998 

Has a nice hint of the exotic. Very sunny and warm and richly welcoming. Top 200 stores.

URUGUAYAN WINE WHITE

Four Corners Sauvignon Blanc 1998 

Crisp, clean and very spry. Top 200 stores.

USA WINE RED

Bonterra Cabernet Sauvignon 1996 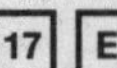

Simply wonderful persistent fruit. It hammers home such brilliance of creamy richness and layered depth. It has great complexity and yet massive, scrumptious quaffability. A wonderful, immediate cabernet. Top 200 stores.

California Old Vine Estate Carignane 1996 

Bit soupy.

California Old Vine Estate Zinfandel 1996 15 D

Fetzer Vineyards Private Collection Cabernet Sauvignon 1995 17 G

If you must spend fifteen quid on a cab style wine, then eschew Tesco's '96 clarets and go for this massively rich, sweet yet deeply serious, tannin-lush specimen. It reaches the levels of drinkability you can enjoy out of a spoon: who needs the convention of a glass? Wine Advisor Stores only.

Robert Mondavi Coastal Cabernet Sauvignon 1995 14 E

Very rich and tarry, more than a touch expensive for what it is, but hugely drinkable and enjoyable for those whose pocket is as deep as their throats.

Stratford California Zinfandel 1997 14.5 C

Tarry and rich and good with food.

USA WINE WHITE

Bonterra Chardonnay 1996 17 E

Voluptuous! Yes, this wine is so – and it's rich, classy, sensual, deep, thought-provoking and utterly sinfully delicious. Top 200 stores.

Columbia Crest Chardonnay 1997 15.5 D

Lovely fruity richness, tempered and never mono-dimensional, encased in a solid coating of mature acidity. A fullish wine, dry yet rounded, it has a deal of charm and striking understatement (that may be a litotes but these days who cares?). Not at all stores.

Fetzer Barrel Select Chardonnay 1997 14 E

Fetzer Viognier 1998 16.5 E

Lovely limpid, lush, lively – a wine of ineffable finesse yet apricot-scented and fruited richness. A rare treat. Fruit to read by, think by, listen by.

Stratford Chenin Blanc NV 14 C

A wine for Thai mussels – rich and spicy.

FORTIFIED WINE

10 Year Old Tawny Port, Tesco 13.5 F

Finest Madeira, Tesco 15.5 E

Mick Morris Rutherglen Liqueur Muscat (half bottle) 17 C

A miraculously richly textured pud wine of axle-grease texture and creamy figginess. Huge, world class.

Superior Oloroso Seco Sherry, Tesco (half bottle) 15 B

Superior Palo Cortado Sherry, Tesco (half bottle) 16.5 C

SPARKLING WINE/CHAMPAGNE

Australian Sparkling Wine, Tesco 14.5 C

Blanc de Blancs Champagne NV, Tesco 13.5 G

Not at all stores.

Blanc de Noirs Champagne NV, Tesco 14 G

Has some elegance and bite and that true suggestion of richness which a Champagne made from black grapes can exhibit. Not at all stores.

Cava, Tesco 16 C

Chapel Down Epoch Brut NV (England) 11 D

Chapel Hill Sparkling Chardonnay (Hungary) 14.5 C

Demi-Sec Champagne, Tesco 13 F

More fruit than normal, and too much for me, but for lovers of the sweet things of life, this will be perfect. Not at all stores.

Douglas Green Sparkling Brut NV (South Africa) 10 E

I find it unconscionably dull and spiritless. Top eighty stores.

Jacob's Creek Sparkling Chardonnay/Pinot Noir NV (Australia) 15 D

Great value.

Laurent-Perrier Cuvee Rosé Brut NV 11 H

Laurent-Perrier Vintage 1990 13 H

Has some class but the price needs to go to Weight Watchers. Top eighty stores.

Lindauer Brut (New Zealand) 13 E

Lindauer Special Reserve NV (New Zealand) 14.5 E

Has finesse and dryness. Class, too.

Moet Vintage 1993 13.5 H

Has some interesting fruit.

Mumm Cordon Rouge Cuvee Limitee 1990 13 H

Too much money for the level of excitement on offer. Top eighty stores.

Mumm Grand Cordon 1990 12 H

Hardly worth fifty quid of anyone's money.

Nicolas Feuillate Brut NV 13.5 G

Premier Cru Champagne Brut NV 15 F

Rosé Cava NV, Tesco 15.5 C

Deliciously dry and gently fruity, it makes many a much-vaunted Champagne blush to its roots at its price.

South African Sparkling Sauvignon Blanc 1998, Tesco 14.5 C

Taittinger Blanc de Blancs Comtes de Champagne 1989 10 H

Rip-off time. Top eighty stores.

Taittinger Champagne Brut NV 12 H

The price is, frankly, difficult to swallow when many Cavas, at a quarter of the price, are no less charming. Not at all stores.

Yalumba Sparkling Cabernet Sauvignon NV 16 E

Yalumba Sparkling Pinot Noir Chardonnay NV 16 E

WAITROSE LTD

Head in the air, a toe in the Midlands.

This retailer seems to have something of a special relationship with British Airways. The world's favourite airline's favourite supermarket is without a doubt Waitrose. BA was among the first companies to subscribe to the Waitrose@work office shopping service, and it has now been given its very own Waitrose store. *Supermarketing* magazine reported in July 1998 that Waitrose was to open a 400 sq ft mini-store in the new British Airways head office at Waterside near Heathrow. It is more or less a convenience store format carrying about 600 lines. Waitrose would not comment on whether it intended to open further outlets of that size, as convenience stores or within other offices.

The retailer subsequently announced the extension of its office shopping scheme to a number of other blue chip companies. Interestingly, among the new subscribers was Virgin Atlantic which among many boasts could claim to being BA's least favourite airline (and vice versa I am sure). Waitrose would probably do well not to get any of their orders muddled up. By April 1999, Waitrose said it had signed up some 27 major corporate clients to the Waitrose@work scheme including the BBC at White City, Capital Radio, Barclaycard and Heinz.

As well as developing its office shopping service, Waitrose has also been expanding its home delivery service. In October 1998, it announced that it intended to extend its home delivery service to 19 more stores by the end of December. The year-long trial it had conducted at its Putney store was successful, the retailer said, with the store making 300 home deliveries a week.

People have strange ideas about Waitrose. In fact, the retailer is concerned that it is rather misunderstood. For instance, people tend to think it is expensive, more expensive than its supermarket rivals. So vexing does Waitrose find this that in May this year, the retailer launched an in-store initiative to communicate that everyday items do not cost more at Waitrose. 'There's a misconception that Waitrose does not care about price and is more expensive – neither of which is true,' marketing director, Mark Price, told *Supermarketing*. Now a retailer that has a director called Mark Price surely has to be particularly careful about what it charges. Mr Price continued that Waitrose's ominous sounding Central Intelligence Department made price checks on a range of 300 popular lines across the supermarket sector. 'We aim to make sure that across that range of goods our prices are competitive with the majors,' he said.

Now with its Price Commitment initiative the retailer aims to communicate this behind-the-scenes work by highlighting shelf-edge labelling for the products that are included in the survey. The Price Commitment message is also being carried on trolleys and baskets and on point-of-sale material at the tills. But the retailer has not lost sight of one important factor. The reason why people think Waitrose is more expensive than other retailers is because, in many people's eyes, it looks more expensive and many of its consumers, I should imagine, rather like this. The last thing the retailer wants to do is spoil its upmarket feel by blazoning messages about how cheap it is everywhere. It's something of a quandary really but Mr Price thinks they have found the answer. He said of the new campaign, 'It's not garish or in your face, but confident and subdued.'

People also think of Waitrose as just a London retailer. True, its strengths are in the M25 area but the retailer is increasingly looking further afield. It has moved into the Midlands with outlets in Birmingham and Newark among its 120-odd stores and last October announced it was moving into the south-west with a store in Okehampton. There are those who feel the Waitrose concept is perfect for many areas beyond its south-east stronghold. 'It is barely north of Birmingham and it should be in Halifax, Chester and other affluent northern areas,' wrote one retail analyst in an article in *Supermarketing* last year. Steady growth appears to be the order of the day for Waitrose. The company reported a 3% rise in sales to £1,782 million in 1998 and said it had nudged up its market share. It said like-for-like sales growth for the first five weeks of the new year was 4% and it planned to open eight new stores in 1999.

Among the other interesting innovations at Waitrose this year was the launch of its own store magazine. In April, the company announced that it was challenging *Sainsbury's* magazine with the launch of its own title, *Waitrose Food Illustrated* which it bought into by adding its name to the already established *Food Illustrated* published by dynamic wine connoisseur and tennis player, Mr John Brown. It will be free to account cardholders and will have an initial print-run of 500,000 copies. Interestingly, it is the first supermarket magazine which will be sold on news stands competing against titles like *BBC Good Food*. New Crane Publishing, which publishes *Sainsbury's* magazine and resolutely refuses to make it available on news stands (it would make the cover price too high), says that its magazine currently has a circulation of 410,000 readers. As consultant wine editor to the latter magazine, my views, however independent from Sainsbury's the magazine is, may carry little weight, but I would comment that advertising agency media departments will not consider free distribution to non-paying account card holders as any big deal (and it doesn't happen with *Sainsbury's* magazine which is only on sale at the retailer's checkouts).

During the past year, some of Waitrose's larger competitors have made dramatic innovations on the new product front with the introduction of own brand computers, mobile phones, pensions and even motor-scooters. Waitrose to my knowledge has made no such outlandish additions to its range but it was reported in *Supermarketing* magazine in February that it had re-introduced a type of potato into the country which has not been sold here for 100 years. The Mr Bresee potato, which has white flesh with a pinkish blush skin, was joined by two other rare types of potato: the Fortyfold and the Shetland Black.

On the wine front, no such startling changes took place. Mr Julian Brind continues his wise and urbane running of the department and its youngest member, Mr Joe Wadsak, continues to surprise old fart wine writers by his fresh face and wonderful enthusiasm. The champagne blends, organised by Ms Dee Blackstock, are masterful and amongst the most delicious and well priced around (the £25 Millennium blend is magnificent). Waitrose also manages to winkle out some superb German bargains. One such was the high-rating Keidricher Grafenberg Riesling Spatlese 1989 which, following my warming words about this wine in a *Superplonk* column, sold out in a few days. True, this caused a tardy *Guardian* shopper to write an angry letter to me, and Waitrose, in the shape of Simon Thorpe MW who buys German wines for this retailer, dealt with the gentleman concerned with style and wit – in passing expressing 'faith in the future of the right type of German wine.' At the right type of price I wanted to add – which was an absurd £4.99.

How then can Waitrose be regarded as an expensive supermarket? If it is true that shoppers do so consider it – and I myself have joked that the supermarket is the rich woman's Harrods – then it is surely amongst the wine shelves that the lie is given to this impression. True, there are some mightily expensive and traditional horrors from Burgundy and Bordeaux, doubtless purchased by the same cobwebby fuddyduddies who have been living and dying on the stuff for the past forty years, but there are some fabulously fruity and inexpensive Italians, Spaniards and southern French wines as well as some trimly priced new world bottles. I once said, in answer to the question 'which supermarket is the best for wine?' that Waitrose was *primus inter pares* with Tesco, Sainsbury, Asda, Morrisons, and Safeway but that if I were to be locked in a supermarket for the night with no electricity and I had to extend my arm in the pitch dark and instantly and successfully locate a terrific wine to lubricate me through my nocturnal ordeal then I would unhesitatingly nominate Waitrose as the one supermarket I would wish to be stuck in. I don't think I feel much different now.

Waitrose
Southern Industrial Area
Bracknell
Berks RG12 8YA
Tel: 01344 424680
Fax: 01344 862584

SEE STOP PRESS SECTION AT END OF BOOK FOR LAST-MINUTE ADDITIONS OR UPDATES TO THIS RETAILER'S RANGE.

ARGENTINIAN WINE RED

Finca el Retiro Tempranillo, Mendoza 1998

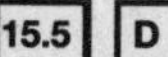

Begins in a plum fresh vein, juicy and frisky, then turns deep and dark and moodily fruity. Lovely drinking.

Sierra Alta Cabernet Sauvignon/Malbec, Mendoza 1998

Meaty, richly perfumed, and dainty on the finish, this is a lithe wine of warm fruitiness.

ARGENTINIAN WINE WHITE

La Bamba Mendoza Sauvignon Blanc 1998

Simple enough in its clean fruitiness but there's a subtle elegance too.

AUSTRALIAN WINE RED

Brown Brothers Barbera 1996

Interesting grape, barbera, for the full-rich-soft Aussie treatment. Italian in feel, yes, but Aussie in chutzpah.

Brown Brothers Tarrango 1998 13 D

They should put it on a lolly stick.

Bushmans Crossing Grenache/Mataro 1998

Bit too juicy and keen to be admired for me. But will chill well (in spite of its tannins).

Fishermans Bend Cabernet Sauvignon 1998

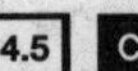

Soft and immensely thick and palate-whopping, this wine will revolt the classicist, charm the revolutionary.

Jacob's Creek Grenache/Shiraz 1998

Raunchy, restless and deeply engaging.

Nanya Vineyard Malbec/Ruby Cabernet 1998

Almonds, plums, and a baked soft-fruit edge make this a plump specimen, food-friendly and mood-friendly.

Penfolds Bin 2 Shiraz/Mourvedre 1997

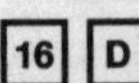

Alert, dry, ripe, firm, full of flavour and personality.

Penfolds Rawsons Retreat Cabernet Sauvignon/Shiraz/Ruby Cabernet 1997

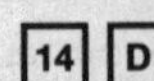

Again the princedom of soft manners sends out its rich, gooey ambassador.

Peter Lehmann The Barossa Shiraz 1997 **17.5** **D**

What a monster of Bacchic depravity! It would convert a celibate nonagenarian teetotal nun to uninhibited acts of fruity abandon. Exciting and rich, hugely appealing and massively deep.

Rosemount Estate Cabernet Sauvignon 1998 **15** **E**

Very juicy and ripe and with a lovely warm but subtle tannic underbelly. It purrs like a cat.

Rosemount Estate Grenache/Shiraz 1997 **13.5** **D**

The usual soft, soupy richness.

St Hallet Gamekeepers Reserve, Barossa 1998 **14** **D**

Smoky and dark.

Tatachilla Cabernet Sauvignon/Merlot 1997 **16.5** **E**

A marvellous mouthful of baked herbs, tight tannins, rich fruit and herby flavoursomeness of great depth.

Wynn's Coonawarra Michael Shiraz 1994 **17.5** **H**

This has come on immeasurably in bottle since I first tasted it. It is now one of the most deftly woven fruit-and-tannin Australians I have ever tasted. It is intensely concentrated but very warm, soft and aromatic, showing a cassis and toffee edge with the texture, divine, of crimped velvet. A magnificent beast. It will age with distinction but not beyond five or six years I believe (Contrary to the maker's ideas of longevity). It is the height of luxury, this wine, for it has an impossibly smug hauteur and sense of superiority. I love it. Available at Inner Cellar stores (0800 188884 for details).

Yaldara Reserve Grenache 1998

Very juicy and thickly textured. The Ribena school will love it.

Yarra Yering Pinot Noir 1991

AUSTRALIAN WINE — WHITE

Bushmans Crossing Semillon/Chardonnay 1998

Great fish wine here but not one which can't be deeply agreeably sipped without food.

Cape Jaffa Unwooded Chardonnay 1998

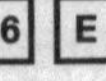

A compellingly concentrated and most individual chardonnay of great untrammelled purity of fruit. Costs, but it delivers.

Chapel Hill Verdelho 1998

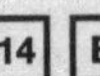

Needs Chinese food.

Chateau Tahbilk Marsanne, Victoria 1997

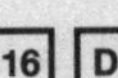

Love it! The sour-faced little puss!

Currawong Creek Chardonnay 1998

Superb gobbets of fat ripe fruit wreak havoc with the taste buds. Lovely oily fruit.

Hardys Stamp of Australia Grenache Shiraz Rosé 1998 14 C

Houghton Classic Dry White 1998 15.5 D

Most accomplished blend: vigour, richness, texture, food versatility and real oomph here.

Lindemans Winemaker's Reserve Padthaway Chardonnay 1995 16 G

A wine classier than many a Meursault at three times the price.

Penfolds Clare Valley Organic Chardonnay/ Sauvignon Blanc, 1997 14 E

Curious over-ripe touches here. Great with rich fish dishes.

Penfolds Koonunga Hill Chardonnay 1998 16.5 D

What a great brand! Stunning richness and balanced, classy finish. If only white Burgundians at three times the price could be this good.

Penfolds Rawsons Retreat Bin 202 Riesling 1998 16 C

Puts riesling on a new plane at this price. Germany please copy!

Petaluma Piccadilly Chardonnay 1997 17 G

So stiff with fruit, gelatinous, bold, emulsive, whipped like thick cream, that it seems the nearest thing to some sacred elixir.

Rosemount Estate Sauvignon Blanc 1998 16 D

Rich, flowing, nutty/fruity, beautifully textured (hint of ripeness firmly controlled). Wit, style, warmth.

Rosemount Show Reserve Chardonnay 1997

16 E

Such style and wit here. And it'll age for two or three years and grow more pointed.

St Hallett Semillon Select, Barossa Valley 1997

Expensive treat which in its polished texture, complexity of fruit and fulsomeness of finish puts burgundies (which are chardonnays) costing five times more to shame.

Tea Tree Estate Colombard/Chardonnay 1998

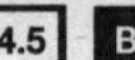

Knockout value here: real rich yet balanced fruit.

BULGARIAN WINE — WHITE

Domaine Boyar Premium Oak Chardonnay 1997

Not remotely woody to my palate – and not rated on this basis – I just like the incisive lemonic lushness.

CHILEAN WINE — RED

Concha y Toro Merlot 1998

Deliciously sweet and rich, if not typically merlot.

Cono Sur Cabernet Sauvignon, Rapel 1998 

Unusually gruff-voiced, gravelly Chilean cabernet – but high class and very accomplished.

Isla Negra Cabernet Sauvignon, Rapel 1998 

Le vin noire! Black liquid, black label, black name, black cork (taint-free plastic)! Immense blue-mood-lifting red fruit, quiet tannins and lingering plummy depths emerge.

La Palmeria Merlot, Rapel 1998 

It combines that wonderful Chilean double-whammy of food fitness and great, concentrated, complex drinking. Gorgeous stuff.

La Palmeria Reserve Merlot, Rapel 1998 

Words fail me. The wine won't let me describe it. I can manage the figure 17-points but my wrist, numb with leathery fruit coursing down my arteries, will not further flicker.

Santa Rita 120 Cabernet Sauvignon, Maipo 1997 

Gorgeous woody dryness and richly textured, bargain fruit.

CHILEAN WINE WHITE

Conch y Toro Sauvignon Blanc 1998 

Simply so much better textured and opulent than Sancerre and more impishly gooseberryish and grassy.

ENGLISH WINE — WHITE

Bacchus 1996 11 C

Grassy and muddy. Not, though, a wine I can admire.

Chapel Down Summerhill Oaked Dry White 

Denbies Surrey Gold 12 C

FRENCH WINE — RED

Boulder Creek Red VdP du Vaucluse 1998 

A simply delicious wine, great chilled, for grilled fish and meat.

Chateau Cazal-Viel, Cuvee des Fees St Chinian 1998 17.5 D

Wonderful damson colour! Like a plump ruby ring on a pre-war Cairo brothel madame's little finger. The texture is richly classy, complex and very deep. The sheer velvet of it is astonishing. A quite lovely, sinfully quaffable construct.

Chateau de Jacques Moulin a Vent 1997 12 E

Chateau Le Tertre Bordeaux 1996 14 C

Chateau Pech-Latt, Corbieres 1997 16.5 C

Superb fruit here – beautifully concentrated and warmly welcoming. Lovely ripe finish – yet it's seriously deep and even a touch dandified.

Chateau Troplong Mondot, St Emilion Grand Cru Classe 1994 12 H

Magnificent tannins here. I'd blend it with a cheap Chilean merlot to bolster the fruit.

Cotes de Roussillon 1998 15.5 C

Richer and juicier version of the Minervois but still lovely and dry on the finish.

Cotes du Rhone 1998, Waitrose 14 C

Terrific value tippling here. Great for grilled meats.

Cotes du Rhone Villages, Domaine de Cantemerle 1997 16.5 C

Deeply smooth and plumply mouth-filling. Lovely polish, great fruit and finely wrought, gentle tannins. Terrific stuff.

Cotes du Ventoux 1998 13.5 C

Cuvee-Eugenie Chateau Capendu, Corbieres 1997 18 E

Ten quid for a Corbieres? Oh yes – when it's better than many a £30 Hermitage. Wonderful texture, perfume and complex finish. An immensely classy wine which even manages to out-box many a much vaunted Aussie shiraz. Thus it is great value.

Domaine du Moulin 'The Cabernets', VdP d'Oc 1998

C

A marvellously dry and richly tannic, excitingly one-in-the-eye for claret blend of consummate drinkability and food versatility.

Domaine du Parc Syrah, VdP de l'Herault 1998 15 C

A smooth yet subtly characterful organic wine (i.e. no herbicides or pesticides touch the vines). It has excellently trim plum fruit, a touch of earth and good harnessing tannins.

Fitou Mont Tauch 1997 

Ripe plums, Gauloises, and juicy cherries, with a dry undertone.

Gallerie Tempranillo/Syrah VdP d'Oc 1998 

The wine behind the Van Gogh label is not so heady a conception as the picture – no bad thing – for it is civilised, level-headed and nicely rich. An unusual blend of style.

Good Ordinary Claret Bordeaux, Waitrose 

Sweeter and richer than previous manifestations.

L'Enclos Domecque Mourvedre/Syrah VdP d'Oc 1998 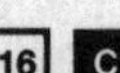

Immensely flavoursome, highly polished (barely a hint of earth or those scrubby Midi herbs) and lovingly well-assembled. The texture is deep and warm. The finish savoury.

La Colombe Organic Cotes du Rhone 1997 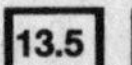 

Le Faisan Syrah Grenache VdP du Gard 1998 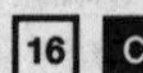

Can you imagine a wine pressed by old leathery souls (and soles), crushed Cuban cigars, hedgerows of ripe blackberries and a pile of herbs? No? Taste this wine!

Les Fontanelles Merlot/Syrah VdP d'Oc 1998

Wonderful coming together of Hermitage and St Emilion – Hermilion, shall we say? – in that the grapes, and the style of the wine, of these two proud plots of vine and soil give definite characteristic fruitiness here joined together in glorious, good value fruit. Wonderful balance to the wine: dry/earthy, fruity/layered, fresh/mature. A triumph for vin de pays rules and New Worldliness.

Maury, Les Vignerons du Val d'Orbieu NV

A sweet red wine for chocolate-based puddings. Did I say sweet? It hardly does this complex wine justice.

Merlot/Cabernet Sauvignon, VdP d'Aigues 1998

Lovely fruit, tannins, herbs and a dry, lingering finish. Considerable class here.

Minervois 1998

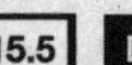

Herby, dry, seriously fruity, great tannins – has personality and purpose.

Saint Roche VdP du Gard 1998 (organic) 15.5 C

An organic wine of great dryness and richness. Has terrific tannin.

Saumur Rouge Les Nivieres 1998

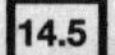

Cherries and wild raspberries and rich tannin. Not as dry as some, it'll take marvellously to chilling.

Savigny les Beaunes Cave des Hautes-Cotes 1996 11 F

Vin de Pays de l'Herault Tempranillo Syrah 1998 16 C

Very plump fruit handsomely riddled with dry tannins. Has a sense of fun with a deep, rich sensuousness.

Winter Hill Merlot/Grenache, VdP d'Oc 1998 15 B

Very dry and richly characterful. Not a pussycat at all. But it still purrs.

Winter Hill Pinot Noir/Merlot VdP d'Oc 1998

Oddly charming marriage which will progressively enrich itself for eighteen months.

Winter Hill Reserve Shiraz VdP d'Oc 1997

Exceptional shiraz for the money which might send a shiver of apprehension up the spine of any Aussie (whose shiraz costs twice this one).

FRENCH WINE WHITE

Alsace Gewurztraminer 1997, Waitrose

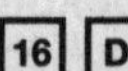

Oh yes! This is a terrifically well-textured, spicy food wine. Wonderful surge of flavour, floral yet dry, on the finish.

Alsace Pinot Blanc, Paul Blanck 1997 14.5 C

Great fruit here for an often plodding grape. Chewy and rich.

Anjou Blanc 1998 12 B

Bergerac Blanc Marquis de Beausoleil 1998 14.5 B

Great value here to make any well-charred fish go down more swimmingly.

Bordeaux Blanc Medium Dry, Yvon Mau 12 B

Chardonnay VdP du Jardin de la France 1998 15 C

Terrific value. Has sour-melon richness and crispness beneath.

Chateau Liot Sauternes 1996 (half bottle) 15 E

Gorgeous marmalade thick waxy texture.

Chateau Terres Douces, Bordeaux 1996 11 D

Don't like its raw woodiness much.

Colombard Sauvignon Blanc, Comte Tolosan 1998 15 C

Terrific fruit here with even a hint of sauvignon seriousness to it.

Cuckoo Hill Chardonnay/Viognier VdP d'Oc 1998 16 C

What a scrumptious blend of two forcefully characterful grapes! Has spice, bite, smoothness and real wit.

Domaine de Planterieu VdP de Gascogne 1998 15 C

Daintily trips down the throat tasting of pears and pineapples.

Gewurztraminer Alsace Les Princes Abbes Domaines, Schlumberger 1995 15 E

Not your all-in-yer-face spiciness but an elegance and ripeness of deft charms. Inner Cellar stores.

L'Enclos Domeque Barrel Fermented Marsanne/Roussanne VdP d'Oc 1998 15.5 D

A fine Rhone blanc taste-alike which will be wonderful paired with river fish – trout, for example.

Le Pujalet VdP du Gers 1998 13.5 B

A pleasant aperitif.

Les Fleurs Chardonnay/Sauvignon VdP des Cotes de Gascogne 1998 16 D

Rather fat at first but then shows an astonishing litheness and freshness as it quits the throat. A bold wine of individuality and style.

Muscat de Rivesaltes, M. Chapoutier 1996 (half bottle) 15.5 C

Muscate de Beaumes de Venise NV (half bottle) 16 C

Superb half bottle of riches and rampantly buttery sweetness. Great for creme brulees and fools.

Rosé d'Anjou 1998, Waitrose

Stickily rich and great for all manner of grilled foods.

Roussanne VdP d'Oc Ryman 1997

Subtle charms with a coating of fruit over some rather classy fresh acids. Lovely restraint.

Saint Roche Blanc VdP du Gard 1998

Most stylishly dry and deft. Accomplished level of blending which totally transcends the usual level of such grapes.

Saint-Aubin Premier Cru Ropiteau 1997

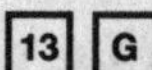

This is a wonderful anachronism: an expensive reminiscence of sullen vegetality and disappointed ducal hopes which recall Lear's 'waterish Burgundy' but also prompts the reflection that in five years' of ageing this wine might have legs.

Sancerre 'Les Marechauds' 1998

Is '98 the vintage to restore Sancerre's affections with me? Maybe. This is almost classic in its keen, crisp fruit and gooseberry richness.

Sancerre Reserve Alfonse Mellot 1998

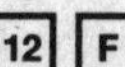

I can't quite see how it justifies a fifteen-pound price tag. It's not as compelling as Waitrose's 'Les Marechauds' Sancerre at half the price.

Sauvignon Blanc 'Les Rochers', VdP des Cotes de Gascogne 1998

Wonderful texture, polished fruit, complex interplay of elements and purposeful finish.

Sauvignon de St Bris 1997 15 C

Delicious country classic of more engaging vegetality and fineness of fruit than most Sancerres.

Tokay Pinot Gris Vendanges Tardives, Hugel 1990 18 H

Butterscotch richness yet calm acidic complexity. A stunning aperitif wine. Inner Cellar stores.

Vin Blanc Sec VdT Francais NV, Waitrose 

Winter Hill Reserve Chardonnay VdP d'Oc 1998 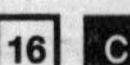

I'd rather touch it than a thousand rancid meursaults. Real class here.

Winter Hill Syrah Rosé, VdP d'Oc 1998 

Great charm for picnics.

Winter Hill VdP de l'Aude 1998 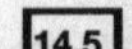

Has a terrific chewy edge to it.

GERMAN WINE WHITE

Avelsbacher Hammerstein Riesling Auslese, Staatsweingut 1989 15.5 D

Bernkasteler Kuesner Weisenstein Riesling Kabinett 1995 

Lovely edge of petrol tickles the nose, and the fruit is in perfect shape: crisp (yet edge of melon/honey), minerals and a swathe of freshness on the finish.

Dr 'L' Riesling, Mosel 1998 14 D

Now here there is three quid's worth more mineral intensity that the Lieb. The fruit is almost sweet but not quite and would benefit from three years of ageing – if not more.

Graacher Himmelreich Riesling Spatlese, JJ Prum 1994 12 G

Langenbach Riesling 1997 13 C

Ockfener Bockstein Riesling QbA, Dr Wagner 1997 13 D

Riesling Kabinett, Robert Weil 1996 12 E

Ruppertsberg Riesling, Rheinpfalz 1996 14 C

The every-day-sipping Nietzsche.

Villa Eden Liebfraumilch Rheinhessen 1998 15 B

One of the best – no, *the* best – Lieb I've tasted. Has developed richness, elegance and it is not remotely sweet or soppily monodimensional.

HUNGARIAN WINE RED

Chapel Hill Cabernet Sauvignon Barrique Aged 1997 15 C

Superb blackcurrant dryness and herb-encrusted richness. Dry but delicious.

Deer Leap Dry Red Zweigelt 1997 16 B

Superb youth, suppleness, cherry/plum fruit, hint of tannin, ripeness and a touch of passion. Brilliant! Knocks Beaujolais for several sixes.

HUNGARIAN WINE WHITE

Chapel Hill Irsai Oliver, Balatonboglar 1998 13 C

Deer Leap Chardonnay/Pinot Grigio 1998 14 C

Delightful fish wine.

Deer Leap Gewurztraminer, Mor 1998 13.5 C

Most effective with light Cantonese food.

Nagyrede Barrel Fermented Chardonnay 1996 13.5 C

Nagyrede Cabernet Sauvignon Rosé 1998 12 B

Tokaji Aszu 5 Puttonyos 1990 (50cl) 16 E

Great dessert richness.

ITALIAN WINE RED

Arcano Chianti Colli Senesi 1997 (organic) 14 D

Touch expensive but the fruit has some elegance to it.

Basilium Alta Vigna Merlot & Cabernet Basilicata 1998 16.5 C

Superb multi-layered richness which proceeds in deliciously textured layers as it courses over the taste buds. Compelling wine.

Cent'are di Sicilia, Duca di Castelmonte 1997 15 C

Individual in taste and texture and splendidly robustly fruity in defence of this singular outlook.

Chianti 1997, Waitrose 14 C

Dry and terracotta fruited.

Chianti Classico, Rocca di Castagnoli 1997

Splendid old-fashioned but modern paradox. A real dinner party wine.

Cordero di Montezemolo Monfaletto Barolo 1995 16 H

Lot of money, lot of wine. Open three hours beforehand (pour it into a large jug) to let the spicy cherries and plums, licorice and almonds to fully flow.

Montepulciano d'Abruzzo, Umani Ronchi 1997 16 C

Wonderful cheroot-scented fruit with great hedgerow richness and firm tannins. Brilliant.

Nero d'Avola/Syrah 1997 (Sicily) 15.5 C

Vivacity, impudence, raffish humanitarian character. Loveable rogue of an edge to it.

Poggio a'Frati Chianti Classico Riserva 1993 16 E

Those who say Chianti is old-hat should chew on this wine. Combines the swagger of a sombrero with the dusty seriousness of a bowler.

Primitivo Merum 1997 16 C

Wonderful cherry/plum fruit, hint of craggy tannicity on the finish, and a full, free-flowing delivery of richness and depth.

Sangiovese Marche 1998, Waitrose 14 B

Cherry-ripe and earthy. The old Italian food-wine trick.

Teroldego Rotaliano, Ca'Vit 1997 16 C

Gorgeous ripe texture, plump and cherry/blackcurrant deep. Very polished but far from all surface.

Terra Viva Merlot del Veneto 1998 13.5 C

Very juicy.

Terre del Sole VdT Rosso (Sardinia) 15.5 C

Deliciously quirky, savoury, herby fruit.

Trulli Negroamaro 1997 14.5 C

Warm, savoury, very polished and almost sedate in its mouthful, it packs a punch of gentility, yet style. Hint of leather to it.

Vino Nobile di Montepulciano, Avignonesi 1995 15 E

Runs fluently over the taste buds leaving behind a herby residue.

ITALIAN WINE — WHITE

Moscato d'Asti, Villa Lanata 1997 16 C

Wonderful honeyed, spicy, floral aperitif. Be different! Drink it with the in-laws!

Pinot Grigio Alto Adige, St Michael-Eppan 1997 13 D

Trebbiano Marche 1998, Waitrose 15.5 B

Superb texture and ripe fruit. Most unusually concentrated trebbiano.

Trulli Dry Muscat 1998 15.5 C

Lovely floral edge, dry as you like it, and not a sissy side in sight. A sophisticated aperitif or to go with minted fish dishes and tomato tarts.

Verdicchio dei Castelli Jesi, Moncaro 1998 16.5 C

An organic wine of stunning richness and class. It is inconceivable that a Verdicchio could score so highly, be so concentrated, without such great grapes. A wine with soul.

MOROCCAN WINE — RED

Le Palmier Merlot/Cabernet Sauvignon 1997 16 C

Easily the most elegant, polished and vegetally complex Moroccan red I've tasted. Astonishing fleet-of-foot fruit.

NEW ZEALAND WINE RED

Church Road Reserve Cabernet Sauvignon/Merlot 1995 15 F

Pricy and accomplished. Wonderful tannins on the finish.

Villa Maria Cellar Selection Cabernet/ Merlot, Hawkes Bay 1996

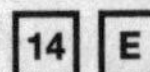

I'd let it age in a dark underground room for another eighteen months or maybe two years.

NEW ZEALAND WINE WHITE

Jackson Estate Sauvignon Blanc, Marlborough 1998 15.5 E

Ripe, fresh and plumply purposeful.

Villa Maria Private Bin Chardonnay, Gisborne 1998 14 D

Villa Maria Private Bin Riesling, Marlborough 1998 15 C

A deliciously subtle and not entirely typical riesling. It will age for a couple of years with distinction and achieve weight and interest.

PORTUGUESE WINE — RED

Sinfonia Alentejo 1997 16.5 C

The sheer polish of this wine as taste-bud-tinglingly rich and well textured. Superb fruit of great class for the money.

Terra de Lobos, Quinta do Casal Branco 1998 16 C

Wonderful richness here, dry (and wry) complexity, earthiness, herbiness, tannins and lovely tenacity on the finish.

Vila Santa Alentejo 1997 17 E

Magnificent classiness from colour through to aroma, fruit in the mouth to finish in the throat. Masterly performer.

PORTUGUESE WINE — WHITE

Quinta de Simaens Vinho Verde 1998 10 C

Terras do Rio Quinta de Abrigada 1998 15 B

Terrific value for grilled fish here.

ROMANIAN WINE — RED

River Route Limited Edition Merlot 1997 15 C

Rather claret-like in its dryness but it has a hint of Romanian sun and a hint of spice. Great food wine.

Willow Ridge Merlot/Cabernet (Oaked) 1997 14 C

Very juicy and fruity but the hint of wry character gives it charm. Terrific blend of grapes.

Willow Ridge Pinot Noir 1998 

Dry, touch earthy, nicely textured, rich, deep and very accomplished.

SOUTH AFRICAN WINE RED

Clos Malverne Pinotage, Stellenbosch 1998 

Always one of the Cape's most accomplished pinotages, the '98 is in fine fettle.

Devon View Cabernet Sauvignon, Stellenbosch 1997 13.5 D

Fairview Malbec, Paarl 1997 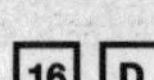

Simply sings along – the fruit is compulsively quaffable.

Kumala Reserve Cabernet Sauvignon 1997 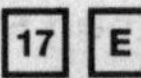

Wonderful one-off marvel of sublime cabernet class: pepper, cheroots, blackberries, tannins – it's got the lot. Plus superb textured richness.

Long Mountain Merlot/Shiraz 1997 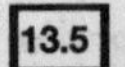

Spice Route Andrew's Hope Merlot/ Cabernet, Malmesbury 1998 16.5 D

What rivetingly rich, dark fruit. Compellingly well textured and the tannin/fruit harness is superb.

Steenberg Merlot, Constantia 1997 13 E

Minty and sweet.

SOUTH AFRICAN WINE WHITE

Culemborg Unwooded Chardonnay, Western Cape 1998 13 C

Fairview Barrel Fermented Chenin Blanc 1998 17 C

Gad, I love this wine. What value for under a fiver. It simply screams with richness and style.

Jordan Chardonnay, Stellenbosch 1997 15 E

Big chewy white burgundy taste-alike. Great wine for chicken and posh seafood dishes.

Long Mountain Colombard/Riesling 1998 14 C

Chirpily cheeky and fresh.

Mission Vale Bouchard-Finlayson Chardonnay Reserve 1997 12 F

Bit gawky for twelve pounds. Inner Cellar branches.

Robert's Rock Oaked Chardonnay 1998 16 C

Fabulous value. You can't quite believe fruit so proud and rich can cost under four quid.

Spice Route Abbotsdale Colombard/ Chenin Blanc 1998 16 C

What lovely clashing of flavours here. It is sprightly yet richly and deeply drinkable. Remarkable balance and style.

Springfield Sauvignon Blanc Special Cuvee 1998 16 D

A very classy Sancerre in style, but not price. It's superb.

Steenberg Sauvignon Blanc 1998 15.5 E

Chewy and grassy. Great with shellfish. Better than many a Sancerre.

SPANISH WINE RED

Agramont Tempranillo/Cabernet Sauvignon, Navarra 1996 16.5 C

Has hints of tobacco, tea-leaf and blackcurrants (with a suggestion of earthy spiciness). It's robust, dry yet richly fruity, complex and bold. Concentrated and calm, classy and complete.

Albacora Tempranillo 1997 16.5 D

What is the remarkable thing is the sheer satiny texture which is beautifully crumpled with tannins.

Espiral Tempranillo/Cabernet Sauvignon 1997 14 C

Very juicy and oriental food friendly.

La Rioja Alta Gran Reserve 904, 1989 13.5 G

Thinning a bit on top, stooping, and not fully fit, this very old softie. Has sound tannins and grip, but it's too much money.

Navajas Rioja 1996 15.5 C

Creamy vanilla-edged fruit of great charm and persistence.

Totally Tinto Tempranillo, La Mancha NV 

Terrific energy and richness here. Great price for such warm hearted fruit.

Vina Fuerte Garnacha, Calatayud 1998 15.5 C

What a lot of life this dry but pertly fruity wine provides. Adventurous, dry, food-friendly.

SPANISH WINE WHITE

Clearly Blanco Penedes NV 14 B

Real character and bite.

Espiral Macabeo/Chardonnay 1998 13.5 C

Las Lomas Moscatel de Valencia 16 C

Superb.

Vinas del Vero Chardonnay 1997 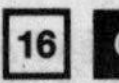

Thunderingly gorgeous (subtle!) bargain. Wonderful grip. Great style on the finish.

USA WINE RED

Bonterra Cabernet Sauvignon 1996 (organic) 

Wonderful herby, sweet/dry fruit I defy even a Venusian not to find totally drinkable.

Fetzer Valley Oaks Cabernet Sauvignon 1996 

Warm, all-embracing, deep, broad, and most charmingly well-textured and ripe on the finish.

Redwood Trail Pinot Noir 1997 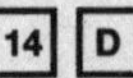

Cherries and soft raspberry-edged fruit with a hint of tannin. Better than a thousand Nuits St Georges.

Stone Bridge Cellars Zinfandel 1996 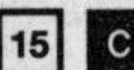

The zin in playful, everyday quaffing mode.

Yorkville Cellars Cabernet Franc 1996 (organic) 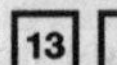

Very sweet.

USA WINE

WHITE

Edna Valley Vineyard Chardonnay 1997

One of the most refined, woody, vegetally charming Californian chardonnays I've tasted. It is like Montrachet would be – if it had sun and sombreros. A truly elegant, hugely classy wine. Thirty Inner Cellar stores.

Fetzer Sundial Chardonnay, 1998

Always as full of sun as the face of a California beachbum, this is fruit modelled on richness, warmth, and the flavours of the tropics. This vintage has a lovely freshness to it.

Fetzer Viognier 1998

Lovely limpid, lush, lively – a wine of ineffable finesse yet apricot-scented and fruited richness. A rare treat. Fruit to read by, think by, listen by. Inner Cellar stores.

Redwood Trail Chardonnay 1996 15.5 D

Redwood Trail Zinfandel Blush NV 10 C

I hate pink zinfandel. It should be outlawed.

FORTIFIED WINE

10 Year Old Tawny, Waitrose 14 F

Apostoles Palo Cortado Oloroso (half bottle) 15.5 E

Comte de Lafont Pineau des Charentes 15 D

Dow's 1977 16 H

Dry Fly Amontillado 12 D

Fino, Waitrose 15.5 C

Fonseca Traditional LBV 1983 15 G

Gonsalez Byass Matusalem Oloroso Dulce Muy Viejo (half bottle) 16 E

The ultimate Everest for the taste buds. Can they climb the peaks of this hugely rich, fruity, acidic, bursting-with-flavour sherry? Or will they wilt?

Harveys Isis Pale Cream Sherry 13 D

Jerezana Dry Amontillado, Waitrose 16 D

A wonderful cold weather cockle warmer. Not remotely austere or molly-coddley fruity, it's simply blood arousing.

Oloroso Sherry, Waitrose 13 C

Pando Fino, Williams and Humbert 14.5 D

Rich Cream Sherry, Waitrose 13 D

Solera Jerezana Dry Oloroso, Waitrose 16.5 D

Fabulous chilled as an aperitif. Dry toffee fruit with a hint of almond.

Southbrook Farm's Framboise (half bottle) 15 E

Vintage Warre Quinta da Cavadinha 1987 17.5 G

A magnificently complete port. It has a chewy texture (vibrant tannins), lovely complex fruit of immense depths and sunny ripeness, and lovely balance. It is a wine to stiffen the sinews, summon up the blood, stun the soul.

White Jerepigo 1979 (South Africa) 14 D

SPARKLING WINE/CHAMPAGNE

Alexandre Bonnet Brut Rosé NV (France) 12 G

Brut Vintage 1990, Waitrose 13 G

Ah! A touch disappointing for eighteen smackers.

Cava Brut NV, Waitrose 16 C

Quite superb.

Champagne Blanc de Blancs NV, Waitrose 15 G

Another brilliant example of Waitrose's superior Champagne buying skills. Other large retailers please copy!

Champagne Blanc de Noirs NV, Waitrose 15 F

The real thing. A fine champagne for the money.

Champagne Brut NV, Waitrose 12.5 G

Toasty and delicious. Has genuine depth of feeling and style Real class here.

Champagne Canard Duchene Brut NV 14 G

Has the tell-tale Duchene fruit yet dryness. Has real character

---

Champagne Fleury Brut NV 18.5 G

A biodynamic Champagne? How did someone wean the vigneron off pesticides and herbicides and onto the astrologic ideas of Rudolf Steiner? In Rheims? With that weird climate? It's a miracle akin to discovering John Major campaigning for the Red Brigade. The wine? Superb. All pinot grapes (fifteen acres of), loads of calm, controlled fruit, immense class (without pretension – no Krug tobacco edging), beautiful fruit, and a lovely finish. It has wonderful texture which as with all outstanding Champagnes, combines a seemingly soft fruitiness (hint of wild strawberry from the pinot noir grapes) with a crisp yet warm finish. One of the best Champagnes I've tasted – ever For the money, it's a steal. Waitrose has only 1600 cases of it, and it knocks Moet (which is pricier) into the most cocked of cocked chapeaux. If you must celebrate the Millennium with bubbles you don't need to spend more than £16.99 on them.

Charles Heidsieck Reserve Mise en Cave en 1993 13.5 H

Clairette de Die Tradition (half bottle) (France) 14 D

Conde de Caralt Cava Brut NV 16.5 D

As elegantly labelled as the superbly polished fruit in the bottle.

Cremant de Bourgogne Blanc de Noirs, Lugny 14 D

Cremant de Bourgogne Rosé NV (France) 15 E

Better than many a Champagne.

Cuvee 2000 Champagne, Waitrose 18 H

Still tasting wonderful. A textbook blending exercise. Far better than many legends.

Cuvee Royale Blanquette de Limoux NV 13.5 D

Green Point Vineyards Brut, 1995 (Australia) 15 F

Rather haughty in its richness and grand champagne-style maturity.

Jacob's Creek Sparkling Chardonnay/Pinot Noir NV (Australia) 15 D

Great value.

Lindauer Brut (New Zealand) 14.5 E

Expressive of nothing but great value for money and utterly charming sipping.

Quartet NV, Roederer Estate (California) 14 G

Saumur Brut NV, Waitrose 14 D

Dry and decisive. Delicious!

Seaview Brut Rosé 14 D

Delicate little rosé.

Seaview Pinot Noir/Chardonnay 1995 (Australia) 15 E

Expands in the mouth on the finish with sesame seeds and some uncategorised fruit. It is dry, very classy and works well from nose to throat.

Seppelt Great Western Brut (Australia) 13.5 D

The *Superplonk* Hotline

A new telephone service giving you speedy access to bargain wines.

I have long been frustrated at a certain inadequacy of my weekly newspaper column and this twice-yearly wine guide. I receive news of bargain offers on supermarket wines on a monthly, sometimes a fortnightly basis. How can I cover *all* these wines? Some aren't up to much and so I don't lose much sleep over their omission, but many are interesting, well-rated, and extremely inexpensive.

And almost always these wines are on offer for a limited amount of time.

How could I contrive to bring these wines to readers' notice on a regular basis? Luckily, I was approached last year by Lines Unlimited (P.O. Box 5426, Leicester LE6 0XG). This company, staffed by enthusiastic *Superplonk* readers so it appears, said they could organise a phone line system which could solve the problem.

The number is 0900 2209209.

What happens when you dial it? You hear about the latest best-buys and well-rated bargain offers at the supermarket of your choice. These are Asda, Morrisons, the Co-op, Safeway, Sainsbury's, Somerfield/Kwik Save, and Tesco.

If you use this service, please let me know what you think. I'm anxious to provide the most satisfactory coverage of UK superplonks it is possible to imagine.

Superplonk 2000

STOP PRESS

ASDA

ARGENTINIAN WINE WHITE

Argentinian Torrontes 1999, Asda 

Delicious floral scented aperitif.

AUSTRALIAN WINE RED

Oxford Landing Cabernet Sauvignon/Shiraz 1997 15.5 C

Rymill Coonawarra Merlot Cabernet 1996 15.5 E

Minty, ripe raspberries and cherries, soft tannins. A jammy ensemble for elegant, spicy food.

AUSTRALIAN WINE WHITE

Andrew Peace Chardonnay 1999 15.5 C

Delicious melon/lemon fruit. Surprisingly well priced for such Aussie richness and style.

Oxford Landing Sauvignon Blanc 1997 14 C

Penfolds Organic Chardonnay/Sauvignon Blanc 1997 

Quite superb level of fruit here: fresh, deep, dry, layered and lush without being remotely ungainly or blowsy.

Rymill Sauvignon 1998 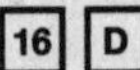

A most elegantly rich and balanced sauvignon of compelling lemon/gooseberry fruit.

CHILEAN WINE — RED

Cono Sur Merlot 1998  

Simply lush leather tannins and richly upholstered fruit. You can relax in it with great pleasure.

Cono Sur Merlot Reserve 1998 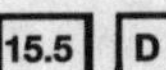 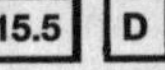

A real food merlot, dry fruit, firm tannins, rich finish. Will age and soften for a couple of years.

CHILEAN WINE — WHITE

35 Sur Sauvignon Blanc 1998 

Superb! The grassiness of the acidity and the richness of fruit, still classic dry sauvignon, make for a wonderful crisp mouthful.

Araucano Chardonnay, Lurton 1997 16 E

Remarkably Californian-style Chilean (i.e. elegant and very classy).

Cono Sur Chardonnay 1998 16.5 C

Utterly delicious, iconoclastic, rich, rivetingly fruity and very modern.

CYPRIOT WINE RED

Ancient Isle Red 1998 15.5 B

Lovely rich fruit, very gently spicy and firm.

FRENCH WINE RED

Chenas 1997, Asda 14 C

Gigondas Chateau du Trignon 1995 15 F

HUNGARIAN WINE WHITE

Badger Hill Hungarian Sauvignon 1998 15 B

A gentle aperitif-style glugging with spicy fruit. Very good with Chinese food.

ITALIAN WINE RED

D'Istinto Nero d'Avola Sangiovese 1997 | 14 | C

Montepulciano d'Abruzzo 1997, Asda | 14 | B

ITALIAN WINE WHITE

D'Istinto Catarratto Chardonnay 1997 (Sicily) | 14 | C

La Vis Trentino Chardonnay 1997, Asda | 15.5 | C

Puglia Chardonnay 1997, Asda | 14.5 | C

PORTUGUESE WINE RED

Bright Brothers Baga 1997 | 14 | C

PORTUGUESE WINE WHITE

Bright Brothers Atlantic Vines Fernao Pires/Chardonnay 1997 | 15.5 | C

SOUTH AFRICAN WINE RED

Long Mountain Red NV 14 C 

Very rubber-necked.

SOUTH AFRICAN WINE WHITE

Cape Muscat de Frontignan NV, Asda 14 C  

SPANISH WINE RED

Conde de Navasques 1997 15.5 C  

Bargain – a vanilla-scented plush wine with soft tannins and ripe fruit which is more velvet-textured than many a much more expensive rioja.

Fuentespina Crianza 1996 15.5 E 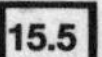 

Tannic yet smooth. Touch spicy. Very rioja-like in feel (and flavour) but superior in mouthfeel.

Jumilla Tempranillo 1997, Asda 14 B 

Mont Marcal Crianza 1996 14 C

Valdepenas Crianza 1995 

Superb freshness and integrated tannins here. Very assertive, cool drinking style.

SPANISH WINE — WHITE

Jumilla Airen 1997, Asda 14.5 B

Spanish Oaked White NV, Asda 15.5 B

Rich, deep, throaty and deeply satisfying. Terrific little quaffing specimen here.

SPARKLING WINE/CHAMPAGNE

De Bregille Vintage 1995 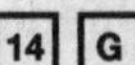

Quaite a naice champers Letitia, don't you think?

CO-OP

ARGENTINIAN WINE RED

Malbec/Bonarda Mendoza Soft Red Wine 1998

AUSTRALIAN WINE RED

Chateau Reynella Basket Press Cabernet Merlot 1996 16.5 F

Interestingly, I saw the grapes for this wine go into the old-fashioned basket press – the device which permits such a sympathetic crush and beautifully evolved tannins to emerge. One of Australia's most civilised cabernet merlots.

Jacaranda Hill Shiraz 1998

Gorgeous rich fruit, fat and slovenly on the tongue like sauce (cassis, leather and plums). A gutsy, unconcerned, unhurried wine of immense quaffing potential.

PORTUGUESE WINE RED

Terra Franca NV

Tame on first opening, it needs a couple of hours to get into some rich, dry, tobacco-edged richness and textured charm.

SOUTH AFRICAN WINE WHITE

Spice Route Chenin Blanc 1998

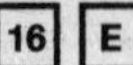

Fat but far from out of condition or flabby. Has a lush peachy ripeness relieved by a lovely texture and nutty-edged acidity. Not at all stores.

SAFEWAY

AUSTRALIAN WINE RED

Mamre Brook Chardonnay, Barossa Valley 1998

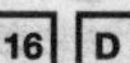

Lovely richness – civilised and not over-ripe. Has real class and individuality. Not at all stores.

CHILEAN WINE RED

Acacias Estate Merlot, Maipo Valley 1998, Safeway

Very untypical, this magnificently dry and tannin-edged wine. Superb with food and difficult books. Not at all stores.

Castillo de Molina Cabernet Sauvignon Reserva, Lontue 1997

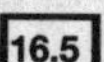

Stunning texture and depth here. The fruit literally hums with high wire tension. Top 129 stores.

Chilean Cabernet Sauvignon 1999, Safeway

Quite superbly meaty fruit. Soft, ripe, perfumed, very deep and warmly textured.

Cono Sur Cabernet Sauvignon, Rapel Valley 1998 16.5 C

Terrific tannins, evolved and vibrant, combined with cassis and tobacco fruitiness.

Errazuriz Cabernet Sauvignon, El Ceibo Estate, Aconcagua 1998 17 D

Beautifully textured, complex, deep, ready and ripe yet ineffably fine and richly integrated. Astonishing price for such poise and power.

Errazuriz Merlot Reserva, Don Maximiano Estate Aconcagua, 1997

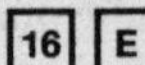

Beautifully tanned, high class leather too soft for belief. Top 129 stores.

Santa Rita Reserva Cabernet Sauvignon, Alto Jahull Vineyards Maipo 1997

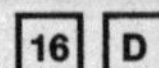

Rampant flavoursomeness and fullness. At most stores.

Villard Estate Cabernet Sauvignon, Central Valley 1997

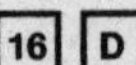

Classic dryness, hint of vegetality, very long, richly tannic finish. Top 121 stores.

CHILEAN WINE WHITE

Casa Lapostolle Cuvee Alexandre Chardonnay, Casablanca 1997 17.5 E

One of Chile's greatest chardonnays. Has superb balance (richness, ripeness, length of flavour) and it's so classy it hurts. Has improved in bottle, too, since I first tasted it. Selected stores.

Chilean Dry White, Lontue 1999, Safeway 

Superb plumpness of fruit, stealth of purpose, calm richness of finish. Terrific price for a terrific wine.

Chilean Sauvignon Blanc Lontue 1999, Safeway 

Superb freshness and compellingly clean yet subtle richness. Lovely fish wine.

Errazuriz La Escultura Estate Chardonnay, Casablanca 1998 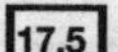

Nuts, touch of smoke, hint of spice, complex soft and hard fruits, lingering finish of polish and satin-textured excitement. A lovely wine.

FRENCH WINE RED

Chateau de Lausieres, Coteaux du Languedoc 1998 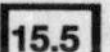

Rustic yet dry and charming. Terrific energy on the finish. Top 129 stores.

Chateau du Piras, Premieres Cotes de Bordeaux 1996 15.5 D

Real claret really cheap. Not at all stores.

Chateau Philippe de Vessiere, Costieres de Nimes 1997 15.5 C

Terrific value for such perky fruit. A dry, delicious red of rusticity yet couth manners. Top 129 stores.

Domaine des Lauriers, Faugeres 1997 17 D

Hedgerows and herbs, earth and orchards – it's got the lot. Plus the magic of tannins and a very low price ticket (for such complexity). Top 129 stores from some time in December 1999.

Enclos des Cigales Syrah, VdP d'Oc 1998 15.5  C

Dry, tobacco-edged, stalky, vegetal – not for lovers of Aussie shiraz but with food it's a wow. Top 129 stores.

Millennium 2000 Syrah/Cabernet Sauvignon VdP d'Oc 1998 16.5 C

Superb example of country fruitiness allied to smart modern winemaking ideas. Full of fruit, yet dry, it offers medium complexity, warmth, herbiness and lovely texture. At around 200 stores.

Mont Tauch Merlot, barrel matured, VdP du Torgan 1998  15.5 E

Very dry, old-style merlot. Great food wine. And will develop well in bottle for a couple of years. Top 129 stores.

FRENCH WINE WHITE

Domaine de la Baume Chardonnay/ Viognier VdP d'Oc 1997 16 D

Rich oils, buttery texture, hint of wood and vegetality. Do Burgundy and Rhone tremble? They should. Selected stores.

GERMAN WINE WHITE

Graacher Domprobst Riesling Spatlese, Mosel Saar Ruwer 1996 16 E

The ultimate Christmas lunch starter wine – with the smoked salmon. The complex acids harness the rich fruit beautifully. An immensely civilised wine. Top sixty-seven stores.

HUNGARIAN WINE RED

Chapel Hill Barrique Aged Cabernet Sauvignon, Balaton 1997, Safeway 16 C

A bargain whizzbang style cab of substance and dry wit. At most stores.

Riverview Kekfrancos, Sopron 1998  C

Loads of stalky hedgerow dryness and richness. Great chilled. At most stores.

ITALIAN WINE WHITE

Pinot Grigio Alto Adige 1998

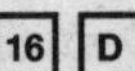

Superbly couth texture, welcoming and civil, and a lovely dry yet warm finish. Very classy. Selected stores.

NEW ZEALAND WINE WHITE

Montana Reserve Chardonnay 1998

Exceptional style of fruit where the depth remains dry, retains complexity, finishes with rich promise. Top sixty stores.

Oyster Bay Sauvignon Blanc 1999

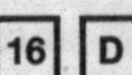

Compressed gooseberry freshness and delightfully controlled richness. Not at all stores.

PORTUGUESE WINE WHITE

Fiuza Sauvignon Blanc, Ribatejo 1998

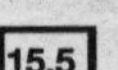

Has a very individual touch to it: fat (yet fresh), full (yet delicate), steely and dry (yet fruity). It's come on a lot since I tasted it last summer (qv the main section of this book). Not at all stores.

SOUTH AFRICAN WINE — RED

Landskroon Cinsaut/Shiraz, Paarl 1999 

Extraordinarily good value. Great balance of soft fruit flavours.

Landskroon Shiraz, Paarl 1998 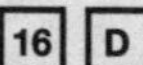

Juicy yet very dry with a charcoal-richness on the finish. Hint of tobacco, too.

USA WINE — RED

L A Cetto Petite Syrah 1997 

Hugely individual and dry – fantastically alert tannins. An exceptional wine. At most stores.

FORTIFIED WINE

Blandy's Duke of Clarence Rich Madeira 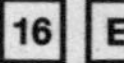

Wonderful old-fashioned plot: Dickensian, warm, sweet, sentimental. Drink it with Christmas cake. At most stores.

SAINSBURY'S

AUSTRALIAN WINE WHITE

Lindemans Cawarra Colombard Chardonnay 1998

Dry, yet hints of rounded richness lurk in the background. Essentially, a big slurpable wine.

Rosemount Estate Show Reserve Chardonnay 1997

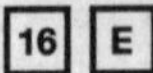

Very impressive acidity which encloses fatness yet freshness. Lovely vegetal hints, wood, leaves, soft fruit and acids. Selected stores.

FRENCH WINE RED

Chateau Agram, Corbieres 1996

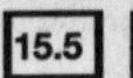

Remarkable value here – a highly civilised quaffing wine from the Midi. It has gentle warmth and soft restrained wit. Selected stores.

Chateau Haut Bergey, Pessac-Leognan 1995

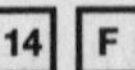

Very smooth and ready. But thirteen quid? Sticks in the throat (like the delicious fruit). Selected stores.

Chateau Tassin Bordeaux Rouge 1998 15.5 C

Superb claret! Great chewy, charcoal-edged fruit with a fine blackcurrant edge. Very dry, very food-friendly. At most stores.

Crozes Hermitage, Cave de Tain l'Hermitage 1997 14.5 D

Roll up, roll up – taste the unique coal-black fruit of Crozes: rugged yet velvety, rich and ready for anything. Most stores.

FRENCH WINE WHITE

Alsace Gewurztraminer 1998, Sainsbury's 16 D

Wonderfully delicate yet potent – it explodes in graduated dollops of spice, lychee, mango and lime. Wonderful heart-lifting quaffing. At most stores.

Domaine de la Perriere Sancerre 1998 15 E

Catch it while it's young and feisty (from the great '98 vintage). A classic dry, mineral-edged, compressed-gooseberry fruited wine. Selected stores.

GERMAN WINE WHITE

Zeltinger Himmelreich Riesling Kabinett 1997  

Will keep for five or six years and get better. Its honey fruit is firmly gripped by fresh acidity making the overall effect dry. 120 selected stores.

ITALIAN WINE RED

Allora Primitivo 1998 15 C

Primitivo in its polished, plump, passion-muted mode. Not at all stores.

Chianti Classico Briante 1997 14 D

Very juicy Chianti – almost sacrilegious.

Nero d'Avola IGT Sicilia, Connubio 1998 15.5 C

Leather and tobacco aroma with the latter flavanoid carried through to the very dry fruit which has a faint echo of dried figs. An unusually characterful, sturdy wine to be so quaffable. Most stores.

Zagara Nero d'Avola Sangiovese 1998 15.5 C

Very bright and firm in its pleasure-providing role – it unites lovely rich tannins with juicy medium-warm fruit. Most stores.

SOUTH AFRICAN WINE RED

South African Reserve Selection Cabernet Sauvignon Merlot 1997, Sainsbury's 16 D

Bold fruit here of great texture and richness. Gorgeous medley of hedgerow fruit flavours plus tobacco and cocoa. Terrific warmth from the evolved tannins. Selected stores.

SPANISH WINE RED

Navarra NV, Sainsbury's 

Superb bargain. Lovely tobacco-edged fruit, classy and rich, with loads of freshness and depth behind it. Terrific quaffing wine.

USA WINE WHITE

Coastal Chardonnay, Robert Mondavi 1997 

Such elegant and forthrightly hedonistic fruit is unusual under ten quid. This makes it with a penny to spare – but it doesn't spare the drinker's huge pleasure. Sixty stores.

Napa Valley Fume Blanc, Robert Mondavi 1997 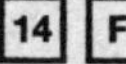

Hint of tropical fruit to what is a dry wine. Very expensive for the style, though. Selected stores.

SOMERFIELD

ARGENTINIAN WINE RED

Argentine Tempranillo 1999, Somerfield 16 C

Outguns rioja with the brilliance of its tannins and creamy richness. Great glugging, great with food.

Santa Julia Sangiovese 1999, Somerfield 15.5 C

Wonderful paradox of dryness and rich, vivacious, plummy fruitiness.

Trivento Syrah 1999 15.5 C

Dry (very dry) but simply superb with robust food.

ARGENTINIAN WINE WHITE

Bright Brothers Argentine Chardonnay 1999 15.5 C

Modern and very modish and great for lifting a blue mood.

Bright Brothers San Juan Chardonnay Reserve 1999 15.5 C

Terrific freshness of fruit and great with food.

AUSTRALIAN WINE RED

Hardys Cabernet Shiraz Merlot 1997 16 D

Bargain Aussie brew of bounce and flavour.

Penfolds Coonawarra Bin 128 Shiraz 1996 15.5 E

Lot of money, ten quid. I'd be inclined to let the wine breathe for three hours, in a jug, and not give the sum a second's thought.

AUSTRALIAN WINE WHITE

Australian Chardonnay 1999, Somerfield 15.5 C

Screwcapped, untainted by cork, fresh and richly melonic.

Lindemans Padthaway Chardonnay 1998 15.5 E

Very warm and sticky – beautiful for diner a deux.

CHILEAN WINE RED

Chilean Cabernet Sauvignon Vina La Rosa 1999, Somerfield 16 C

Dry and dainty, yet powers home a rich, handsomely textured finish.

Chilean Cabernet Sauvignon/Merlot Vina La Rosa 1998, Somerfield 15.5 C

Hugely gluggable and friendly.

Cono Sur Pinot Noir 1999 14.5 C

Needs time to get the aromatic posture of the '98.

CHILEAN WINE — WHITE

Isla Negra Chardonnay 1999 16.5 C

Even more energy and richness to the new vintage.

FRENCH WINE — RED

Beaume de Venise Cotes du Rhones Villages 1997 15.5 D

Hugely juicy (quite unusually so for this co-op) but the tannins are there and they strike beautifully on the finish.

Chateau Cazal Cuvee des Fees Vieilles Vignes, St Chinian 1997 17 D

Superb syrah! Better than any Aussie at the price. It has superb suppleness to its texture and very elegant harmony of elements. Coming along brilliantly in bottle (qv main section of this book).

Chateau Valoussiere, Coteaux du Languedoc 1997 15.5 C

Tobacco, hints of the Midi scrub, good alertness to the tannins.

Domaine de Courtilles Cote 125 Corbieres 1998 15.5 D

Starts like a baby, mewling with soft fruit, then goes gruff and generous on the finish.

Domaine Haut St George Corbieres Rouge 1996 15.5 C

Very fresh-faced yet hint of antique cigar, touch of old sock.

Gouts et Couleurs Syrah Mourvedre VdP d'Oc 1998 15.5 C

Full of flavour and fully-charged fruit. Dry, compelling, food friendly.

James Herrick Cuvee Simone VdP d'Oc 1998 16 C

Elegant, voluptuous, very posh edge to what is essentially a country bumpkin.

ITALIAN WINE RED

Bright Brothers Negroamaro Cabernet, Conti Zecca 1998 15.5 C

Lovely softness to the vibrant fruit.

Calissano Barbera d'Asti, Calissano 1997 15.5 C

Throaty, dry yet bullishly fruity, great tannins on the finish which undercut perfectly.

Caramia Primitivo del Salento Barrique 1997 16 D

Very plummy and ripe (very modern), but there are tannins here and they will grip food beautifully.

L'Arco Cabernet Franc, Friuli 1998 15.5 C

Superb ripeness yet characterful dryness and richness.

ITALIAN WINE WHITE

L'Arco Chardonnay, Friuli 1998 15.5 C

Very elegant and beautifully textured. Lovely fruit.

SOUTH AFRICAN WINE RED

Kumala Reserve Cabernet Sauvignon 1998 16 E

Curious ambivalence here: youthful exuberance with seasoned mellowness. The wine offers ripe plum, subtle tobacco nuances, hint of chocolate and tea (lapsang souchong) and a smoothness of almost smug hauteur. For all that, nine quid is a lot of money. It can be opened and decanted five to six hours beforehand.

South African Cabernet Sauvignon 1999, Somerfield

A lovely specimen of Cape warmth and wit. A dry, tobacco-edged red of huge charm and commitment.

SOUTH AFRICAN WINE WHITE

Bellingham Sauvignon Blanc 1999 15.5 C

Very grassy and fish-friendly.

TESCO

ARGENTINIAN WINE RED

Alamos Ridge Malbec 1997 16 D

Throbs with purposeful fruit and gently pulsates with soft tannins. The result is a very moving experience.

Bright Brothers Barrica Syrah 1998 16 D

Outguns many a fancy Aussie with the same grape. Loads of jammy rich fruit but it's the tannins which pull the whole wagon-load of flavours along. Not at all stores.

Catena Cabernet Sauvignon 1996 17 E

A quite compellingly concentrated amalgam of very comely cabernet vegetality and subtle spiciness and big tannins. An excellent bottle for festive lunch (or dinner) where its presence at table will be more amusing, and more explosive, than the funniest Christmas cracker. Available at the twenty-five Wine Advisor Stores only.

AUSTRALIAN WINE RED

Penfolds Bin 2 Shiraz/Mourvedre 1998 (1.5 litre) 15.5 E

Dry, subtle-rich, not as vibrant as previous vintages. Good for

Christmas lunch. Price bracket adjusted to the equivalent of 75cl. Not at all stores.

AUSTRALIAN WINE WHITE

Langhorne Creek Verdelho 1998, Tesco 15.5 C

Operates gradually on the taste buds from a spicy start, to a soft fruity phase, then a deft creamy finish.

Limited Release Barramundi Marsanne 1998 16.5 D

I love the big oily richness of this thickly-textured, tautly-designed wine. The fruit is dry peach with a hint of waxy pineapple.

Penfolds Yattarna Chardonnay 1996 17 H

It explores every nuance of its flavour scheme from sesame seeds (roasted lightly) to ogen melon, wood and a hint of spicy pear. Yes, £35 is a lot of money but this is a lot of wine – more elegant, more rewarding than many a Montrachet. Available at the twenty-five Wine Advisor Stores only.

Rosemount Chardonnay 1998 16 D

Utterly scrumptious fruit. Also available at most stores in a terrific sexy 1.5 litre bottle for big tables of thirsty friends. Improved a bit since I tasted it last spring, too.

CHILEAN WINE — RED

Valdivieso Malbec Reserve 1997 — 16.5 E

Gorgeous baked fruit texture which hardens – encrusted with superb tannins. Very rich and deep, full of stylish edges, and hugely elegant overall. Selected stores only.

FRENCH WINE — RED

L'Autre Obsession Corbieres NV — 15 

Rustic charmer. Flowing, earthy, rich cherries and soft tannins. Simple but tasty.

Millennium Red VdP d'Oc NV, Tesco — 15.5 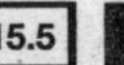

Dry, fruity, characterful, gluggable, food-friendly, brilliant value. Also available in 5 litres. Not at all stores.

FRENCH WINE — WHITE

Domaine Cazal Viel Viognier 1998 

Most subtle. The dry apricot fruit is classy, restrained and elegant and very delicious. More impressive than some Condrieus I could name, where the viognier grape is soi-disant KING (or QUEEN), for it has real texture and ingenuity. Selected stores.

ITALIAN WINE RED

Terra Viva Vino da Tavola Organic Red 1998 15.5 C

The best, for the money, I've tasted organically from Italy. It's dry, very dark, and terrific with food.

NEW ZEALAND WINE RED

Villa Maria Reserve Cabernet Merlot 1996 15.5 G

A lovely soft blend of calm fruit which though too delicate for spicy foods is rather splendid with a fruity novel. Top eighty-five stores.

PORTUGUESE WINE RED

Bright Brothers TFN Douro 1997 16 D

Loads of juicy richness but this is beset by rich tannins. A terrific dinner party, roast food wine. Top eighty-five stores only.

SOUTH AFRICAN WINE RED

Beyers Truter Pinotage 1998, Tesco 16.5 C

Stunning bargain for Christmas lunch. Really hums with aromatic richness, hint of spice, touch of chocolate and cassis, but it's fresh, the tannins are alert, the whole surging flavoursome construct is eager to delight the palate. At most stores.

Goats Do Roam Fairview, Paarl 1999 15.5 C

Great pun, great fruit. Though it isn't so much Cotes-du-Rhone as juicy Bandol-style. Great quaffing style. Not at all stores.

SOUTH AFRICAN WINE WHITE

Thelema Chardonnay 1998 15.5 F

Expensive Christmas treat. Very sophisticated under-strung fruit of style and subtle richness. Available at the twenty-five Wine Advisor Stores only.

SPANISH WINE RED

Finca Lasendal 1998 15.5 C

Lovely soft, rich, textured ripeness and earthiness. Not at all stores.

Vina Montana Monastrell/Merlot 1998 

Wonderful vibrancy of texture and resounding richness of corduroy-tufted fruit – finely cut, touch raffish, great with food or mood.

WAITROSE

ARGENTINIAN WINE RED

Sierra Alta Shiraz, Mendoza 1999 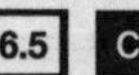

Brilliant richness and smoothness and with plenty to occupy nose and throat. A gently throbbing undertone of excitement here.

AUSTRALIAN WINE RED

Church Block Cabernet Shiraz Merlot, Wirra Wirra Vineyards 1997 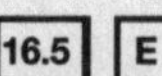

A wonderful blend of striking richness and very stylish tannins. Aromatic, all-action and endearing (but not *too* dear).

Wrattonbully Cabernet Sauvignon, Limestone Coast 1998 

Very juicy but brilliantly balanced tannins, alcohol and acids. Lovely surge of flavour as it strikes so purposefully home.

Yaldara Reserve Grenache 1998 

Creamy, soft-fruity, very rich and goody-goody – but brilliant with a richly-stuffed Christmas turkey. Improving marvellously in bottle (qv the main section of this book).

AUSTRALIAN WINE — WHITE

Chapel Hill Verdelho 1998 15.5 E

Lovely lime/pear/melon spicy wine for Thai food. Coming along very nicely in bottle (qv the main section of this book).

Jacob's Creek Chardonnay Limited Release 1997 (magnum) 16 C

Brilliant magnum for the festive table full of oily rich fruit and compelling fruitiness (melons, waxy limes and pineapples). Price bracket is for the 75cl equivalent.

BULGARIAN WINE — RED

Domaine Boyar Merlot/Gamza, Iambol 1998 15.5 B

Superb class for the money.

CHILEAN WINE — RED

Cono Sur Cabernet Sauvignon, Rapel 1998 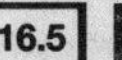 C

Terrific tannins, evolved and vibrant, combined with cassis and tobacco fruitiness. It's improved in bottle, too, since the summer (qv the main section of this book).

CHILEAN WINE WHITE

35 Sur Sauvignon Blanc, Lontue 1998 15.5 C

Fresh and green, lovely grassy undertone.

FRENCH WINE RED

Cabernet Sauvignon La Cité VdP d'Oc 1998 

Better than many a claret at three times the price.

Clos de Gleize Cuvee Aurore VdP des Bouches du Rhone 1998 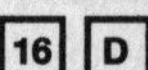

Brilliant organic fruit. Superbly rich, vigorous tannins.

Clos St Michel Chateauneuf-du-Pape 1998 

Those wonderful tannins!

Domaine de Courtille, Corbieres 1998 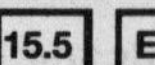

Nine quid for a Corbieres? When it's this tongue-lashingly fruity and textured, yes.

Domaine de Rose Syrah/Merlot, VdP d'Oc 1998

Fantastic bargain. Full of hints of the Midi sun, herbs and landscape. A colourful, rich, yet far from rustic wine.

Ermitage du Pic Cuvee Classique, Coteaux du Languedoc 1998

Aromatic, ripe, deep, balanced, hugely food-friendly (yet no over-hirsute tannins) and a surge of flavour on the finish.

Saint-Joseph, Cave de Saint-Desiderat 1996

Characterful, gently rugged, shy – a delicious conundrum.

Special Reserve Claret, Cotes de Castillon Limited Edition Millennium Magnum 1996 (magnum)

Bargain claret in a big sexy bottle – the fruit is subtly sensual too, and wears a thick winter coat of nicely-knitted tannins. Price bracket shows the 75cl equivalent.

Winter Hill Reserve Shiraz VdP d'Oc 1998

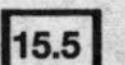

Very civilised and restrained.

FRENCH WINE — WHITE

Alsace Gewurztraminer 1998, Waitrose

Superb plumpness and vivacity of fruit. Not too spicy but oodles of flavour.

HUNGARIAN WINE RED

Chapel Hill Cabernet Sauvignon Barrique Aged 1997

Wonderful woody fruit, improving marvellously in bottle (qv the main section in this book).

HUNGARIAN WINE WHITE

Deer Leap Gewurztraminer, Mor 1998

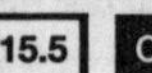

Not as thickly textured as Alsace, but deliciously subtly spicy and fresh. Improving nicely in bottle (qv the main section of this book).

ITALIAN WINE RED

Allora Aglianico, Puglia 1998

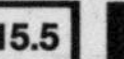

Hugely drinkable, combining warm fruit and even warmer tannins.

Bonarda Sentito, Oltrepo Pavese 1998

Montepulciano d'Abruzzo, Umani Ronchi 1998

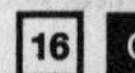

Gorgeous tannins and rich red fruit.

Nero d'Avola/Syrah 1998 (Sicily) 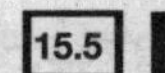 C

What a drop-dead fruity bargain.

ITALIAN WINE — WHITE

Castello della Salla Chardonnay 1998 16 D

Very different, creamy fruit – stunningly delicious.

Mezzomondo Chardonnay 1998 15.5 C

Gorgeous freshness with a hint of fat melon and waxy lemon.

Soave Classico Vigneto Colombara 1998 16 C

Soave made on a different planet.

SOUTH AFRICAN WINE — RED

Fairview Cyril Back Reserve Shiraz, Paarl 1997 15.5 E

Immensely juicy but the tannins and acids keep it from going gooey. Very modern.

Goats Do Roam Fairview, Paarl 1999 15.5 C

Great pun, great fruit. Though it isn't so much Cotes-du-Rhone as juicy Bandol-style. Great quaffing style.

Kumala Reserve Cabernet Sauvignon 1998 16 E

Curious ambivalence here: youthful exuberance with seasoned mellowness. The wine offers ripe plum, subtle tobacco nuances, hint of chocolate and tea (lapsang souchong) and a smoothness of almost smug hauteur. For all that, nine quid is a lot of money. It can be opened and decanted five to six hours beforehand.

Savanha Merlot 1998 16 D

Lovely throaty richness and impactful leathery texture here.

Spice Route Cabernet Merlot 1998 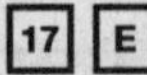

Sheer unadulterated richness of such texture and finesse, yet power and depth, the drinker waits as each act unfolds. A dramatic wine of huge class.

SOUTH AFRICAN WINE — WHITE

Fairview Barrel Fermented Chenin Blanc 1999 16 C

Superb style and acidity meet Cape richness and fruity depth.

Jordan Chardonnay, Stellenbosch 1998 15.5 E

Creamy, almost-yoghurty richness to the deeply textured fruit.

Springfield Sauvignon Blanc Special Cuvee 1999 15.5 D

Very grassy and rich. A superb fish wine.

SPANISH WINE RED

Cosme Palacio Tinto, Rioja 1991 (magnum) 

Big bottle of vanilla-edged fruit of perfect maturity – excellent with the Christmas fowl. Price bracket shows the 75cl equivalent. (Small parcel only – limited availability.)

SPANISH WINE WHITE

Espiral Macabeo/Chardonnay 1998 

Superb food wine. Simply terrific and life giving for dead fish dishes. Has come on tremendously in bottle since I tasted it last spring (qv the main section of this book).

Vinas del Vero Chardonnay 1998 

Sheer charm and coolness here, lovely restrained richness and balance. Very classy.

USA WINE WHITE

Cuvaison Carneros Reserve Chardonnay, Napa 1997 

G

A big, big twenty quid Christmas treat. It's better than Montrachet.

SPARKLING WINE/CHAMPAGNE

Champagne Blanc de Noirs NV, Waitrose 15.5 F

Superb champagne of great class and concentration. Tasting even better than it did last spring (qv the main section of the book).

Sparkling Burgundy NV (France) 15.5 D

A superb clean bubbly for the money.

NOTES

NOTES

NOTES

NOTES

DON'T MISS:

STREETPLONK 2000

Gluck's guide to High Street wine shops

Millennium? What Millennium? STREETPLONK 2000 is about bargain wines NOW!

Gluck covers them all: **Fullers, Majestic, Oddbins, Spar, Thresher (including Wine Rack and Bottoms Up), Unwins, Victoria Wine and Wine Cellar.** Malcolm Gluck's annual guide to the best-value wines available at our top high street wine shops is without equal.

* Completely rewritten every year

* The most up-to-date wine guide you can swallow

* 'Gluck's descriptive vocabulary is all his own, and some of his judgements turn convention on its head' *Time Out*

DON'T MISS:

THE SENSATIONAL LIQUID

Gluck's Guide to Wine Tasting

Britain's bestselling wine writer shows – with wit and without pretension – how to get the most pleasure from wine in his first fully illustrated hardback.

For too long, the world of wine tasting has been the preserve of a select few. Now Malcolm Gluck cuts through the pretension, and explains all the mysteries, from how to spot a corked bottle to what kind of glass to select. He shows how wine tasting involves each of the senses, and only when we have tuned all of these can we truly appreciate a wine. Innovatively written, illustrated and designed, THE SENSATIONAL LIQUID will be indispensable to all those who want to learn how to take their enjoyment of wine drinking to even greater heights.

HODDER AND STOUGHTON PAPERBACKS